LIVING ARRANGEMENTS AND HEALTH CONDITIONS OF ELDERLY IN RURAL INDIA

Living Arrangements and Health Conditions of Elderly in Rural India

S. Muthukrishnaveni

SERIALS PUBLICATIONS
NEW DELHI (INDIA)

First Published - 2010

ISBN: 978-81-8387-388-8

Published by

SERIALS PUBLICATIONS
4830/24, Prahlad Street, Ansari Road
Darya Ganj, New Delhi-110002 (India)
Phone : 23245225 Fax : 91-11-23272135
E-mail: serials@satyam.net.in

CONTENTS

PREFACE

India is the second largest country in the world, sharing 15 percent of world's population. Over the years, as a result of the improvement in public health and medical services, there has been considerable decline in fertility and mortality. A significant impact of this demographic change is the increase in the number of elderly persons. The 2001 census has shown that the elderly population of India accounted for 77 million. While the elderly constituted only 24 million in 1961, it increased to 43million in 1981 and to 57 million in 1991.The proportion of elderly persons in the population of India increased from 5.63 per cent in 1961 to 6.58 per cent in 1991 and to 7.5 per cent in 2001. The census also revealed that the percentage of elderly was much higher in rural than in urban areas.

Indian aged population is currently the second largest in the world. The absolute number of elderly population aged 60 years and above is expected to increase from 77 million in 2001 to 137 million by 2021. Majority of older persons in the world today are women and they are the most vulnerable group and are prone to socio-economic, psychological and health problems.

Traditionally age and wisdom are very much respected in India. Family is expected to play an important role in providing care and support to elderly. Younger generations must and should realise and concern for their parents and give respect towards elderly members in the family. Modernisation and globalisation has brought tremendous changes in the family structure. When young people leave their villages for the towns and cities, the elderly are left uncared. The joint family system is the backbone of 'old age care', as the elderly need 'socio-psychological and emotional support'. As majority of families become nuclear, the social safety net availed by the elderly in the joint family system is eroding fast. But the norms and values attached to the family still retain its place in most cases. The government has initiated a number of programmes to take care of the aged. Besides the governmental efforts, non-governmental organisations (NGOs) have also involved in the care and support of elderly in India.

It is in this context, the present book emerged from my Ph.D. thesis is based on the data collected for the university Grants Commission Major Research Project on 'Changing Living Arrangements, Health Conditions and Care of Elderly in TamilNadu'. I had the opportunity to work as a project fellow in this project implemented by the Department of Applied Research of the Gandhigram Rural Institute-Deemed University and I have used the data collected for the study for my Ph.D. thesis. Besides the data collected from the elderly to assess their living arrangements and health status , information were also collected from various secondary sources and complied to present the levels and trends in population ageing at global, national and state level. Thus the book is based on the data collected through both secondary and primary sources. I hope this book will immensely useful for the researchers, students, teachers, programme planners and policy makers who are involved in the study of aging.

Dr. S. Muthukrishnaveni

LIST OF ABBREVIATIONS

ADL	–	Activities of Daily Living
CHD	–	Coronary Heart Disease
FGD	–	Focus Group Discussion
HDI	–	Human Development Index
ICMR	–	Indian Council of Medical Research
IMR	–	Infant Mortality Rate
LDC	–	Less Developed Countries
MDC	–	More Developed Countries
MFLS	–	Malaysian Family Life Survey
MMR	–	Maternal Mortality Rate
NSSO	–	National Sample Survey Organization
OBC	–	Other Backward Caste
PHCs	–	Primary Health Centres
RA	–	Rheumatoid Arthritis
SC	–	Scheduled Caste
SEAR	–	South East Asia Region
SPSS	–	Statistical Package for Social Sciences
ST	–	Scheduled Tribe
TFR	–	Total Fertility Rate
UN	–	United Nations
WHO	–	World Health Organization

GLOSSARY

Activities of Daily Living (ADL)—The things we normally do in daily living including any daily activity we perform for self-care work (such as feeding ourselves, bathing, dressing, grooming), homemaking and leisure. The ability or inability to perform ADLs can be used as a very practical measure of ability/disability in many disorders.

Ageing—Proportion of people aged 60 years and above reaches 7 per cent.

Census—A canvass of a given area, resulting in an enumeration of the entire population and often the compilation of other demographic, social and economic information pertaining to that population at a specific time.

Health—Is a complete state of physical, mental and social well being and not merely the absence of diseases or infirmity.

Index of Ageing—Number of persons aged 60+ per 100 aged 0-14.

Index of Oldest Old to Young Old—The population aged 80 years and above per 100 population aged 60-64.

Index of Parents to Children—The population aged 60-74 per 100 population aged 40-44.

Old Dependency Ratio—Number of persons aged 60+ per100 aged 15-59.

Population—A group of objects or organisms of the same kind.

Sample—A part or subset of the population used to supply information about the whole population.

Sex Ratio—Number of females per 100 males in a population.

Survey—A canvas of selected persons or households in a population usually used to infer demographic characteristics or trends for a larger segment or all of the population.

Total Dependency Ratio—Number of persons aged 0-14 + Number of persons aged 60+ per 100 aged 15-59.

Young Dependency Ratio—Number of persons aged 0-14 per 100 aged 15-59.

ACKNOWLEDGEMENTS

I wish to express my deep sense of gratitude to *Dr. S. Gunasekaran,* Reader, Department of Applied Research, Gandhigram Rural University, Gandhigram, for his able guidance and invaluable advice to complete this research work. His keen interest, continuous encouragement and valuable suggestions were of immense value without which it would not be possible to make this research work a success.

I am indebted to Dr. M.A.Sudhir, Professor and Head, Department of Applied Research, Gandhigram Rural University, Gandhigram for his continuous support and encouragement at various stages of the work.

I acknowledge my sincere gratitude to the University Grants Commission (UGC), New Delhi, for the opportunity given to me to work as Project Fellow in the UGC Major Research Project and complete the research work successfully.

My grateful thanks are also due to the respondents for their kind cooperation in responding to the questions during the personal interview and also during the focus group discussions.

I express my sincere thanks to all the faculty members and non-teaching staff of the Department of Applied Research for their support at the various phases of this research work.

I take this opportunity to place on record of my profound love and sincere gratitude to my father, mother, brother and sister for the cooperation and moral support extended to me throughout my studies.

(Dr. S. Muthukrishnaveni)

1

INTRODUCTION

Ageing of the global is one of the biggest challenges facing the world in the 21st century. From a demographic point of view, population ageing is a result of both mortality and fertility. Fewer children are born and more people reach old age. Over the last fifty years, with the modern and advanced medical facilities, mortality rates in developing countries have declined dramatically raising the average life expectancy at birth from around 41 years in the early 1950s to almost 66 years in 2007. Sharp falls have also been observed in birth rates in nearly all developing countries (World population data sheet, 2007).

The improvement in mortality and reduction in fertility have made the population age structure much older than before and by 2025, the elderly are expected to reach 15 per cent of the world total population. So far the issues related to ageing have figured mainly in the context of developed countries. However of late the demographic scenario of more and more developing countries is changing from high fertility to low fertility besides the demographic transition in the developing countries has proceeded at a much faster pace than it did in the developed ones involving large absolute numbers. This is resulting in a much faster pace of ageing and large absolute size of the elderly population in many of the developing countries.

The continued growth of elderly population both in absolute terms and in relation to other segments of the society is the most significant demographic trend of the twentieth century. Throughout the twentieth century, the proportion of people aged 60 and older has increased in all countries of the world. This trend started earlier in the industrialized countries, but countries in the developing world are experiencing the same changes in population structure. Population ageing is expected to have a major impact on life in the twenty first century (United Nations, 1998).

The number of persons aged 60 years or older in the world is projected to grow to nearly 2 billion by 2050. It is estimated that about 10 per cent of the world population are aged 60 or older. It is about 20 per cent in developed countries and is about 8 percent in developing countries, which are at an early stage of the demographic transition. The United Nations long range population projections (United Nations, 1999a) show that future populations will reach a significantly older age structure than the populations of the present or even of the populations of 2050.

The tempo of ageing is more rapid in the less developed regions than in more developed regions. The rapid growth of the elderly population and increase in the proportion in older groups imply a decrease in the sex ratio (number of females per 100 males) for the total population and greater number of older women than of older men. At ages 60 or older, there were an estimated 81 men for every 100 women globally in 2000 and at ages 80 or older there were only 53 men for every 100 women. The sex ratios of older age groups are lower in the more developed regions than in the less developed regions, since there are large differences in life expectancy between the sexes in the more developed regions (United Nations, 1998).

The rapid increase in the older population and the changes in the family system and life style of younger generation lead to changes in the living arrangements of elderly both in developed and developing countries. Throughout human history, the family has been the safest heaven for the aged. Its ties have been the most intimate and long lasting and on them the aged have relied for greatest security (Simmom, 1945).

Living arrangements are influenced by a variety of factors, including marital status, financial well being, health status and family size and structure, as well as cultural traditions such as kinship patterns, the value placed on living independently or with family members, the availability of social services and social support and the physical features of housing stock and local communities (Victoria et al., 2001).

At older ages, women are less likely to be married and more likely to be widowed than men, not only because they survive on average to higher ages, but also because most women marry men several years older than themselves. According to the United Nations estimate (United Nations, 1999b), 79 per cent of older men in the world are married compared to only 43 per cent of older women.

Women in developed countries are much more likely than men to live alone as they aged, mainly because women are more likely to be widowed. There has been an increase in the proportion of the older population living alone in developed countries; in developing countries both older women and men usually live with adult children; and the use of institutional care for the elderly varies widely among countries but is relatively low everywhere (Victoria et al., 2001).

For a comprehensive picture of support provided within family, it is important to investigate the role of kin living elsewhere. Since relatives and non-relatives living nearby may be an important source of essential support and assistance and even distant kin may provide significant financial assistance. There is also a need for a better understanding of the nature of intra-family transfers and their relationship to the welfare of the elderly. The younger old are more likely to be healthy can still be economically active and may provide substantial assistance to their children and grand children with advancing age and with the onset of chronic disease or disability, the older generation becomes more likely to depend on others for both financial support and personal care (United Nations, 2001).

Changes in age distribution have complex social and economic implications at the social and individual levels. If changes are slow, countries can more easily adopt. As the experience of developed countries have shown, despite an ageing process that has occurred over many years, adjustment to the challenges posed by the population ageing has not been smooth. Given that large shifts in age structure are being compressed into a relatively short period in developing countries, these countries have less time than the developed countries to adapt to the problems posed by the changing age structure (Barry Mirkin and Mary Weinberger, 2001).

In India, the number of elderly people aged 60 years or older is steadily increasing. The significant reduction in the death rates and the improvements in the life expectancy have lead to more number of elderly in the country. Though the percentage of elderly to the total population is estimated around 7 percentage, their numbers increased from 12.0 million in 1901 to about 76 million in 2001.

Ageing in India is described as a process of change in human roles throughout life. Culture is transmitted between generations. Social changes in India have impacted on the elderly through shifts in lifestyles, housing shortages, migration of youth, increasing female employment, high cost of living and changed priorities in the distribution of income within families and the breakdown of the system of common ownership of land. The net demographic result of change is increased longevity and an increased proportion of elderly among total population. The Indian Constitution assures the protection of the elderly with public assistance. Children are obliged to care for elderly or infirm parents according to the 1973 criminal code and a 1956 Hindu act. The Indian approach to the care of the elderly has been guided by religious beliefs and philanthropic ideals. Economic support is provided by states to some extent for the destitute and the uncared-for aged. The national medical care system is available in the formal sector for organized, urban wage earners. There is a deficit in program support for the elderly poor that are recognized by central government. A new challenge in India is the small family's ability to meet the economic demands of support for parents (Gokhale, 1994). The trend in the size and growth of elderly population in the country indicates that ageing will become a major social challenge in the future when vast resources will need to be directed towards the supported care and treatment of the old (Sivaraju, 2002). In this context, the present study is undertaken to assess the living arrangements and health conditions of elderly in rural TamilNadu.

CHAPTERIZATION

The present book contains the following seven chapters

- Introduction
- Review of literature
- Objectives and methodology
- Levels and trends in population ageing
- Survey results
  - Background characteristics of elderly
  - Living arrangements
  - Familial relationship
  - Personal life style behaviour of elderly
  - Physical disabilities
  - Psychological problems
  - Health status of elderly
  - Expectations of elderly
- Focus group discussion
- Summary and conclusion

In chapter two, an in-depth review has been made on the ageing of population at global, national and state level with special emphasis on rural India. The review of literature mainly focused on trends in population ageing, their living arrangements, psychological problems, health problems, disabilities and care and support available to elderly.

Chapter three focuses on the methodology of the study. In this chapter, objectives, study area, study design, variables included in the study, data collection method and data analysis is presented in detail.

Chapter four presents the levels and trends in population ageing at global, national and state level.

Chapter five discusses the results of the survey. The survey findings are presented in eight sections. In the first section of chapter five, the background characteristics of elderly such as age, education, religion, caste, marital status, occupation and economic status are presented in detail. The housing characteristics of elderly such as type of house, ownership of house, electrification, toilet facilities and number of rooms are also included in this section.

Section two of chapter five focuses on the living arrangements of elderly in rural areas. The topics mainly covered in this section include place of living, reasons for not staying with their son, availability of separate room for elderly, reasons for separate room, place of sleeping and reasons for not sleeping inside the house. The χ^2 test of significance is used to see the association between background characteristics of elderly and their living arrangements. The logistic regression analysis has also been carried out to see the effect of each of the background characteristics of elderly on their living arrangements.

Section three of chapter five focuses on the familial relationship of elderly. The topic covered in this section include extent of freedom available to use household facilities, maintenance of cordial relationship with other family members, participation in family ceremonies, reasons for not participating in family ceremonies, involvement in decision-making process on various family matters, role of elderly in solving family disputes, abusive/violence behaviour of family members, type of abuse, frequency of taking food, adequacy of daily in take of food, requirement of special food, availability of special food at home, reasons for not getting special food at home, need of money to meet their personal needs, availability of finance, sources of finance and sufficiency of money to meet their personal needs.

In section four of chapter five, the life style behaviour of elderly is presented in detail. In this section the topics related to the daily activities of elderly and their support to household activities are covered. The leisure time activities of elderly are also covered in this section.

In section five of chapter five, the physical disability, difficulties in their activities of daily living (ADL), physical mobility status and physiological status of elderly are presented in detail. The χ^2 test of significance is used to see the association of the background characteristics of the elderly on their physiological status. The logistic regression analysis is used to see the effect of various background characteristics of elderly on their physiological status.

Section six of chapter five, deals with the psychological problems of elderly. The psychological problems of elderly are related to the age, sex and living arrangements. The χ^2 test of significance has been used to see the influence of age, sex and living arrangements of elderly on their psychological problems. The overall psychological status of elderly is grouped in to three categories as good, moderate and poor and it is related to the background characteristics and living arrangements to see the influence of the background characteristics and living arrangements on the psychological status of elderly.

Section seven of chapter five focuses on the health status of elderly which was assessed based on the self reported symptoms on a set of chronic diseases. The morbidity pattern of elderly during the past two weeks prior to the survey was also assessed and presented in this section. The χ^2 test of significance has been used to see the significance of the association of the background characteristics of the elderly with their health status.

The last section of chapter five covers topics on the expectations of elderly from family and government. Suggestions for the youth, opinion on increased longevity and availability of basic needs to lead a healthy life have also been covered in this section.

In chapter six, results of the Focus Group Discussions (FGDs) are presented in detail.

In chapter seven, results observed in chapter four to six are summarized and the significant findings are highlighted. Based on the findings, recommendations are made and policy implications are suggested for a comprehensive measures to care and support elderly in rural areas.

At the end, the list of references quoted in the text, district-wise Human Development Index (HDI) values, sample area and a copy of interview schedule are annexed.

2

REVIEW OF LITERATURE

This chapter deals with the existing literature on the trends in ageing at global and national level, living arrangements of elderly, psychological and health problems of elderly, disability status of elderly and care and support available to elderly. The review gives a clear perspective of the overall situation in ageing.

POPULATION AGEING–GLOBAL PERSPECTIVE

Ageing is an inevitable phenomenon in all biological species. It is a rent-less process in life, leading to its extinction. One of the upcoming issues in the global demographic situation is the population ageing. By the sheer magnitude of their number, the next century society can be rightfully termed as the society of aged.

Virtually all nations are experiencing growth in the numbers of elderly residents. Comparatively, there is a great increase of elderly populations in lesser developed countries than in more developed ones. Even in nations where the elderly percentage of the total population remains small, absolute numbers may be rising steeply. Such growth poses challenges to social institutions that must adapt to changing age structures (Kinsella, 2000).

The elderly used to account for only 5 per cent of total population. The numbers have increased dramatically in some countries to about 10 per cent and many will be increasing to these and higher proportions. The proportion of elderly people was expected to increase by 32.5 per cent in developed countries between 1980 and 2025, but in developing countries the rate of increase was expected to be as high as 88.6 per cent. In developed regions, by 2025, the numbers will be low at 257 million and 19 per cent of total population. In developing countries, the percentage of elderly will average 8.07 per cent, but the numbers will be large (571 million). Ageing will be rapid in Eastern Asia and slow in Western Asia. The stage in demographic transition has affected the speed of ageing. Southern countries were the farthest behind. Early and quick demographic transition will result in rapid ageing. A more rapid fertility decline will result in a longer period of a very low age dependency ratio, which would be advantageous to economic growth (Kuroda, 1993).

The world's elderly population, 60 years and older, reached 251.6 million by 1950, 488 million by 1990 and, according to United Nations projection estimates, it will reach 1205.3 million in 2025. These figures mean an increase of 94 per cent between 1950 and 1990 and of 146 per cent between 1990 and 2025. Asia accounted for the highest number of elderly persons (49.2 per cent, in 1990). Europe reported 19 per cent, Africa 6.3 per cent and Latin America 6.5 per cent. On the other hand, over the next 35 years, the European region figure will decrease to 12 per cent while other regions will show increased percentages: 58 per cent for Asia and around 8 per cent for Africa and Latin America. Fertility and mortality decreases in developing countries will result in the elderly population constituting 12 per cent of the total population in the year 2025. In this same year, Latin America will have the same high proportion of elderly persons as the world will have in the year 2020. On the other hand, some of the developed regions, such as Northern America and Europe, will reach figures around 27 per cent. Below the average value for these regions in the year 2025 will be the former Soviet Union with 20 per cent and Oceania with 19.2 per cent. Another way to confirm population ageing is by computing the median age of a population. Thus, while in 1950 the world median age was 23.4 years, it increased up to 24.2

years in 1990 and is estimated to be 31.1 years by the year 2025. Developed regions show higher population ageing than the less developed ones. In fact, in 1990, developed countries had a median age of 33.7 years and developing countries had a median age of 22 years. While the median age will be 40.7 years for developed countries in the year 2025, it will only be 29.7 years for less developed countries. Nevertheless, this relatively high median age indicates that the ageing process has already started in less developed countries (Hernandez, 1992).

One of the major features of demographic transition in the world has been the considerable increase in the absolute and relative numbers of elderly people. This has been especially true in the case of developing countries like India, where ageing is occurring more rapidly due to the decline in fertility rates combined by increase in life expectancy of people achieved through medical interventions. About 60 per cent of the elderly live in the developing world and this will rise to 70 per cent by 2010. Further the older population itself is ageing, with the oldest old being more than 10 per cent of the world's elderly (Indirani Gupta et al., 2003).

The rise in the proportion of the ageing population represents one of the most significant demographic shifts in history. In 1950, there were 205 million people who were over 60, in 2000, there were 606 million and by 2050, there will be two billion. The number of elderly trebled over the last 50 years and an encore is expected in the next 50 years. As a proportion of the total world population, the number of elderly will double in the next 50 years. This demographic change is fast turning the hair of policymakers prematurely grey throughout the world, especially in developing countries, where the growth of the aged population is happening at a more rapid pace (Ashakrishnakumar, 2004).

While world population is growing at a rate of 1.7 per cent per year, the proportion of those aged 55 years and above is increasing at 2.2 per cent per annum and the number of aged 65 and above at 2.8 per cent per year. Every month, the world's older population increases by 1.2 million persons. More than 80 per cent of the increases occur only in developing countries whose growth rate of the aged (3.1 per cent) is 3 times as high as in developed countries (Lakshmi Pathi Raju et al., 2002).

The elderly population over age 60 amounts to about 540 million in the world and about 330 million of them is in developing countries. The average life expectancy in developing countries is estimated to be around 72 years in 2020. By 2020 there will be over 1000 million elderly people in the world and 710 million in developing countries. Europe will be the oldest region in the world with 19 per cent of elderly out of total population and 24 per cent in 2020. By 2020, Japan will have the most elderly with 31 per cent, followed by Greece, Italy and Germany with above 28 per cent and Switzerland with 27.4 per cent. Regional distribution of elderly in 2020 will be 23 per cent in North America, 17 per cent in East Asia, 12 per cent in Latin America and 10 per cent in South Asia. By 2020, seven developing countries will have the largest elderly populations: China (231 million), India (145 million), Brazil (30 million), Indonesia (29 million), Pakistan (18 million), Mexico (15 million) and Bangladesh (14 million). Population ageing in developing countries is associated with persistent poverty and misery. The population of elderly doubled in France in 115 years and in China in 27 years. Colombia, the Philippines, Kenya and Thailand will experience a 300 per cent increase in elderly in 40 years. By 2020, 75 per cent of all deaths in developing countries will be age-related and due to non-communicable causes. Mental health problems are expected to increase. Senility among the elderly in Africa, Asia and Latin America may exceed 80 million in 2025. Cataracts account for over 50 per cent of all blindness in Asia and Africa and over 40 per cent of all low vision cases (Population Ageing: a public health challenge, 1996).

The concept of population ageing is viewed differently by demographers and policy makers. During demographic transition, population growth depends on declining mortality and constant fertility. Population ageing is dependent on the intensity and speed of fertility decline. It is suggested that countries be grouped into three stages for the timing of fertility decline: started before 1950, started during 1950-90 and not started by 1990. Countries above a fertility rate of 5.0 during 1950-90 are pre-initiation countries. Countries with a decline of over 1.5 children in fertility, which was over 5.0 during 1950-90, are late-initiation countries. Early-initiation countries are ones where fertility was below 5.0 during 1950-55. These countries include Australia, Japan and New Zealand in Asia. Late-initiation countries include India, Sri Lanka, Cambodia, China, Fiji, Hong Kong, Indonesia, Malaysia, Myanmar, Philippines, the Republic of Korea, Singapore, Thailand and Vietnam. Pre-initiation countries include Afghanistan, Bangladesh, Bhutan, Iran, Laos, Mongolia, Nepal, Pakistan and Papua New Guinea. Early-initiation countries experienced a continuous ageing of their population during 1950-90. Population projections during 1990-2025 according to the UN medium variant suggest a decline of the percentage of the population aged under 15 years from 44 per cent to 28 per cent in pre-initiation countries of the ESCAP region, from 32 per cent to 21 per cent in late-initiation countries and from 19 per cent to 15.5 per cent in early-initiation countries. The percentage aged 60 years and over is expected to increase during 1990-2025 from 5 per cent to 8 per cent in pre-initiation countries, from 8 per cent to 15 per cent in late-initiation countries and from 17 per cent to 29 per cent in early-initiation countries. In early-initiation countries the percentage aged 75 years and older will change from being 17 per cent of the population aged 60 years and older in 1950, to 27 per cent in 1990 and 41 per cent in 2025. The rate of growth among the elderly will accelerate in pre-and late-initiation countries and will slow in early-initiation ones after 2010 (United Nations, 1994a).

In Asia, the elderly population is growing in both absolute number and as a proportion of total population. The speed of population ageing and the absolute size of the elderly population among countries with low levels of economic development pose challenges. Rapid urbanization and industrialization, which increase the flow of young and female population to urban areas, has the undesirable consequence of the separation of the elderly in rural areas without sufficient support. Fertility decline results in a reduced number of caregivers in a family. Modernization brings changes in values, perceptions, attitudes and expectations that impact on the elderly. Life expectancy and health improvements increase the potential for self-reliance and for contributions to social and economic development among the elderly. This "young old" group (aged 60-69 years) in 1990 constituted 62.65 million persons in China, 38.39 million in India and 7.37 million in Indonesia. These "young old" continue to work in self-employment or non-organized sectors without pensions or social security until they cannot. The "old old," aged over 70 years, are likely to suffer from physical or mental disabilities of old age and require care (United Nations, 1994b).

By the age of 85 years and older in Japan, female elderly are double the number of male elderly. The female-male ratio at 60 years is almost equal. One out of 10 elderly live alone and 80per cent of those living alone are women. Single-only and couple-only elderly households increased over time. More women are admitted to nursing homes. The greatest problems of the elderly are dementia and being bedridden. Japanese women's health differs from Western models, due mainly to dietary habits. The ageing process of women after menopause differs from that of men in all countries. In Japan, there are differences in the elderly born before and after the World War II. Before the war women were trained to become a "good wife and a wise mother" and to sacrifice. It is difficult to train these women now to exercise their rights to self-determination, or to accept being cared for by a husband. A major issue for elderly women is poverty. Wives may not be protected by any pension plan. Legal changes in Japan allow transfer of house ownership to a spouse with taxation under certain circumstances. Employment opportunities narrow for older women (Higuchi, 1996).

It is noted that 1 out of every 16 persons in Nepal is now aged 60 years or older. It has been estimated that Nepal will have an ageing population by the year 2010. On a global perspective, the proportions of the elderly differ from region to region. 1 out of every 5 Europeans, but 1 out of every 20

Africans, is aged 60 years or older. In the Asian and Pacific region, more than 300 million elderly persons are aged 60 years or older. In China, there are more than 114 million elderly people, while Japan is home to 25.1 million elderly persons, the largest age group of its population and the largest proportion of elderly people among all of the countries in this region. The steady increase of older age groups both in absolute numbers and in relation to the working-age population holds significant implications for many countries. The economic and social impact of ageing populations presents both an opportunity and a challenge to all societies (Bisht, 2000).

The increasing trend in the ageing population of countries in the South-East Asia Region (SEAR) transforms these countries from "mature societies" to "ageing societies". The elderly population in this region would be increasing from 18.1 per cent in 1995 to 21.4 per cent of the world elderly population in 2025. Since women have a longer life expectancy than men, the proportion of elderly women in the region would increase to 13.2 per cent by 2025, while the proportion of elderly men would be 11.6 per cent. In SEAR, 11.8 million people reportedly suffered from blindness in 1998; 50-80 per cent of these cases are caused by cataract, which is most common in those aged 60 years and above (Wibowo, 1999).

It was argued that rural elders have smaller number and narrower range of community-based services available to support independent life. However, application of advanced telecommunications services to health care may significantly improve efficiency, quality and access to services and may even lower the health care cost. In general, rural populations are characterized by: the exodus of young generations; eroding traditional family systems and networks; limited access to existing health and social infrastructures; and socioeconomic and environmental hardships and challenges (Hermanova, 1998).

In Hong Kong, the population has been ageing rapidly over the past 15 years. It has been projected that the percentage of the population aged 65 and over will increase from 10 per cent in 1996 to 12.5 per cent in 2016. In addition, there will also be a rapid increase in both the number and proportion of people aged 85 and over. In effect, there has been a progressive reduction in average household size and the nuclear families have been largely replaced with extended family. Furthermore, the reduction in labor force participation of the elderly highlights their employment and income insecurity. It is noted that the family continues to provide most health care and support services to older persons, especially through daughters and daughters-in-law. In this respect, professional assistance, financial aid and counseling services need to be available to families caring for disabled or chronically ill ageing members. With respect to the provision of health care services, the elderly should have free choice and accessibility (Phillips, 1999).

In Asia, the last decade of the 20th century is marked by significant changes in the age structure due to the process of population ageing. The implications of this ageing population on the life of Asian countries have to be addressed since demographically the current situation is changing rapidly and there lie the future challenges that have to be answered. Due to the growing size of the elderly population, Asia will need better plans to prevent these elderly groups from turning into the socio-economically vulnerable group of society (Suyono, 1999).

According to the UN standards, China will soon become an ageing society. The ageing population poses several challenges to the country with the greatest challenge being the increasing social responsibility to care for the aged. With the undeveloped legislative framework to protect the interests of the aged and the serious drawbacks in the pension system to cater only to the income part and not the service part of the aged, China is not yet ready for the advent of ageing. Violation of the rights of senior citizens is still very rampant despite enactment of the law on Protection of the Rights of the Elderly in 1996. Moreover, China is not economically ready to become an ageing society. China faces this challenge by adopting a three-pronged approach to solve the problem namely: family support, establishment of nursing homes and creating a social security framework that addresses the needs of the society suited to the Chinese condition. It is believed that with the growing economy of the country and the rising income of its people, a comprehensive social security net will be created to take care of the aged (China Population Today, 1999).

The trends in population ageing during 1982-2000, 2000-2025 and 2025-2050, in China, indicated that ageing began in the early 1970s when fertility began to decline. The adult population grew and the dependency ratio declined. By 2025, the elderly will number 278 million, or 18.5 per cent of total population. The increase during 2000-2025 constitutes a net increase of 150 million persons in 25 years. The ageing problem will have a greater impact in rural areas with a large number of young and adult migrants to urban areas. The elderly will reach 389 million in 2050, or 25.8 per cent of total population. The dependency ratio will be the maximum and age distributions will stabilize. Every 100 working-age persons will support about 40 elderly persons and 30 children. Elderly laborers will comprise over 33 per cent of the total working-age population. Labor resources will be insufficient by 2050. The traditional function of the family as a primary supporter of the elderly is gradually becoming weakened. China must develop a development plan that balances population ageing and socioeconomic development. China must rapidly develop the economy with its current abundant labor resources. China must devise a unique social security system. China must improve community services and social welfare programs (Li and Zhang, 1998).

Little is known about the health status of the elderly in Sri Lanka. There is a question about whether health care should be integrated or age specific. Alternative care systems are viewed as necessary and integrated with the Ayurvedic system. Surveys have revealed that the reduction in family size has not reduced the availability of care givers to the extent that the elderly are being abandoned. Family care givers would be better providers of the elderly with proper training, recognition for their devotion to elderly care and incentives.

The expectation is that increases in the number of elderly will increase the demand for old age homes. State-run homes are strictly operated at present, but future needs are identified as homes with greater flexibility and better trained staff. The institutional environment should shift from the drab to the more appealing and from low to high quality care. Ready access to health care is needed for elderly persons in old age homes. There is no employment guidance or placement service for the elderly, who may retire in their early or mid-fifties as healthy, productive adults. The increase in longevity and the marriage squeeze may increase the number of single elderly females, who do not receive as much support as married couples and are considered the most vulnerable group. The increase in marriage age results in retirement with child dependency. Decision makers have not yet become aware of population ageing. In 2011 the population aged 60 years and older could be 10.52 per cent. The rapid increase in the aged is expected to result in a higher demand for health and social security services by the elderly. The household is the traditional support system. Voluntary organizations are active in provision of services for the elderly. Pensions are available, even for farmers, if they have 10 acres of cultivatable land. The health care system provides free primary care regardless of age. The homeless and the poor regardless of age have priority in the housing program (Perera, 1994).

The aged population in Bangladesh is expected to increase from 4.90 million in 1980 to 17.62 million in 2025 (1 out of every 10 persons). Retirement age from the formal sector ranges from 57 to 65 years. In the informal sector the elderly work for as long as health permits. The elderly population aged 60 years and older will show an increase in the old age dependency ratio from 8.7 in 1990 to 16.2 in 2025. The burden will increase for young wage earners and the government. Currently social security programs for the aged apply to retired military, government and industrial workers. The family is the primary source of care among most of the population, 85 per cent of who live in rural areas. The literature on the aged in Bangladesh is still quite limited. The most important baseline

lived alone. Among those living alone, a high proportion was separated or divorced women. About 1 in 4 elderly believed that the widowed should live alone. About 1 in 3 believed that a widow should live with a child. About 40 per cent of married persons believed that the best arrangement was living by themselves, even though few did so. The elderly living with a child tended to own the house. 69.2 per cent co resided with a child and 76.8 per cent co resided or lived next door to a child. Co residence with a child was unaffected by the number of living children. Co residence increased with age and was more common among males, married and urban residents. 28.6 per cent lived with a single son and 21.7 per cent lived with a single daughter. More parents received money from a non-co resident child. The proportion of parents who gave money to children was lower than the proportion who received money from children. 92.5 per cent of the elderly cared for a grandchild. A large proportion of elderly both accepted the concept of homes for the aged and would live in an institutional setting (Natividad et al., 1997).

An analysis of the Public Use Micro data Samples of the 1960 and 1980 Brazilian Census of Population, revealed that the distribution of households in Brazil showed an increase in the proportions of smaller households and single parent households. Correspondingly, the prevalence of both horizontally and vertically extended family households declined between 1960 and 1980. Comparisons revealed similarities between the United States and Brazil in the association of kin availability with the likelihood of living alone. Analysis also revealed that much of the age effect in predicting co residence with children in Brazil can be explained by the correlation between parent and child ages. Multinomial logit models confirmed the importance of demographic factors: many of the social and economic predictors became less significant once the sample was stratified by kin availability (Agree, 1993).

Western culture has affected the financial support of the elderly in Taiwan. This finding is based on the December 1988 monthly labor force survey in Taiwan. Respondents were grouped into 1) dependent (dependence on their children for living costs); 2) independent (economic self reliance), 3) supplementary (partial assistance provided from children); and 4) semi-dependent (primary dependence on children and little respondent income). Dependent types comprise 43.2 per cent independent types 11.9 per cent, supplementary types 18.2 per cent and semi dependent 17.2 per cent of the sample. Living costs are the only results reported since medical costs followed a similar pattern of results. When secondary sources are considered, 75 per cent receive support for living costs. Living arrangements are considered an intervening variable. Sex, social class and health are determinants for the direction of flow of intergenerational wealth. Economic support is related to living arrangement and socio-demographic variables. In the analysis of health and types of support where living arrangement is the control variable, percentage distribution differences between the poor and good health status for the four types of support disappear. The relationship between living arrangements and types of economic support is unchanged when health status is controlled. Living arrangements are a specifying variable in analyzing the relationship between economic support and sex, marital status and education and between economic support and age. Polytomous logit analysis is performed to test the independence of the socioeconomic variables and living arrangements. The result was that younger, healthy, male elderly who are married and better educated and not living with children have a greater likelihood of being independent. Living arrangements has the largest coefficient followed by age and education. The likelihood of being supplementary is related to older female elderly in poor health with less education and unmarried. The general conclusion is that the society is in transition from depending on offspring in old age to being independent or less dependent. Society must prepare to meet the change (Chen, 1992).

The temptation to equate the status and well being of the elderly with their living arrangements is resisted. Micro rather than macro correlates of living arrangements in the Philippines,

Singapore, Taiwan and Thailand are examined specifically to determine the extent to which the elderly live alone, live only with their spouse, or live with at least one of their children. Factors affecting the choices are the availability of kin with whom to reside and the relative costs and benefits of different living arrangements, which are measured indirectly. Both within country and between country comparisons are made. The data were available from country specific household surveys, which are national probability samples. Measures selected were reasonably similar across countries even though countries differed. The social and cultural differences reflect patrilineal Chinese societies with son's caring for the elderly in Singapore and Taiwan. The Philippines has a bilateral kinship system and Thailand is flexible and resource oriented. All countries stress the children's obligation to care for the elderly. Although the assumption is that living arrangements are directly affected by the explanatory variables, it is also quite clear that prior decisions about childbearing, joint decision making by children and parents and the instability of living arrangements are important also. The data are indirect measures of the elderly at one point in their lives and on one particular date. The results based on regression analyses indicate that with the exception of Taiwan <10 per cent live alone or with a spouse. Isolation from children is not in evidence since 50 per cent of the elderly in the Philippines and Thailand live near a relative and 25 per cent in Taiwan. The five demographic factors selected for analysis include sex, age, number of living sons, number of living daughters and marital status with each having an effect on the elderly living arrangements. The results are, for example, that each of the 3 dependent variables is associated with the availability of children. Living alone or with a spouse is strongly related to no children. The number of sons or just one son differs across countries, with Taiwan the most dissimilar. In general, the relative strength of sons vs. daughters is similar, but sons are more important in Taiwan and daughters in the Philippines and Thailand. Singapore is mixed. Sex of the elderly only affects living alone arrangements. Societal effects, which are reflected in the analyses, will be investigated in later work (Casterline et al., 1991).

Considering that the proportion of the population over 55 years of age is growing 3 times faster in developing than in developed countries, data from the 2nd Malaysian Family Life Survey (MFLS-2) were used to analyze living arrangements of the older population in Peninsular Malaysia. Specifically, factors influencing the probability of seniors to co reside with an adult child were considered. Factors include housing costs, income and rural-urban location, along with senior and adult child characteristics such as health, age, marital status, education and ethnicity. The MFLS-2 data came from a senior sample of 1359 respondents 50 years of age and older and was conducted between August 1988 and January 1989. The logistic regression analysis was conducted under the hypothesis that co residence is affected by costs and benefits of co residence, opportunities for co residence and preferences of seniors and their adult children. Analysis supports the hypothesis of association (Chan et al., 1991).

Analysis of data from surveys of the elderly conducted in 1984 on the socioeconomic, cultural and demographic determinants of living arrangements of the elderly in Fiji, Korea, Malaysia and the Philippines revealed that the availability of kin—spouse and children—plays an important role in determining the living arrangements of the elderly. Models estimated include a logit model of living with children or not and a multinomial logit model with 4 outcomes: living alone, living with spouse only, living with children and living with other. Being male raises the probability of living with children, but, surprisingly, living with children declines with age. Living in an urban area in Philippines is positively associated with living with children, but home-ownership and being self-supporting are negatively associated with living with children in several countries. Education and health of the respondent have little effect on living arrangements, but variables such as religiosity and ethnicity do (Martin, 1998).

The foreign-born elderly in Canada include persons who immigrated as young adults but have now grown old as well as persons who have immigrated late in life, usually under the auspices of family reunification. Considerable diversity exists among the elderly as a result of these echoes of past and current migration flows. Yet, the implication of such diversity has not been extensively researched. Previously married elderly women who arrived as children or as young adults are less likely than other groups including the native born to live with family. The percentage living with family instead of living alone or with non relatives is highest for women immigrating at age 65 or later (Boyd, 1988).

Japan is known to have had extended families throughout its history. Before the industrial revolution, the prevalent family system in Japan was the stem family in which a married couple lived with their unmarried children, the eldest son, his wife and their grandchildren. 3 surveys in the 1980s now show that roughly 50 per cent of people aged 60 or older lived with their married children, about 20 per cent lived with their unmarried children, another 20 per cent lived with their spouses only and 10 per cent lived alone. In the US, before the turn of this century, the nuclear family dominated. Only 1/6 of the American elderly lived with their adult children. However, extended family systems were once more prevalent in the US than they are today. In 1952, 1/3 of the aged lived with their children, 1/4 by 1957 and 1/5 by the mid-1960s. The dominant view of current social science seems to be that industrialization is the driving force behind change in family systems; industrialization requires geographical mobility and weakens the kin network. It lets public and voluntary systems instead of kin groups solve problems. Recent changes in Japan's family structure suggest that the effects of industrialization are so strong in Japan that the status of the elderly is steadily being undermined in favor of nuclear families. Care for older people is becoming an urgent problem, as it has become in the US and in most other industrialized countries (Kamo, 1988).

A study on the living arrangements of people 60 and over in Mexico, Costa Rica, the Dominican Republic, Panama, Colombia and Peru found that a majority of older people live in complex family households, but that this is considerably more probable for unmarried people than for married people. In addition, a significant number of both married and unmarried older people still live in simple family households with one or more never-married children. Unmarried older people are much more likely than currently-married people to live in complex family households. Among the married, people 70 years and older are generally less likely than people 60-69 to live in a complex family household rather than with a spouse only. Finally, women are more likely to live in complex family households than are men, but this depends both on marital status and on the alternative to complex family living. Although unmarried women are much more likely than unmarried men to live in a complex family household instead of a non-family household, married women are less likely than married men to live in a complex family household rather than an empty nest. Overall, complex family living is greater in rural areas among the married but less among the unmarried. For education, there was an overall negative relationship among married people in the major urban areas, but not among unmarried older people. The relationship appears clearest in Costa Rica, in contrast to Peru. Results from all 6 countries tend to be similar, though some differences are noted. Colombia and Peru follow an extended family system most closely whereas the Dominican Republic and Panama tend to have the lowest incidence of husband-wife-children or single-parent households. Costa Rica and Mexico follow the most conjugal of the extended family systems. The implication is that change in Mexico and Costa Rica might be most similar to that which occurred in the US-change toward more separate living among older people (De Vos, 1987).

The analysis of data from the study on "A Multi-dimensional, Diachronic Study of Ageing in Beijing" conducted between 1992 and 1994 found that during a period of 2 years; the living arrangements of the elderly underwent dramatic changes. Elderly people who used to live in two-generation households were now living in three-generation or single households. A higher percentage of elderly people chose to live separately from their children to avoid family conflict. Despite the reform of social security systems and promotion of elderly care in the Chinese society, a rising percentage of elderly people still believe that "one raises children in order to have support in old age." The changes in the family structure of the elderly calls for certain practical measures geared at consolidating the role of the family and society in caring for the elderly (Du, 1998).

Results from two research projects, supported by the Administration on Ageing, provide an appropriate framework for discussing possible changes in patterns of living arrangements among the elderly over the next 20-30 years. Foremost among the conclusions are that 1) living arrangements of older persons are not randomly distributed and 2) the housing behavior of the elderly reflects both their current status and characteristics and their previous life history. Research findings with respect to the determinants of aggregate changes in living arrangements show that the factors influencing individual decisions have temporally constant effect. Changes in population composition were identified as the major factors responsible for generating changes in observed patterns of living arrangements. Changes in the sex-ratio, racial composition and marital status composition of the older population proved to be relatively minor and had comparatively inconsequential effects on aggregate changes. There is no single residential environment that is "good" for all older people or for the same persons at different ages. Efforts need to be made to define the types of living arrangements and housing most appropriate for specific levels of functional ability. A wider range of alternatives should be made available to older persons who want to sustain independent living as long as possible. The orientation of current service programs targeted at older persons also must be seriously evaluated (Soldo, 1978).

The results of the study on the demographic and socioeconomic correlates of living arrangements of women aged 60 years and over in Lesotho show that a majority of elderly women in the country are widows, live in the rural areas, have had little education and dwell in extended family households of which a significant proportion of them are the head. The findings further indicate that the age of the women's surviving children and advancing age of the elderly themselves are important factors contributing to kin co residence of the Lesotho elderly female population. The propensity of co residence is found to increase with advancing age, while higher levels of educational attainment have significant negative correlation with the likelihood of kin co residence. A combination of fertility decline, migration and urbanization puts the older women in a disadvantaged position since there are fewer adult children available to provide support and care and there is no universal non- familial social security system (Mba, 2002).

In India, gradually the sex ratio is getting evened out. India was one of the few countries with the dubious distinction of having an unfavorable female to male ratio in the population with demographic changes. Now there will be older women in India too. But the bad news is that they are likely to be more vulnerable due to socio-cultural reasons. Older women are likely to have more health problems, less likely to be financially independent and have less power and status compared to old man. India lives in her village, old people in rural areas face several hard ships while being deprived of basic amenities that take granted with migration and urbanization depriving rural areas of its able bodied empty young people, rural areas will become packets of poverty living arrangements also change leading to problems in providing security to elderly (Indira Jai Prakesh, 2001).

A study on the living arrangements of elderly revealed that except a few (7 per cent), all most all elderly live with their children. These few are living by themselves in single household because of not having any children. Among the others, 73 per cent live with their sons whereas 20 per cent with their daughters (Dharmalingam et al., 2001).

More elderly are now living in joint households, with one or more married sons and some other relatives than about 50 years ago. However, the rest of the older persons either live alone or with spouse and also in pilgrim centres and old age homes (Shah et al., 1997).

A comparative study of living arrangement of elderly conducted in TamilNadu, revealed that a remarkably large percentage of respondents (40 per cent) from Chennai lived with their spouse independently whereas in Coimbatore, 35 per cent of the sample lived in joint-family setup (Hema Nalini et al., 2002).

The results of a study on the living arrangement of elderly revealed that only 9.16 per cent of respondents lived alone and 18.33 per cent lived with spouse only. Majority of respondents (77.50 per cent) lived with their children (38.34 per cent as couples and 34.17 per cent as widows) and 95 per cent lived in their own house (Sundhar et al., 2004).

Majority of the oldest old women (68–88 per cent) and men (59-83 per cent) aged 80-105 lived with their children. The higher the age, higher the proportion of the oldest old living with their children. Female oldest old of all age groups are more likely to live with their children because they are more likely to be widowed and economically dependent (Zengyi et al., 2002).

Most of the elderly stay with their unmarried children, when it comes to sharing their inner feeling of life, like joys and sorrows. They preferred and considered their wife as their close and intimate person in the family. It is also pointed out that the respondents have maintained friendly relations with their grown-up-children (Jayashree, 1999).

In a study on Living arrangement of elderly found that on an average the Indian elderly are residing in a household where at least seven members are living. Interestingly, Only 2.4 per cent of the elderly are living alone and another 3.5 per cent are residing with other relatives or non-relatives. More elderly female (3.49 per cent) are living alone compared with males (1.42 per cent). In other worlds, only 6 per cent of elderly in India are living in a family where their immediate kinship is not present in the household (Irudaya Rajan et al., 2003).

Another study on the Living arrangement of elderly both in rural and Urban areas found that 7.31 per cent of the elderly in rural areas as against 5.54 per cent of the elderly in the urban areas are living alone. Living with children is more common among the urban elderly (50 per cent) than the rural elderly (48.57 per cent). On the other hand, percentage of elderly living with spouse is more in the rural areas (37 per cent) than in the urban areas (35.26 per cent) (Ilango Ponnuswami, 1987).

The National Sample Survey Organization (NSSO) report of 1991 indicates that there is no significant difference in the living arrangements in both rural and urban areas. Elderly mostly stay with their adult children and about 7 per cent of men and 11 per cent of women were supported by their spouses. Approximately three-fourths were supported by their own children and about 8 per cent and 12 per cent of elderly men and women, respectively were supported by others (National Sample Survey Organization, 1991).

A study on the level of life satisfaction among the elderly people according to their age and type of family found that the younger respondents had greater life satisfaction and the respondents who were living separately from their children were more satisfied than those who were living with their married or unmarried children (Hosmath et al., 1993).

Old people living with their families have cordial relation with their children and spouse, their social interaction are good and they have a positive frame of mind. But this cannot be said about people living in institutions as they do not have cordial relations with their children and spouse, they do not feel good about themselves and they do not have peace of mind (Sudha Katyal et al., 1999).

PSYCHOLOGICAL PROBLEMS

Older people are often victims of mental disorders on account of their fear about death and feelings of dependency, anxiety, boredom, loneliness and helplessness. The treatment and the diagnosis of psychological problems are not yet prioritized. Many old people suffer from mental illness, which their families may not even be aware of them.

Every human being has emotional attachment to their own kins and creeds. The socio-biological view considers the phenomenon of social support to be deeply rooted in our biological inheritance, providing a central influence in our success of life form (Richard E. Pearson's, 1999).

One of the major psychological problems of elderly women is loneliness as most of them are widowed and also due to mobilization. The concepts of loneliness with particular reference to old age suggested that successful treatment of loneliness in life reduces the risk of more serious complication, such as feelings of meaninglessness, decrease in social contacts, self esteem and trust (Asgarali Patel et al., 2000).

In Kerala, which has the highest proportion of elderly in India and has several social security schemes, 73.6 per cent of the rural females and 76 per cent of the urban females are fully dependent on others. This shows that vulnerable elderly women are even in Kerala, known for its high order of social investment.

Aged face psychological problems like decreased vitality, loss of work, reduced income, isolation, age associated disability, lack of protection and supervision, deteriorating mental function which often leads to psychological problems (Sunil Goyal et al., 1999).

Changing society had an over all negative impact on their well being of aged. A negative impact of changing times a mental well being was evident from views expressed by respondents and strongest feeling was increasing loneliness and alienation in lives of elderly due to changing orders of society, elderly are more sad and depression in the materialistic world and feeling of mental insecurity is due to lack of moral support from adult children due to emotional and physical distancing from them (Sundhar et al., 2004).

The rural aged were found to suffer from anxiety, alienation, maladjustment, fear, tension, feeling of insecurity, worthlessness, dependency, loss of memory, vision, hearing, giddiness and body pain (Selvi, 2001).

Successful treatment of loneliness in old age reduces the risk of more serious complications, such as feeling of meaninglessness, decrease in social contacts, self-contacts, self-esteem and trust. Loneliness among the aged can be reduced by acceptance, reflection, social interaction and increased activity. Loneliness has been conceived as a problem for every one and the elderly experience more loneliness because their spouse might be deceased, their friends might have either moved away or died. Their children might be in distant places and they themselves might be subject to physical disabilities. Industrialization and urbanization have weakened the traditional joint family set up in India and elderly persons are least or not wanted in the social set up of a family or society at large resulting in loneliness and anxiety about death (Weeks, 1994).

An old person begins to feel that even his children do not look upon him with that degree of respect which he used to get some years earlier. The old person feels neglected and humiliated. This may lead to the development of psychology of shunning the company of others; loneliness in turn may give risk to depression and may eventually lead to worsening of sickness (Chowdhry, 1992).

A study on the psycho-social problems of the retired concluded that age had a significant positive relationship with psychological distress and significant negative relationship with attitude towards physical changes (Prema B. Patil, 2000).

After retirement there is a feeling of loneliness, perception of void in life, financial problem, loss of status accompanied by a sense of alienation and helplessness (Majumdar, 1985).

Psychological problems such as loss of job, anxiety, depression, loneliness, loss of social support, neglect, abuse and exploitation were faced by the elderly (Hema Nalini et al., 2002).

In a study on aged, the percapita income was found to have negative and significant relationship with depression and the number of children was found to have positive and non-significant relationship with depression (Patil et al., 1998). Gradually elderly people develop a feeling of uselessness and purposelessness. Opportunities should be made available to the aged to fulfill their varied kind of needs adequately (Surendra Singh, 1997).

In a study on the psychological problems of elderly, it is found that 88 per cent old people were found suffering from mental tension. 74.5 per cent were found suffering from fear of death, 71.7 per cent were found suffering from the feeling of dependency, 70 per cent were found suffering from anxiety, 62.5 per cent were found suffering from the feeling of loneliness, 60 per cent were found suffering from the feeling of helplessness, 52.5 per cent old people were found suffering from depression, 52 per cent were found suffering from the feeling of uselessness. In this study 70 per cent old people did not know whether they were suffering from whims, 16 per cent said that they were not suffering from whims where as 14 per cent old people were suffering from whims 80 per cent old people felt that they have mental freedom (Hitesh Patel, 1997).

It is observed in a study that a sizable majority of the aged suffer from loss of memory, lack of proper vision, no sleep and losing teeth. Psychologically a maximum number of the aged feel isolated, frustrated and depressed. A good number of the aged feel separation of children as a major set back in their life. Majority of them feel that there is no respect and importance in the family. Sizable number feels lonely following death of spouse (Siva Raju, 2002).

Depression increased with aged people. Gender wise comparison revealed that females had low level of depression compared to males. The depression level of the respondents living in joint family was less (Prema D. Patil, et al., 2000).

A study on the psycho-social problems of aged in the Indian perspective based on 160 retired people from central and state services belonging to urban and rural area of Ratna district highlight that elderly people are facing multitude of problems. As people grow older, they usually become less interested in life and more concerned about death. When health deteriorates, they tend to concentrate on death and become preoccupied with it. This is in contrast with the perception of life by younger people. The study found that habit, gender and caste play significant role in the adjustment of aged people. It was also found that rural aged was more adjusted than urban aged (Ratique Alam et al., 1997).

A study on the role of adjustment and status it aged conducted among the Bengali Population of Meghalaya found that feeling of isolation was high in female and they had poor life satisfaction. Income seems to be a very important factor influencing adjustment. Widowed older women being dependant on families, face several problems in adjusting to others (Bannerjee Mrinmayi Tyagi et al., 2001).

A study conducted in two places to estimate the prevalence of dementia, one in a rural and other in an urban area of Madras, India found that the prevalence of dementia was 3.5 per cent in the rural and 2.7 per cent in the urban sample and increased exponentially with age. Rural prevalence estimates were higher than the urban estimates. Though gender differences were negligible in the rural setting, dementia rates were significantly higher among urban males in contrast to urban females. The authors compare the findings of the two studies and discuss their implications for India's growing elderly population in the context of age, literacy and gender (Rajkumar et al., 1998).

Most of the studies reviewed in this section indicate that all most all elderly had one or the other psychological problems and the psychological problems tend to increase with age.

HEALTH PROBLEMS

Human organs gradually diminish in function overtime although not at the same rate in every individual by itself, this gradual diminution of function is not a real threat to the health of most old people unless they fall prey to some disease. Disease are the chief barriers to extended health and longevity and when they accompany normal changes associated with logical ageing maintaining health and securing appropriate health care becomes especially problematic for older person. Health in simplest term is defined as the absence of disease or illness. Health is not only a biological or medical concern, but also a significant personal and social concern. In general, with declining health, individuals can lose their independence, lose social roles, become isolated, experience economic hardship, be labeled or stigmatized, change their self-perception and some of them may even be institutionalized (Ketshukietuo DzuvichÜ, 2005). Morbidity pattern among the elderly varied from country to country. Chronic conditions which produced infirmity and disability became more common in old age.

The major problems of elderly are health care and economic hardship. Furthermore these problems will increases with increased industrialization and modernization. It is also deduces that (1) a large majority of India's aged do not have any problem or are indifferent to them. (2) in the lower socio-economic classes, poor health and poverty are elderly's major problems (3) elderly persons from the upper strata of society have expressed more concern for social problems such as social obligations and law and other (4) a significantly large proportion of elderly males are economically active. However probably due to industrialization this proportion has shown a declining trend. This would add further to the economic hardship of the aged and would make them more dependent on their children (Goyal, 1989).

Old age in general is associated with multi-dimensional problems. The problems which are associated with age and the care of elderly are not exclusively the problems of social, cultural and economic ramifications, rather they include health and medical problems also that affect the life of a community as well paradoxically, it is the advance technology of medicine, which in turn facilitating contraception and reducing morbidity during the second half of life has eventually increased the prominence to the needs of the elderly. Health status is an important factor in deciding the quality of life of the rural elderly along with certain related factors such as service availability, awareness and accessibility (Vijaya Kumar, 1998).

The extension in life expectancy has been accompanied by an increase in the level of chronic diseases, including heart disease, diabetes, hypertension and arthritis. Also of concern is the weakening of traditional informal support systems, both community and family and the marginalization and elimination of the elderly's social and economic roles (Eldermire, 1997).

Analysis of data on persons 65 and over years of age drawn from National Sample Survey, Sample Registration System and Censes of India revealed that, gender is a very important variable that influences quality of life at all ages. Of the population over 70 years of age, more than 50 per cent suffer from one or more chronic conditions. Lack of social support, breaking up of joint family system, changing life-styles; all aggravates health and nutritional problems in elderly age group. While elderly people in India may have reasonable access to family care, they are inadequately covered by economic and health security (Susuman, 2005).

As part of a broader study of ageing and health conditions in rural India, 267 persons over 60 years old from Uttar Pradesh's Varanasi district were interviewed in 1990. Overall, 37 per cent of men and 70 per cent of women rated their health condition as "bad." The incidence of illness after age 60 years was 77 per cent among women and 61 per cent among men. Most common were chest problems such as asthma, tuberculosis and bronchitis. The percentage of unhealthy persons was slightly lower among illiterates and those with a university education than men and women with primary or middle school educational levels. These educational differences are presumed to reflect class-based occupational histories. In general, those with middle levels of education were employed in household industry or businesses with high exposure to disease. Men and women with unsatisfactory, conflictual family relationships also experienced increased health problems (Yadava et al., 1996).

The analysis of data on persons 65+ years of age drawn from the 42nd Round of the National Sample Survey found that, among population over 60 years of age, 10 per cent suffer from impaired physical mobility and 10 per cent are hospitalized at any given time, both proportions rising with increasing age. Of the population over 70 years of age, more than 50 per cent suffer from one or more chronic conditions (Reddy, 1996).

A survey conducted in 29 randomly selected villages in Jaipur to determine the incidence of chronic bronchitis among persons aged 60 or over found that 70 per cent had chronic bronchitis. The prevalence of the disease increased significantly with age among the males and was unrelated to socioeconomic status or smoking. Chronic bronchitis was also more common among males (85.9 per cent as compared to 50.1 per cent). While the incidence of the disease was not related to marital status, it was inversely proportional to economic status and significantly related to smoking. More men were smokers and chronic bronchitis occurred twice as often in the smokers as in nonsmokers, being especially prevalent in smokers of 45 years duration (Purohit et al., 1974).

A study conducted on a sample of Assamese- and Bengali-speaking populations of the Hindu and Muslim religions in Assam found that due to low education, poor economic conditions and rural backgrounds, the scheduled caste people reported poor access to health care facilities. Moreover, elderly persons having sanitary latrines and tapped or tube well water were healthier than those without proper sanitation and tapped/tube well water. Use of electricity is also associated with good health among the elderly. In addition, elderly persons who have a separate sleeping room with their spouses have better health than the elderly who share sleeping quarters with other family members. The findings revealed that socioeconomic, demographic and ecological factors have an important role in the health of old people. Most elderly people could have better health if they received better health care and followed healthy life styles (Nath et al., 2000).

A study on the socioeconomic and health status of the aged in the rural areas of Karnataka, India revealed that the incidence and prevalence of chronic as well as non-chronic diseases is obviously high among the elderly. The major chronic diseases are 1) respiratory diseases, 2) loco-motor illnesses and 3) blood pressure. The duration of illness is comparatively longer among males. The majority of the aged have been treated by private physicians. Since the social and health problems of the elderly are peculiar and considering their growing population size, a huge infrastructural development will be necessary to take care of their health and social needs. This is even more important in view of the reduction in family size, the nuclearization of families and the erosion of family kinship ties even in rural areas of the country (Nair, 1989).

There are more women than men at any elderly age group. Depression and osteoporosis are the commonest problems in elderly subjects. Some problems specific to males are hypogonadism, erectile dysfunction and enlargement of prostate and to females are post-menopausal disturbances, urinary incontinence and breast and lung cancer. However, problems of special concern in both male and female elderly are malnutrition, falls and cognitive dysfunction. Men and women in general suffer from the same sorts of health problems but the frequency of these problems as well as the speed of the onset of death distinguishes them. In fact cultural and social forces act to separate the sexes in their personal health ethos and their sick propensity. The impact of old age on women is different from that of men because of differences in their status and role in society. This is specially so because proportion of widows in 60+ age group is considerably higher than of widowers. Sexuality is often overlooked as a health status particularly in elderly women. Clinicians should recognise the importance of sexual functions to the overall health of older persons particularly women. Religious participation and involvement are associated with positive mental and physical health. Family life is the key to the health of elders' especially older men. Lack of social support increases the risk of mortality and supportive relationships are associated with lower illness rates, faster recovery rates and higher levels of health care behavior (Dhar, 2001).

Morbidity due to cancer, coronary heart disease (CHD), diabetes, hypertension and arteriosclerosis had increased while there was a decline in morbidity among the elderly from conditions like skin diseases, visual and hearing handicaps and multiple orthopedic problems (WHO, 1989).

A study of 658 elderly in a rural area found 20.15 per cent of males and 68.1 per cent of females widowed. The women were found to be poorer, suffering a lot having more morbidity than the men, in spite of their greater life expectancy. The diagnosed illness included hypertension (18.4 per cent), arthritis and joint complaints (12.1 per cent), chronic bronchitis (11.7 per cent), diabetes (9.5 per cent) and coronary heart disease (5.7 per cent). Chronic bronchitis and diabetes were more among the males whereas hypertension was more among the females. 20.9 per cent of men and 32.8 per cent of women were habituated to chewing of betel leaves. Perceived morbidity was higher among the females than men (Vijayakumar, 1994).

A study on the problems of the oldage people conducted in a village in Dindigul District of TamilNadu found that only 22.36 per cent accounted for overall good health and the remaining suffered with bone disorders, digestive problems, ulcers, headaches, respiratory problem, etc. Better the health is better the adjustment to retirement and life (Kesavan, 1998).

A study on psycho-social perspectives, problems and strategies for the welfare of the rural female aged found that a majority suffered from joint pain, blood pressure and chest pain. A few complained of asthma, piles, loss of weight, diabetes and skin disease. Only 30 per cent among the rural aged were in good health (Pappathi et al., 2005).

A study on the nutritional and health problems of the aged found that the rural aged suffered from nutritional, psychological and other problems, when compared to urban aged. The aged employed privately and those self-employed had more of health problems than not gainfully employed persons. In general, the male members were found to be literate, economically independent and had less physiological and nutritional problems when compared to the female counter parts, when the literacy level, income level and employment status improved; they seemed to have better health (Vasantha et al., 1998).

A study on rural aged found that disengagement from work is very rare among the young aged (60-70 years) males. The most prevalent illness among the aged are loss of eye sight, arthritis, tuberculosis, asthma, skin diseases, urinary infections and general body pain. Very few have reported that they are living in good health (Lalitha, 1998).

Joint problems are a common feature among the elderly in Kerala while the disease like cough and blood pressure was also reported by a sizable section of elderly population. The prevalence rates are 480, 204 and 170 for joint problems, cough and blood pressure respectively. The chronic disease such as piles (53 per cent), heart disease (40 per cent) and urinary problem (37 per cent) are also prevalent in the population. The age wise differential showed that the chronic diseases such as cough, joint problem are common in the old-old category. Heart disease and blood pressure are more frequent among the young old. Sex wise differentials are clear with the burden of joint problems and blood pressure being more among economically dependent persons than their counter parts who are independent or partially dependent on others for their livelihood (Dillip, 2001).

Another study found joint pain as the number one problem followed by failing eyesight and cardiac problems. It is interesting to note that in spite of high level of prevalence of diseases among the elderly at most 63 per cent of them reported that their health status was good (Hema Nalini et al., 2002).

A study on the general physical health of Brahmin women aged 60 and above found that 5 per cent of elderly suffered from major diseases. Almost a quarter of them suffered from cardiovascular problems and an equally high frequency was observed for maturity on set diabetes and four each had asthma and cancer. Increasing trend in the incidence of various so called minor health complaints commonly associated with advancing age was observed. Eye ailments ranked highest (55 per cent). Half of them suffered from gastric disorders. 44 per cent from urinary incontinence and nearly one third had hearing problems of varying degrees. Statistically significant increase in sensory impairments such as hearing and eye ailments, arthritis and urinary incontinence from young-old to old-old was well demonstrated in them (Bagga et al., 1999).

A study conducted to find out the health problems of the aged in Nagaland found that a majority of the aged suffer from one or a combination of ailments but many of them either regard themselves to be in excellent condition or are indifferent to their health and consider it as common in old. Despite of all ailments and handicaps, the medical facilities available for the aged are inadequate and many aged are compelled to seek help from private practitioner's inspite of their poor economic status (Ketshukietue DzuvichÜ, 2005).

A study on health conditions of the aged population of Allahabad city found that the health of the aged male is better than that of his female counterpart. Most of them suffer from more than one health problem. The most common illnesses are abdominal problems, cold, cough and fever. Almost all the respondents of this study have gone for allopathic treatment for their major ailments more than half the patients obtained treatment from private hospitals, three fourth from government hospitals and only a very small minority from other sources (Tripathi, 2001).

In a study conducted in Kerala, it was found that only 6 per cent of the aged were in good health while 6.9 per cent in moderate health, 20 per cent in poor health and 5 per cent were in very poor health. The attitude, both professional and general seems to be that the illness was an essential part of old age and most of the illness of the old have no cure but only palliative (Nayar, 2000).

A study of health status of the rural aged in Andhra Pradesh, found that health problems tend to increase with advancing age and very often the problems aggravate due to neglect, poor economic status, social deprivation and inappropriate dietary intake. It was found that a higher proportion of the total respondents (sample of 300 elderly) stated that they were suffering from serious illness and lack of medical facilities in the village and poor economic condition might be responsible for the lower health status of the village (Rao, 2003).

The health problems of elderly tend to increase with advancing age and very often the problem aggravated due to neglect, poor economic status, social deprivation and inappropriate dietary intake. Hence a large majority of landless rural aged were suffering from one or the other health problem and physical disabilities. Indigestion, anemia, blood pressure, skin diseases, poor eye sight, respiratory problems, urinary/ kidney troubles and diseases of joints with varying degrees of affliction were some of the physical ailments with which the landless rural aged were suffering (Chandra Paul Singh, 2005).

With the advancement of age, the illness of elderly becomes more chronic. It is evident that many of the elderly are suffering from more than one combination of ailments. Cough, cold, fever and abdominal problems are common illness reported by the elderly (Vijayakumar, 1998).

Out of the total elderly living in rural India, about 45 per cent are suffering from chronic disease and 5.4 per cent are immobile. The elderly suffer from problems like ophthalmologic, bone and joints, hearing, gastrointestinal, cardiovascular, respiratory, nervous system, skin, endocrinal and nutritional disorders (NSSO, 1991).

A study on the morbidity pattern of aged found that multiple morbidities were common in 89.62 per cent of aged. Amongst men, the leading symptoms are visual impairment (65 per cent), chronic cough with (or) without expectoration and difficulty in breathing (58.06 per cent), joint pains (51.86 per cent), hearing problems (18.36 per cent), gastrointestinal problems (9.98 per cent) and 4.2 per cent experienced problems of isolation, loneliness and felt depressed. Amongst female, the predominant prevalent morbidities comprised of visual impairment (56.2 per cent), joint pain (55.2 per cent), cough and breathing problems (27.95 per cent), hearing problem (22.5 per cent), gastrointestinal problems (7.14 per cent), followed by loneliness and depression (5-8 per cent) (Sunder lal et al., 1999).

In a study on the disease pattern of the retirees, blood pressure is rated the highest (19.25), diabetes is rated second (14.18) and problems with ears and eyes as third (8.64). It is followed by muscular pain, frequent colds, insufficient sleep, dental, throat and heart problems (Jayashree, 2004). Another study on the health status of elderly revealed that only 20 per cent of senior citizens did not suffer from any disease, 22.5 per cent each were suffering from hypertension and arthritis, 7.5 per cent each were suffering from asthma and diabetes mellitus, 5 per cent were found to have heart disease and anemia and 10 per cent of elderly were suffering from other disease (Suresh, 2002).

Health problems of the aged widows are also important. A study conducted in the urban setting of West Bengal found that 41.82 per cent widows are with inadequate treatment facilities and unbalanced diet and 21.43 per cent widows are free from chronic disease as well the problem of senility. Out of 55 widows (78.57 per cent) of various types of diseases, the highest percentages are subjected to suffer chronic diseases which are neglected at their early stage (Samita Manna et al., 1990).

The Indian Council of Medical Research (ICMR) has attempted to compile data on morbidity from different sources. The total number of blind persons among the older population was around 11 million in 1996, eighty per cent of them due to cataract (Angra et al., 1997). The consequences of blindness are not limited only to physical disability that ensues, but also impinge on economic, social and psychological domains of the affected individual's life. Nearly 60 per cent of older people are said to have hearing impairment in both urban and rural areas. The hearing loss and resultant communication problems adversely affect the well being of older people (Kacker, 1997).

In 1996 the number of hypertensive among the elderly population was nearly nine million. The prevalence rate of coronary heart disease among the urban population was nearly three times higher than rural population and the estimated number of cases was around nine million in 1996 (Shah et al., 1997).

An estimated five million were diabetic and the prevalence rates were about 177 for urban and 35 per 1000 for rural elderly people. Crude prevalence rate of strokes is estimated to be about 200 per 1,00,000 persons. Older persons surviving through peak years of stroke (55-65 years) with varying degrees of disability are already a major medical problem (Dalal, 1997).

Age related changes in immune system render people susceptible to a variety of infections and tumors. Though tuberculosis related mortality has declined, it is still not eradicated effectively and the prevalence rate is reported to be higher in the older age group (Dey et al., 1997).

Adverse reactions and major side effects to anti-tuberculosis therapy have been reported in as much as 40 per cent of the cases. Disabilities arising from ageing assume greater significance as a large segment of this population is below the poverty line. Under nutrition is also common in this population (Srivastava et al., 1996).

The nutrients least adequately supplied in the diet of the aged Indian are calcium, iron, vitamin A, riboflavin and niacin. Health is a key contribution factor to quality of life and is therefore closely associated to low socio-economic conditions (Bali, 1997).

The analysis of data obtained from a 1987-88 special survey conducted in the 42nd round of the NSSO, the 1981 NSSO on disabilities and death surveys in rural areas, found that the elderly suffer from conditions specific to this population that are accumulated over the life cycle. The major causes of death for persons aged over 50 years are respiratory diseases (18-19 per cent), diseases of the circulatory system (10 per cent), disorders of the central nervous system (12 per cent), senility (almost 50 per cent) and other causes (12 per cent). 75 per cent of respiratory deaths are due to bronchitis and asthma. Air pollution causes chronic respiratory damage. The most vulnerable people are the elderly, children, smokers and those with chronic respiratory problems. Almost two-thirds of circulatory system deaths are due to heart attacks. Paralysis is a common cause of central nervous system deaths. Cancer accounts for almost 50 per cent of other diseases. Medically certified deaths among those aged over 55 years show the major causes as heart attacks, ill-defined conditions, infectious and parasitic diseases, respiratory system diseases and neoplasms. Senility causes are unknown causes. Compared to mortality among the working-age population, the elderly suffer more from respiratory diseases and paralysis, especially men. Senility is higher among women. 45 per cent of the elderly have some chronic disease. 80 per cent of the chronically-ill suffer from joint problems, coughs and high blood pressure. Elderly morbidity follows a residence and gender pattern. Around 10 per cent suffer from disabilities. Blindness is highest among the elderly, especially women. Women experience conditions related to menopause (Rao et al., 1998).

The prevalence of the inflammatory joint disorder in elderly is underestimated at present time. Rheumatoid arthritis (RA) was commonest rheumatologic disorder observed. 41 patients of RA who developed disease at or after 60 years were compared with 100 younger adult with RA. A relatively higher male to female ratio was observed in late onset category (p is equal to 0.05). The pattern of joint involvement revealed that shoulder joint was more often first affected (26.82 percent versus 6.42 percent). However, on statistical comparison between all large and small joints involved, no significant difference was noted. Deformities were more common in elderly (39.02 percent compared to 29 percent, p is equal to <0.01). Surprisingly erosive type of RA was less frequently observed in the elderly (p is equal to<0.041). The ESR was significantly higher in elderly RA patients (p is equal to >0.004). The rheumatoid factors' positivity was comparable in both groups (Meena et al., 1995).

Studies show that health problems of the elderly shift from communicable and infectious diseases to non-communicable disease. Poor nutrition and lack of clinical care are known to be important factors explaining the health profile of the persons. The health conditions of elderly are making a great demand for geriatric services. There is an unmet need for health care and social security services for elderly. Hence there is a need for a community based health care strategy to care and protect the welfare of the aged in the country. Old age manifests different diseases and these diseases have a compound effect with each other. Hence there is a need to assess the living conditions of the older population and the care and support available to them in order to develop appropriate social security and health care measures for the vulnerable elderly population.

DISABILITIES

Measuring the prevalence of functional disability among older people is extremely important. The number of older people is projected to increase in both the developed and the developing countries. The incidence and prevalence of functional disability are high among older people and they are higher at older ages (Kovar, 1991).

A study on the prevalence of physical disabilities, their differentials and determinants based on the data collected from 750 old persons (aged 60+ years) selected from nine rural (450) and six urban (300) clusters of TamilNadu State, in India found that half of the elderly population in the study areas is suffering from one or the other forms of physical disability. Logistic regression analysis shows that the likelihood of physical disabilities increases significantly with an increase in age. Elderly persons who live in urban areas have significantly lower proportion of physical disability as compared to their rural counterparts. It was also observed that elderly people who belong to the higher socio-economic class were found to have lesser disabilities (Audinarayana et al., 2002).

In the old-old group, there is likely to be a minority with no or mild disability in any domain of functioning. The majority, however, will have multiple disabilities, while a sizable group will have difficulties with instrumental activities of daily living (Zarit et al., 1993).

Visual impairments are reported in 11 million Indians, while 38 million have hearing impairments. Hypertension among the urban elderly was twice as high as among the rural elderly. Older subjects had nearly 20 times higher prevalence of hypertension compared to total population (Shah et al., 1997).

A study conducted on the burden of ill health among elderly in Kerala found that visual disability was the most prominent form of disability among elderly followed by locomotors, hearing, senility and speech disability. Sex wise differentials showed that the conditions like visual, hearing and speech disabilities to be predominant for females than males. The prevalence of all these forms of disabilities was found to be much higher in rural areas than in urban areas and for elderly from poor household than their counterparts with better economic status (Dillip, 2001).

The prevalence of disability in at least one of five ADL items (6.6 per cent in those aged > or = 65) appeared lower than elsewhere, including China, but higher than reported past prevalence within the country. Functional disability on at least one of the 10 ADL items was independently associated with female sex, Indian ethnicity, older age, poor self-rated health, specific chronic diseases, cognitive impairment, sensory impairment and living with others(Ng et al., 1988).

Elderly people needed care because of physical disability more often than behavioural disability. Those with physical disability received more formal services and more help from health professionals than those with behavioural disability. Contact with general practitioners was high for both disabled and non-disabled subjects. Carers of the physically disabled had raised levels of anxiety and symptoms of depression and poorer self-rated health, but carers of the behaviourally disabled did not. Wives, daughters and husbands made up the biggest categories of carers and around two-thirds of carers were women (Jorm et al., 2001).

The extent of mobility and changes in living arrangements associated with disability were studied using data from the Longitudinal Study of Ageing for 1984-86. It was hypothesized that persons with significant limitations in their ability to perform normal daily activities (ADLs and IADLs) in 1984 would be more likely to move, more likely to be living with others in 1986 and more likely to have entered an institution between 1984-86 than those without limitations. When only those variables which were measured in 1984 were used as predictors, this turned out to be true for institutionalization and for living with others in 1986. However, residential mobility showed little relationship to disability when other variables were controlled. When the change in disability between 1984 and 1986 was added to the prediction equation, there were strong relationships between changes in disability and all three types of adjustment in living arrangements (Speare et al., 1988).

In a study of disability among elderly, it was found that less than 4 per cent experienced difficulty with self-maintenance activities of daily living, but 30 per cent had difficulty with instrumental activities. The former were all visually impaired and both visual and mobility problems contributed to the latter. Elderly people experienced many symptoms but had inadequate access to health services and used medication infrequently. Subjects were mainly self-sufficient for financial income and 60 per cent still worked. They had declining resources with age and received little help from the social welfare department. Their health and functional abilities deteriorated with age but it was older subjects who had most difficulty getting to the clinic. Simple measures such as cataract surgery and analgesics were available only to the minority or not at all (Allain et al., 1997).

A study on the physiological status of elderly found that up to 53 per cent of the elderly (61 per cent of males and 47 per cent of females) were disability-free. Greater disability was associated with higher age, lesser education, worse subjective health, worse subjective vision and worse subjective hearing. No association of disability with female gender and cognitive deficit was found when including age and education in the logistic model (Ania Lafuente, 1985).

Throughout the world all populations are seeing burgeoning numbers of "elders", defined as persons aged 65 year and older. In many countries, including Japan, the United States, Norway, Sweden and the United Kingdom, those aged over 65 are at or approaching 15 per cent of the population. As their numbers have increased, so have their health care expenses, leading to extensive research on the health, well being and life expectancy of these increasingly older elders. Today this group is further sub-divided: the young-old ages 65-74, the old-old ages 75-84 and the oldest-old ages 85+, for both health care and research purposes. However broad variation still characterizes even these groupings. Rates of frailty and disability increase with increasing age among these elders. For example, inabilities to complete at least one activity of daily living increased from about 5-7 per cent at ages 65-69 years to about 28-36 per cent at ages 85+ in 1987. Death rates continue to decline at all ages in the past 50 years and rates of disability seem to be doing the same. For the foreseeable future, we may expect increasing numbers of older, frail elders than in previous decades. Thus, people are not only living longer, they generally are healthier at advanced ages than were previous cohorts, thus "old age" disabilities of the 20th century will be put off to even older ages during the 21st century. As yet there is no clear way to assess senescent changes in humans, although activities of daily living and frailty indices have all been suggested. One future need is greater development and use of universal and accessible design in all aspects of the built environment (Crews et al., 2006).

CARE AND SUPPORT

Population ageing is an inevitable phenomena experienced by many countries and regions in Asia. Until recently, population ageing was not given the right view and interpretation. Population ageing is the change that occurs within the family setup. It is evident that the structure, function and values that are traditionally held by families are rapidly changing. With the social, economic and cultural changes occurring in the society, families are faced with a difficult challenge concerning the position and responsibilities of families towards their elderly relatives. Although, changes are good indicators of development, dilemma for support capacity of the family towards the elderly is inevitable. With many women entering the work force, available support for the elderly has significantly reduced. As a consequence, the International Year of the Family has appealed to the world to maintain, strengthen and protect the family to ensure continuity of its vital role in preserving dignity, status and security of its ageing members. (Achir, 1998).

In most industrial and pre-industrial societies, the family was the main provider of care of their elderly relatives. In many cases, family is merely euphemism used for women who shoulder the main burden of caring for the intimate aspects of personal care and are engaged in taking care for longer period of time (Walker, 1992).

In the developing world, the household is a critical institution for older adults, who often require social, economic and physical assistance. Most industrialized countries have public pension and health systems to support the elderly, but in many developing countries little or no such public support is available. As a result, older adults in Africa, Asia and Latin America tend to rely heavily on household members and family for their well-being and survival. It was noted that as countries become more developed, extended families weaken and families become more nuclear. Therefore, countries with higher levels of education tend to experience more internal migration and to have more extensive government-funded social security and health programs for older adults (Population Briefs, 2001).

Throughout Asia, the proportions of national populations aged 65 years and above are predicted to grow rapidly over the next 50 years. While this process of ageing is already well underway in the more economically developed countries in East Asia, it is just beginning to accelerate in Southeast Asia. This increase in the proportion of the elderly population creates new demands for social and economic support and simultaneously brings to the forefront the concern that changing household structures will translate into a decline in support for the elderly (Beard et al., 2001).

India is a country with the tradition of respecting, loving and supporting the aged. The extended families of several generations under the same roof were the basic unit of production and livelihood in the traditional agricultural society in ancient India. As a result of economic development and westernization, instead of living in joint families, living in nuclear families is becoming the way of the day and this type of transformation brought more difficulties in supporting and taking care of the aged. In India, certain recent developments such as industrialization, high cost of living, migration of children to other places, disintegration of joint family, etc. have given rise to some stresses and strains which have made the position of the aged more problematic. The status of the aged women has been further affected due to less importance being assigned to socio-religious ceremonies in which her knowledge and advice were valuable and less use of her knowledge and experience in child rearing due to greater reliance on modern medicine technology and information. The problem of old age has become a social problem in society like in any other country of the world (Help age India, 2002).

India has been in the past and remains today a predominantly agrarian society. The concentration of older people in the country side was even more striking with over 80 per cent in rural areas. However, the process of urbanization in India is accelerating. It is not surprising that the rural population is older than that of the urban areas. The social implications of this migration can be profound. The combined effects of changes at the level of the community and the gradual rural decline and the corresponding increase in urban areas are presenting great challenges to India's grey population. At an individual level, the process of migration usually begins with a single person often a man moving in to the city. His wife and children, often leaving his parents behind join him later. Thus a new households is formed which grows into a joint-household with the arrival of sons, wives. Meanwhile the elderly parents are left to tend for themselves without the social and emotional support of their children (Shubha Soneja, 2000).

The agricultural economy, the patriarchal joint family system and traditional values such as reverence for age that bound parents and their adult children are the distinguishing characteristics of the ancient Indian culture. In the patriarchal joint family system, the oldest male member of the joint family is the head of the family. Property inheritance is matrilineal (from father to son to grandson). In a joint family, all members of the family live, cook and eat together and share the responsibility of managing common land holdings a business. The oldest male member may also live with his siblings and their children and grand children under the same roof. In such a joint family, its elderly members, even if disabled, are easily taken care of by the other members. Elder care was not a problem (Suryanarayana, 1998).

Indian women are rapidly purling professional career for self-fulfillment as well as joining the work force out of economic necessity. She further adds that with limited help from the men in the family, the care of the elderly adds significantly to her workload. Currently, there is no data to indicate that Indian women's employment has influenced the care of the elderly. However with the passage of time, the potential for abuse, neglect, abandonment of the elderly is likely to increase (Vaswani, 1996). The elderly considered their family as the major support system because they preferred to approach the family in case of any problems and only in absence of the family they sought help from the neighbours. The relatives were approached least because it was not easy to reach them (Bhamini Mehta el al., 2003).

In India, the elderly are playing effective roles in the joint family system which provides them security and emotional support. In a study, it is found that nearly half of the elderly depend financially on their families. In addition 86.16 per cent are being supported by the government through pension scheme which raised their self-esteem and self-reliance to some extent (Sunder Lal et al., 1999).

The youth provided personal care to the elderly in all the possible ways. The men gave medicine to them regularly and accompanied them when they need to go out, whereas the girls and women washed the clothes of the elderly. They also served them food, gave them medicines and cleaned their room (Amirtha Gowri et al., 2003).

The older people are the custodians of our rich cultural heritage. They adhere to universal values and their treasure of practical knowledge and experience guides them to wisdom. They are conserving firm in ideas, slow to adopt new ideas, meticulous in observing rituals and following traditions. They are dogmatic in their approach. There is always a gap between the young and the old. To bridge the gap the parents should socialize their children to promote psychological bonds with old, particularly the traits of love, compassion and obedience towards the elderly. A constructive reciprocity between the aged and the young can mould their attitude and perception in restoring their love and concern for each other and bringing about personality and mental development (Bajpai, 1998).

Evidences showed that the traditional means of support - sons are becoming less reliable. The experience of the elderly, on the other hand, shows that the elderly were in a worse economic situation that would be expected from the Indian Cultural ideal. In particular, the poor and women are most affected in terms of old-age support. The evidence about the link between fertility and old-age support suggests that while existing living conditions make children the main source of support in old age, they are becoming less reliable as a result of recent economic and social changes (Dharmalingam, 1994).

The trend in the size and growth rate of the elderly population in the country will become a major social challenge in the future when vast resources will need to be directed towards the supported care and treatment of the old. To solve the emerging problems of the elderly effectively, a holistic approach has to be followed considering the social, economic and cultural changes that have taken place in Indian society (Sivaraju, 2002).

Researchers and international organizations frequently suggest that elderly women are broadly disadvantaged in comparison to elderly men. An analysis of data from Thailand, however, indicates a far more complex association between gender and various aspects of ageing. The analysis of data from the one per cent sample of the 2000 Thai census and two national surveys of the elderly in Thailand conducted in 1994 and 1995, found that elderly Thai women do face certain disadvantages in comparison to their male counterparts, including lower education and literacy, far greater chances of experiencing widowhood and living alone and lower likelihood of receiving formal retirement benefits. Elderly Thai men, however, face other disadvantages compared to women, including worse survivorship, a lower likelihood of receiving money from adult children and a greater probability of debt and other financial problems. Men are also less likely to feel satisfied with their financial situation. Many other demographic, psychosocial and economic measures are not significantly associated with gender. The analysis provides some support for a life course perspective that relates gender differences in old age to differences in earlier life experiences, roles and reward structures, particularly in terms of access to retirement pensions and the type of support elderly men and women provide to their co resident children. The analysis highlights the importance of marital status and age distinction, which often mediate gender differences in elderly well-being (Sobieszczyk et al., 2002).

Traditionally Indian society has looked after its elderly citizens through the family and community support systems. The social and economic security of elder people, rested in the hands of the younger generation of individual families, which considered such a duty to be sacrosanct and a part of their socio-cultural heritage. However as in other parts of the world urbanization and large scale migration for economic reasons are changing societies and family systems. The average family size is shrinking due to lower birthrates and socio-economic reasons resulting in fewer caregivers. The family activities which required more people providing engagement for healthy elders to some extent are being gradually and very definitely replaced by technology. Women are increasingly stepping, outside the home for employment and higher education, consequently the marginalization of the elder persons within and outside the families is on the rise. Although family ties in India are still live with their family members, the position of an increasing number of older persons is becoming vulnerable. In the present scenario they cannot take it for granted that their children will be able to look after them when they need care in their old age, keeping in view the longer life span which implies an extended period of dependency. The changing roles and expectations of women have also had the impact of reducing the availability of caregivers to discharge the traditional family responsibility of caring for the older members (HelpAge India, 2002).

In the traditional Indian society, the aged occupied position of power and prestige. In the pre-industrial agrarian Indian society, most of the aged people remained financially independent throughout their life. The traditional social and cultural values did not permit the grown up children to leave their parents financially dependent on others and physically insecure. Moreover the prevailing economic, political and social value systems which were based on the preservation of inherited in equality enabled the aged people to enjoy leadership roles in the joint family, caste group and the village community, this traditional system provide social, economic and emotional security to the aged. But, industrialization, urbanization and modernization have changed the values of traditional Indian society. This change in social structure and value system does not seem to be in harmony with the changes in the demographic structure of society. Due to the advances in medical science, improved health standards and better living conditions there has been a steep rise in the population of elderly in India (Chandra Paul Sigh, 2005).

The UN estimated the proportion of the population in Lebanon which was aged 60 years and older at 7.4 per cent in 1970, 7.8 per cent in 1985 and 8.3 per cent in 1995. However, social security systems for the elderly are lacking and there are no technical and administrative units responsible for planning specific services for them. Health professionals, including social workers, receive no formal training in the care of the elderly and no reliable data exist on the supporting role of the family. While cultural and ethical values continue to protect the majority of older people in Lebanon, it is likely that changes in family structure, the declining numbers of children and the increasing numbers of women who work outside of the home have weakened the family as a care giving institution. Warfare and foreign intrusions over the period 1975-91 produced deaths in families, injuries, property destruction, kidnappings and associated threats. During that period, many older people were left homeless and jobless while their savings were eroded. Younger relatives more likely to have migrated out of the country provided little support. Studies have shown that constant exposure to the stresses of war has a long-term impact upon the health of middle-aged and elderly people. Support is needed for Lebanon's elderly (Sibai, 1997).

3

OBJECTIVES AND METHODOLOGY

The Objectives and Methodology followed in this study is presented in the following sections.

OBJECTIVES

- To study the living arrangements and health conditions of elderly in Rural TamilNadu;
- To study the physical mobility status and the ability of elderly to perform activities of daily living;
- To study the physiological, psychological and health problems of elderly in Rural Tamilnadu; and
- To suggest a comprehensive health care strategy and social security measures to provide needed care and support to elderly in rural areas.

HYPOTHESES

1. Increase in age, increase the health, physiological and psychological problems of elderly.
2. The physical movement of elderly decreased with the increase in age.
3. Increase in financial security decrease the psychological problems of elderly.
4. Female elderly are having more health problems than male elderly.

5. The increase in the physical mobility status decrease the psychological problems of elderly
6. The psychological problems of elderly are more among male than female.
7. Female elderly are contributing more to household activities than male elderly.
8. Increase in education decrease the health problems as well as psychological problems of elderly.
9. Elderly living with their children feel more comfortable than those living elsewhere.
10. Disability problems are more among male than female.

METHODOLOGY

Sample Design

The study was carried out in two stages. In the first stage, informations were collected on the levels and trends in ageing at global, national and state level. These informations were collected from various secondary sources such as journals, books, census publications and internet. The data collected were compiled and compared to study the variation in the levels and trends in ageing among the developed and developing countries of the world as well as among different states of India.

In the second stage, an interview survey was carried out in the rural areas of three districts of TamilNadu viz., Thiruchirapalli, Vellore and Villupuram. The sample for the study was selected based on the multistage random sampling procedure. First, all the districts in TamilNadu were arranged in descending order based on the district Human Development Index (HDI) reported in the TamilNadu Human Development Report, 2001 and were then classified in to three groups as high, medium and low development districts. Among the districts arranged in descending order, the first ten districts were considered as highly developed, the next ten districts were considered as moderately developed and the rest were considered as low development districts. In the next stage, one district was selected at random from each of these three groups. (The details of districts with HDI status are given in Annexure-I).

After the selection of districts, three Primary Health Centers (PHC) were selected from each of the selected districts based on their distance from the district Head Quarters. This yardstick was used because of the fact that people living away from district Head Quarters will deprive of many of the basic amenities including transport, communication and health care services. In the next stage, one sub-centre was selected at random from each of the selected PHCs. All the elderly persons aged 60 years or more in the selected sub-centre area were listed and a sample of 100 elderly were selected using systematic random sampling procedure from each of the sub-centre areas. Thus the sample consisted of 300 elderly aged 60 years or more in each of the selected districts. In all, 900 elderly were selected for interview from all the three districts of TamilNadu. (The list of PHCs and sub-centres selected for the study are given in Annexure–II).

Besides the data collected through personal interview, one Focus Group Discussion (FGD) was conducted in each of the selected districts to collect qualitative data on the living arrangements and health conditions of elderly in rural TamilNadu.

Data Collection

A structured interview schedule was developed for the study. The interview schedule consisted of simple and short questions which could be easily understandable and answered by the elderly. The interview schedule, covered a range of subjects which include the living arrangement of elderly, their social and economic status, physiological status, Activities of Daily Living (ADL), psychological and health status and societal, community and governmental support available to elderly in rural TamilNadu. The interview schedule was pre-tested by administering the schedule to elderly living in the near by areas of Gandhigram. Based on the results of the pretest, the quality and content of the schedule were improved. Further, the pre-tested interview schedule was given to experts and the opinion and suggestions made by the experts were incorporated in the schedule. Thus, the interview schedule was finalized based on the results of the pretest and on the basis of expert's opinion and suggestions.

The research scholar had collected the data during the period from January to June 2006 by personally contacting the elderly at home. Besides the data collected from the elderly through personal interview, the research scholar had also collected qualitative data on the living arrangements, health conditions and care of elderly through Focus Group Discussions (FGDs).

Data Analysis

The data were office edited and entered in to the computer. The analysis was carried out using Statistical Package for Social Sciences (SPSS). Both univariate and multivariate analysis were carried out to assess the determinants of living arrangements and health conditions of elderly in rural areas and also to assess the effect of various socio-economic variables on the living arrangements and health conditions of elderly in rural areas. The statistical techniques used in the analysis of data are χ^2 and logistic regression.

VARIABLES

Dependent Variables

1. Living Arrangements
2. Activities of Daily Living (ADL)
3. Physiological status
4. Psychological status
5. Health status

Independent Variables

1. *Demographic Variables*– Age, sex, marital status and number of children.

2. *Socio-economic Variables*– Religion, caste, education, main, occupation, monthly family income, individual income, type of family and property ownership.
3. *Housing Characteristics Variables*– Type of house, ownership of house, electricity facility, toilet facilities, size of family, number of rooms and access to public amenities.
4. *Familial Relationship Variables*– Freedom to avail household facilities, cordial relationship with family members, participation in family ceremonies, consultation on important family matters, role in solving family disputes, abuse behaviour of family members, adequacy of daily in take of food, personal needs, availability of finance, sources of finance and sufficiency of money to meet their personal needs.
5. *Personal Life Style Behaviour Variables*– Activities of Daily Living (ADL), support to household activities, leisure time activities and personal habits.
6. *Physical Disability Variables*– Difficulties in performing Activities of Daily Living (ADL) and Physical mobility status.
7. *Expectation Variables*- Expectations from family members, expectations from government, suggestions for the youth, opinion on increased longevity, opinion on their living condition and availability of basic needs.

4

LEVELS AND TRENDS IN POPULATION AGEING

Population ageing refers to an increase in percentage of all extant persons who have lived to or beyond certain age. The United Nations defines a country as 'ageing' where the proportion of people over 60 reaches 7 per cent. In this chapter, the levels and trends in population ageing in the developed and developing countries of the world are discussed in detail.

GLOBAL TREND

Growth of Elderly

The decline of fertility and increased survival has resulted in the population ageing both in developed and developing countries of the world in the 20th century. Although all the countries in the world are experiencing ageing, the levels and trends in ageing vary enormously from country to country. The number and percent of elderly people aged 60+ presented in Table 1 and Figure 1 showed that during the period from 1990 to 2000, the world elderly population aged 60+ has increased from 8.9 per cent to 10 per cent. The proportion of elderly was substantially highest at 19.4 per cent in more developed regions compared to 7.7 per cent in less developed regions of the world. However in terms of absolute numbers, there are significantly more number of elderly aged 60+ in developing countries than those in developed countries. The estimated elderly population aged 60+ during 2000 was only 229,182 million in More Developed Countries (MDC) compared to 368,040 million in the Less Developed Countries (LDC) of the world.

Table 1
Number and Percent of Elderly People (60+) in More Developed Countries (MDC) and Less Developed Countries (LDC) of the World (1990-2000)

	Number of Countries	*Population 1990*	*Population 2000*	*Age 60+ 1990*	*Age 60+ 2000*	*%Age 60+ 1990*	*%Age 60+ 2000*
World	187	5,900,322	5,988,845	528,224	597,221	8.9	10.0
MDC	45	1,175,908	1,180,425	207,843	229,182	17.7	19.4
LDC	142	4,724,414	4,808,420	320,380	368,040	6.7	7.7

Data Source: http://www.who.int/whr/2001/annex/en/
Division of countries made into more/less developed from US Census database categorization. Several countries are not categorized, so this table excludes countries for which US Census didn't assign a category.

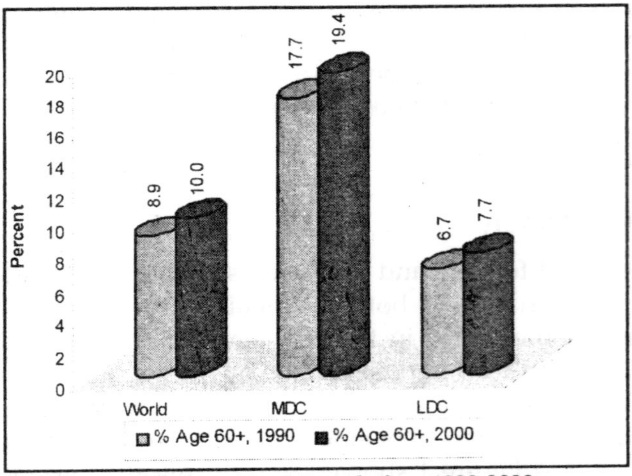

Figure 1: Percent Elderly to Total Population, 1990-2000

In 2006, almost 500 million people world wide were 65 and older. By 2030, that total is projected to increase to 1 billion – 1 in every 8 of the earth's inhabitants. Significantly, the most rapid increases in the 65 and older population are occurring in developing countries, which will see a jump of 140 per cent by 2030 (U.S. Department of State, 2007).

Young and Old Population

Population with high fertility tends to have low proportions of older persons and vice versa. The percent distribution of child (0–4 years) and elderly population (65+) presented in Table 2 revealed that the world child population has decreased from 11.8 per cent in 1990 to 9.9 per cent in 2001, while at the same time the elderly population has increased from 5.9 per cent to 6.9 per cent. Similar trend has been observed for both MDCs and LDCs. In the MDCs, the child population has decreased from 7.1 per cent in 1990 to 5.7 per cent in 2001 while at the same time the elderly population has increased from 11.8 per cent to 13.9 per cent. In the LDCs, the child population has decreased from 12.9 per cent in 1990 to 10.9 per cent in 2001 while at the same time the elderly population has increased from 4.5 per cent to 5.4 per cent. Thus, both declining trend in fertility and increasing trend in the elderly population are observed in recent times in all countries of the world.

Table 2
Number and Percent Distribution of Child (0-4 year) and Elderly Population (65+) in More Developed Countries (MDC) and Less Developed Countries (LDC) of the World (1990-2001)

	N	*Total Population*	*Population Over 65*	*Population Age 0 to 4*	*Percentage 0 to 4*	*Percent Over Age 65*
			2001			
World	177	4,471,479,856	310,648,311	444,166,103	9.9	6.9
LDC	149	3,660,895,326	197,916,972	398,056,979	10.9	5.4
MDC	28	810,584,530	112,731,339	46,109,124	5.7	13.9
			1990			
World	177	3,829,788,186	227,864,249	450,657,484	11.8	5.9
LDC	149	3,059,751,995	137,232,301	395,880,922	12.9	4.5
MDC	28	770,036,191	90,631,948	54,776,562	7.1	11.8

Data Source: U.S. Census Bureau, International Data Base

The proportion of total population aged 0-14 and 60 and over in more and less developed regions of the world presented in Figure 2 showed that in more developed countries, the proportion of elderly population aged 60+ has become more

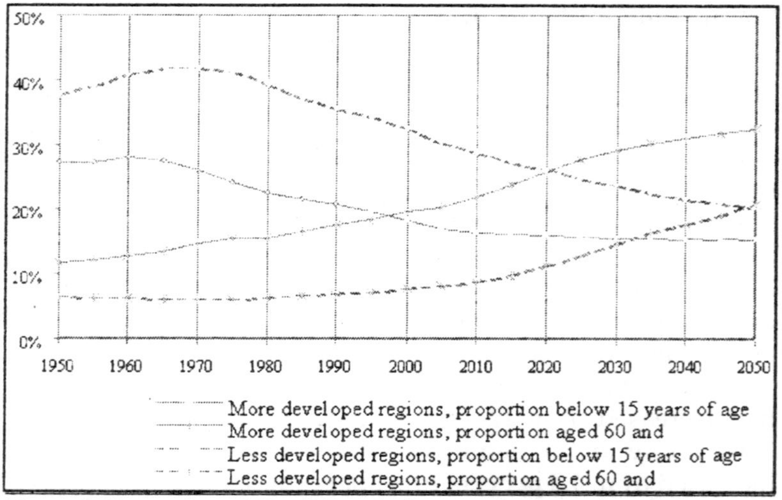

Figure 2: Proportion of Total Population Aged 0-14 and 60 and Over in More and Less Developed Regions, 1950-2050. (Medium Variant Projections)

Source: World Population Prospects, the 1998 Revision, Volume II: Sex and Age. The Population Division, Department of Economic and Social Affairs, United Nations Secretariat

than the younger population aged 0-14 by the year 2000 while similar trend is expected to occur in developing countries by the year 2050.

Thus the reduction in fertility and increased longevity result in more number of elderly aged 60+ than the younger population aged 0-14 in the developing countries by the years 2050.

Trends in Population Ageing

Increase in Population Age 65 and Over

The projected figures for the elderly population (65+) for the period from 1950 to 2025 presented in Table 3 and Figure 3 revealed that the elderly population is expected to reach 10 per cent of the total population by 2025 for the world as a whole. While the proportion of elderly is estimated at 19 per cent for the developed countries, it is estimated at 8 per cent for the developing countries.

Table 3
Number of Elderly People (65+) in Developed and Developing Countries, 1950-2025

	Developed Countries		*Developing Countries*		*Total*	
Year	*Total (000)*	*Percent*	*Total (000)*	*Percent*	*Total (000)*	*Percent*
1950	63566	7.6	64262	3.8	127808	5.1
1960	80250	8.5	76817	3.8	160067	5.3
1970	101007	9.6	99129	3.7	200137	5.4
1980	130858	11.5	133129	4.0	263986	5.9
1990	145614	12.1	182018	4.5	327633	6.2
2000	172820	13.7	251696	5.0	424516	6.8
2005	185644	14.4	290319	5.3	475962	7.1
2015	210735	15.9	387136	6.1	597804	7.8
2025	257028	19.0	571136	8.0	828164	9.7

Source: Asian Population Studies Series No.131-c, (1994).

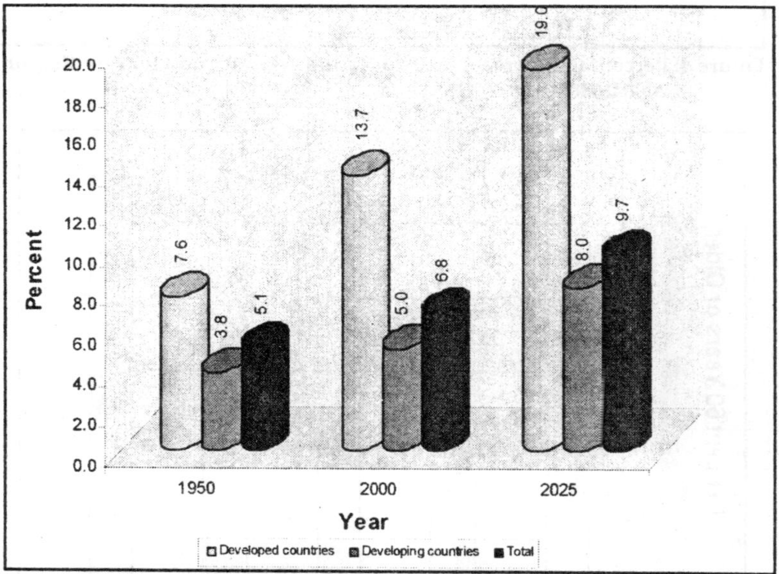

Figure 3: Projected Population Aged 65+, 1950 - 2025

Increase in Population Age 60 and Over

The percentage increase in population age 60 and over by region for the period 2000–2050 presented in Figure 4 showed that the proportion of elderly population aged 60 years and over has increased significantly in all the regions of the world.

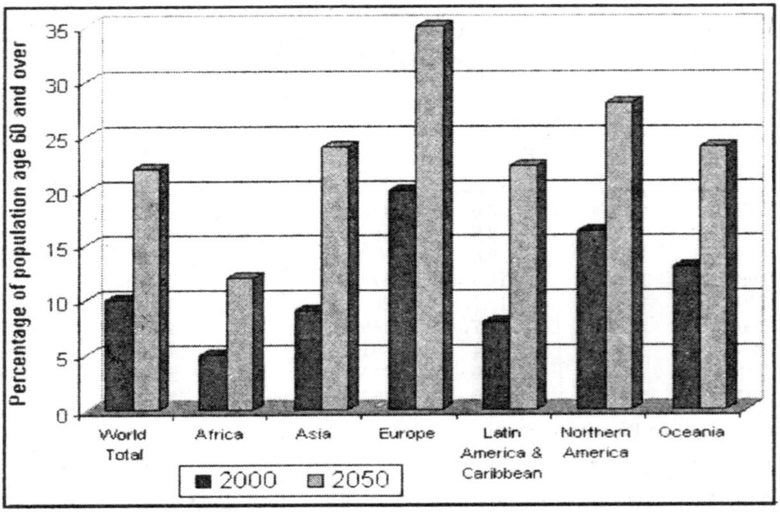

Figure 4: Percentage Increase in Population Age 60 and Over by Region, 2000-2050

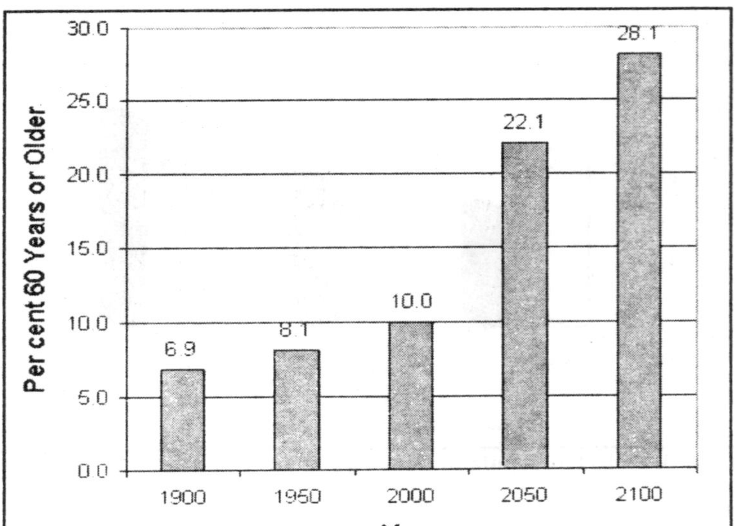

Figure 5: Three Centuries of World Population Ageing (60+)

Source: Long-Range World Population Projections: Based on the 1998 Revision. The Population Division, Department of Economic and Social Affairs, United Nations Secretariat

While Europe has witnessed a very high proportion of elderly, Africa has witnessed a very low level of elderly population by 2050.

Three Centuries of Population Ageing (60+)

The three centuries of world population ageing presented in Figure 5 revealed that the elderly population aged 60 years or more is projected to reach the level of 28.1 per cent by the year 2100.

Summary

The analysis of secondary data on the global trend in population ageing revealed that the proportion of elderly is substantially more at 19.4 per cent in more developed regions compared to only 7.7 per cent in less developed regions of the world. However in terms of absolute numbers, there are significantly more number of elderly aged 60+ in developing countries than those in developed countries. The world child population has decreased from 11.8 per cent in 1990 to 9.9 per cent in 2001, while the elderly population (65+) has increased from 5.9 per cent to 6.9 per cent during the same period. Similar trends have been observed for both more developed countries and less developed countries of the world. Elderly population (65+) is expected to reach 10 per cent of the total population by 2025 for the world as a whole. Europe has witnessed a very high proportion of elderly and Africa has witnessed a very low level of elderly population by 2050. The elderly population aged 60 years or more is projected to reach 28.1 per cent by the year 2100. Reduction in fertility and increased longevity results in more number of elderly aged 60+ than the younger population aged 0-14 in the developing countries by the year 2050.

POPULATION AGEING IN INDIA

Trends in Population Ageing

In India, the number of elderly population aged 60 years or older is steadily increasing. The significant reduction in death rates and the improvement in the life expectancy have lead to more number of elderly in the country. The percent distribution of persons aged 60 years and above by age, sex and residence in India presented in Table 4 revealed that the proportion of elderly has increased from 5.63 per cent of the total population in 1961 to 7.44 per cent in 2001. The increase in the proportion of elderly was more in rural than in urban areas.

The increase in the elderly population aged 60 and over is observed in all age groups. The elderly population aged 70-79 years has increased from 1.39 per cent in 1961 to 2.06 per cent in 2001 and the elderly aged 80 and over has increased from 0.57 per cent in 1961 to 0.78 per cent in 2001. It is also to be noted that there are more number of female than male in all age groups.

Major State-Wise Elderly Population in India

The major state-wise percentage of population aged 60 years and above presented in Table 5 indicates the ageing of population in many of the states in India. Population ageing was highest at 9.9 per cent in Kerala followed by Himachal Pradesh (9.2 per cent), Punjab (8.6 per cent), TamilNadu (8.5 per cent), Maharashtra (8 per cent), Orissa (7.7 per cent), Andhra Pradesh (7.6 per cent), Gujarat and Karnataka (7.4 per cent each) and Haryana (7 per cent). In all the states where population is ageing, the proportion of elderly was comparatively higher in rural than in urban areas. It is also observed that in all the states the proportion of elderly was more among female than male.

Age Structure

The percent distribution of elderly population by broad age group presented in Table 6 and Figure 6 showed that the proportion of young age population (0-14) has decreased from 42.02 per cent in 1971 to 35.34 per cent in 2001 and the proportion of elderly aged 60+ has increased from 5.97 per cent in 1971 to 7.45 per cent in 2001. The results indicate a speedy ageing process in India.

Table 4

Percent Distribution of Persons Aged 60 Years and Above by Age, Sex and Residence in India* (1961–2001)

		Total			*Rural*			*Urban*		
Age Group	*Year*	*Total*	*Male*	*Female*	*Total*	*Male*	*Female*	*Total*	*Male*	*Female*
60–69	1961	3.66	3.61	3.72	3.78	3.78	3.79	3.15	3.01	3.32
	1971	3.89	3.92	3.88	4.06	4.44	3.99	3.26	3.16	3.39
	1981	4.16	4.12	4.20	4.38	4.38	4.38	3.48	3.32	3.58
	1991	4.24	4.22	4.26	4.46	4.47	4.44	3.62	3.53	3.73
	2001	4.60	4.33	4.88	4.78	4.51	5.05	4.14	3.87	4.43
70-79	1961	1.39	1.33	1.46	1.46	1.39	1.51	1.13	1.03	1.24
	1971	1.48	1.47	1.18	1.55	1.55	1.53	1.22	1.17	1.29
	1981	1.71	1.68	1.73	1.80	1.80	1.80	1.39	1.30	1.49
	1991	1.75	1.76	1.75	1.85	1.87	1.82	1.48	1.42	1.54
	2001	2.06	2.02	2.11	2.15	2.14	2.16	1.85	1.75	1.96
80+	1961	0.57	0.52	0.62	0.59	0.55	0.63	0.48	0.38	0.55
	1971	0.58	0.55	0.62	0.61	0.59	0.63	0.48	0.41	0.57
	1981	0.61	0.59	0.64	0.64	0.64	0.65	0.53	0.46	0.60
	1991	0.76	0.76	0.76	0.80	0.82	0.78	0.65	0.60	0.70
	2001	0.78	0.74	0.83	0.81	0.78	0.84	0.70	0.62	0.80
60+	1961	5.63	5.46	5.80	5.82	5.70	5.94	4.73	4.42	5.11
	1971	5.97	5.94	5.99	6.21	6.26	6.17	4.97	4.73	5.26
	1981	6.32	6.23	6.41	6.83	6.83	6.85	5.36	5.08	5.69
	1991	6.70	6.69	6.71	7.10	7.17	7.05	5.75	5.55	5.96
	2001	7.44	7.09	7.82	7.74	7.43	8.06	6.70	6.25	7.20

Contd.

		Total			Rural			Urban		
Age Group	*Year*	*Total*	*Male*	*Female*	*Total*	*Male*	*Female*	*Total*	*Male*	*Female*
All age	1961	439234771	226293201	212941570	360298168	183504095	176794073	78936603	42789106	36147497
	1971	548159652	284049276	264110376	439045675	225319943	213725732	109113977	58729333	50384644
	1981	665287832	343930414	321357418	507607666	260054014	247553652	157680167	83876401	73803766
	1991	838567936	435208158	403359778	622796324	321271205	301525119	215771612	113936953	101834659
	2001	1028610328	532156772	49643556	742490639	381602674	360887965	286119689	150554098	135565591

Note: * Excludes figures for Assam in 1981 and Jammu & Kashmir in 1991 where the census was not conducted due to disturbed conditions

Source: Ageing population of India, an analysis of the 1991 census data and 2001 census data, Registrar General, India.

Table 5

Major State-wise Percentage of Population Aged 60 years and Above to Total Population by Sex and Residence in India, 2001

India and Bigger States	*Total*			*Rural*			*Urban*		
	Total	*Male*	*Female*	*Total*	*Male*	*Female*	*Total*	*Male*	*Female*
Andhra Pradesh	7.6	6.8	8.3	8.1	7.3	8.9	5.8	5.3	6.4
Assam	5.1	5.2	5.0	5.0	5.1	4.9	5.8	5.7	5.8
Bihar	6.4	6.2	6.6	6.5	6.3	6.7	5.7	5.4	6.0
Gujarat	7.4	6.6	8.3	8.1	7.1	9.0	6.1	5.5	6.8
Haryana	7.0	6.5	7.6	7.2	6.8	7.7	6.1	5.4	6.9
Himachal Pradesh	9.2	9.5	8.8	9.3	9.8	8.9	6.9	6.8	7.0
Karnataka	7.4	6.9	7.9	7.5	7.0	8.0	7.1	6.7	7.6
Kerala	9.9	9.3	10.5	10.0	9.4	10.5	9.8	9.0	10.6
Madhya Pradesh	6.5	5.9	7.1	6.7	6.1	7.3	5.9	5.2	6.7
Maharashtra	8.0	7.2	8.7	8.7	7.9	9.5	6.8	6.2	7.4
Orissa	7.7	7.4	8.0	7.9	7.6	8.2	6.1	5.8	6.5
Punjab	8.6	8.3	9.0	9.0	8.7	9.3	7.4	6.9	8.0
Rajasthan	6.4	5.6	7.3	6.4	5.7	7.3	6.1	5.1	7.1
Tamil Nadu	8.5	8.1	8.8	8.7	8.4	9.0	8.0	7.6	8.3
Uttar Pradesh	6.8	6.5	7.0	7.0	6.8	7.3	5.5	5.2	5.9
West Bengal	6.7	6.3	7.2	6.1	5.7	6.6	8.3	7.9	8.8
India	7.1	6.6	7.6	7.3	6.8	7.7	6.5	6.1	7.0

Source: Sample Registration System Statistical Report 2001, Registrar General of India.

Table 6

Percent Distribution of Total Population by Broad Age Group, India, 1901-2001

Census Year	*Age Group (years)*		
	0-14	*15-59*	*60+*
1901	38.60	56.35	5.05
1911	38.45	56.40	5.15
1921	39.20	55.55	5.25
1931	40.00	55.95	4.05
1941	38.25	56.85	4.90
1951	37.50	56.85	5.65
1961	41.00	53.36	5.64
1971	42.02	52.01	5.97
1981	33.16	53.92	6.49
1991	37.24	55.43	6.76
2001	35.34	56.93	7.45

Source: Census of India, Registrar General of India

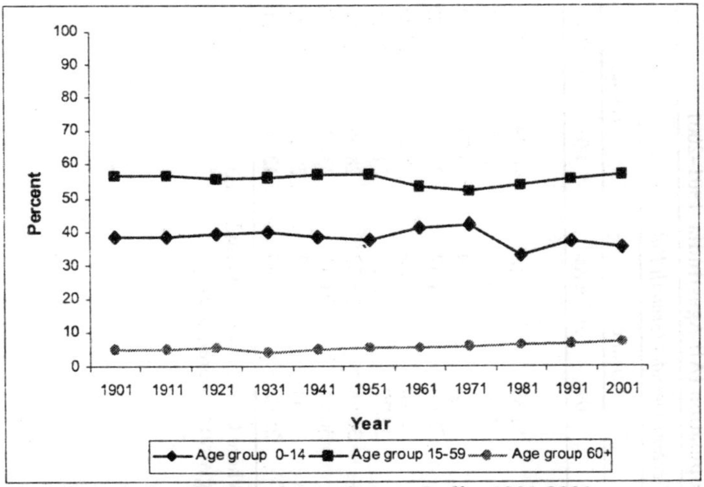

Figure 6: Population by Broad Age Group, India, 1901-2001

Decadal Growth Rate

The percent decadal growth rate of elderly in India presented in Table 7, 8 and Figure 7 showed a substantial increase in the decadal growth rate of elderly from 26 per cent in 1961 to 35.18

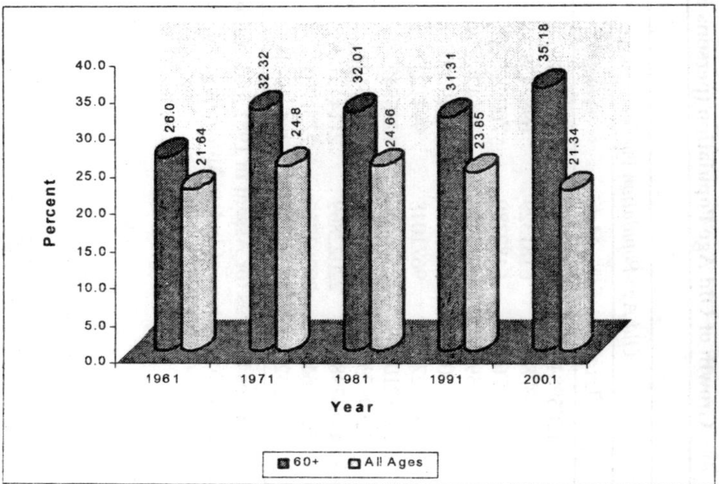

Figure 7: Percent Decadal Growth Rate of Elderly (60+) and All Ages, India 1961-2001

Table 7

Growth of Old Age Population (persons 60+ years) and Total Population (All Ages)India, 1901-2001

	Old Age Population by Sex			Percent Decadal Growth Rate					
				Total		Male		Female	
Year	*Total*	*Male*	*Female*	*60+*	*All Ages*	*60+*	*All Ages*	*60+*	*All Ages*
1901	12059846	5501791	6558055						
1911	13168787	6181329	6987458	9.20	5.75	12.35	6.18	6.55	5.30
1921	13484764	6482389	7002375	2.40	0.31	4.87	0.13	0.21	0.75
1931	14208391	6944128	7264263	5.37	11.00	7.12	11.29	3.74	10.71
1941	18040000	8890700	9149300	26.97	14.22	28.03	14.52	25.95	13.92
1951	19612270	9671048	9941222	8.72	13.31	8.78	13.25	8.66	13.38
1961	24712109	12356687	12355422	26.00	21.64	27.77	21.97	24.28	21.29
1971	32699731	16874325	15825406	32.32	24.80	36.56	25.52	28.08	24.03
1981	43167388	22022869	21144519	32.01	24.66	30.51	24.41	33.61	24.93
1991	56681640	29363725	27317915	31.31	23.85	33.33	24.30	29.20	23.37
2001	76622321	37768327	38853994	35.18	21.34	28.62	17.90	42.21	31.20

Note: * Excludes Figures for Assam in 1981 and Jammu & Kashmir in 1991 where Census was not conducted.

Source: Ageing Population of India: An Analysis of the 1991Census Data, Registrar General, India.

Table 8
Percent Decadal Growth of Population Aged 60+ and Total Population (All Ages) by Age, Sex and Residence, India, 1961- 2001

Age Group		*Total*			*Rural*			*Urban*		
	Period	*Total*	*Male*	*Female*	*Total*	*Male*	*Female*	*Total*	*Male*	*Female*
60-69	1961-71	32.83	36.05	29.50	30.94	34.55	27.23	43.20	44.10	42.23
	1971-81	29.50	27.41	31.78	24.96	23.00	27.10	52.22	49.49	55.20
	1981-91	28.63	29.77	27.43	24.83	26.01	23.58	44.24	45.22	43.22
	1991-01	32.90	25.31	41.02	27.65	19.78	36.08	51.59	45.07	58.50
70-79	1961-71	32.42	39.10	25.98	29.40	36.35	22.73	50.17	55.01	45.39
	1971-81	39.81	38.30	41.42	34.92	34.02	35.89	64.64	60.20	69.30
	1981-91	29.41	31.92	26.81	25.70	28.21	23.07	44.85	47.79	41.92
	1991-01	44.63	41.27	48.26	38.63	35.63	41.93	66.28	66.22	70.48
80+	1961-71	28.78	33.57	24.55	25.76	31.27	20.81	46.54	47.87	45.47
	1971-81	28.95	31.72	26.32	23.29	26.21	20.44	57.54	62.16	53.72
	1981-91	54.47	61.92	47.09	51.23	58.78	43.50	67.27	75.39	60.20
	1991-01	26.11	18.88	35.08	20.81	12.80	29.89	45.02	37.63	52.04
60+	1961-71	32.32	36.56	28.08	30.03	34.68	25.40	45.18	46.97	43.34
	1971-81	32.01	30.51	33.61	27.28	26.03	28.61	55.80	53.22	58.50
	1981-91	31.31	33.33	29.20	27.56	29.67	25.36	46.67	48.63	44.68
	1991-01	35.28	28.62	42.23	29.73	23.12	36.91	54.61	48.67	60.83
All Ages	1961-71	24.80	25.52	24.03	38.25	37.27	39.41	21.85	22.78	20.88
	1971-81	24.66	24.41	24.93	44.46	42.77	46.43	19.74	19.62	19.86
	1981-91	23.85	24.30	23.37	38.01	37.00	39.16	19.60	20.34	18.82
	1991-01	22.66	22.28	23.08	19.22	18.78	19.69	32.60	32.14	33.12

Note: * Excludes Figures for Assam in 1981 and Jammu & Kashmir in 1991 where Census was not conducted.
Source: Ageing Population of India: An Analysis of the 1991Census Data, Registrar General, India

per cent in 2001. At the same time, the decadal growth rate of population of all ages has decreased from 24.80 per cent in 1971 to 21.34 per cent in 2001. The percent decadal growth rate of elderly was substantially higher in urban than in rural areas.

Sex Ratio

The sex ratio (number of females per 1000 males) of elderly population and general population presented in Table 9 and Figure 8 revealed that the women's share of oldage population increases with age in recent years. The gender specific differences in mortality play an important role in determining the sex ratio at older ages. Because women tend to marry men who are several years older than themselves, percent widowed are much higher among women than men until old age. As a consequence, the sex ratio increased with age for elderly population aged 60 years or older. The sex ratio of elderly population was highest at 987 females per 1000 males

Table 9
Sex Ratio of Elderly Population and General Population by Place of Residence, India, 1961-2001

		Age Group (years)				
Year	*Place of Residence*	*60-64*	*65-69*	*70+*	*60+*	*All ages*
1961	Rural	975	971	1062	1000	963
	Urban	939	916	1072	947	845
	Total	969	962	1064	1000	941
1971	Rural	926	921	957	936	949
	Urban	908	895	978	928	858
	Total	923	916	961	937	930
1981	Rural	937	984	958	949	951
	Urban	933	994	1051	1000	878
	Total	936	986	976	950	935
1991	Rural	904	954	1025	958	958
	Urban	957	1009	1084	1016	897
	Total	916	966	1038	971	941
2001	Rural	956	952	1008	968	964
	Urban	1005	1000	1060	1039	913
	Total	969	965	1022	987	947

Source: Sharma S.P and peter xenon "Ageing in India. Demographic background and analysis based on census materials." Occasional paper No.2 of 1992, office of the Registrar general and census commissioner India, New Delhi.1992 and census of India, 2001.

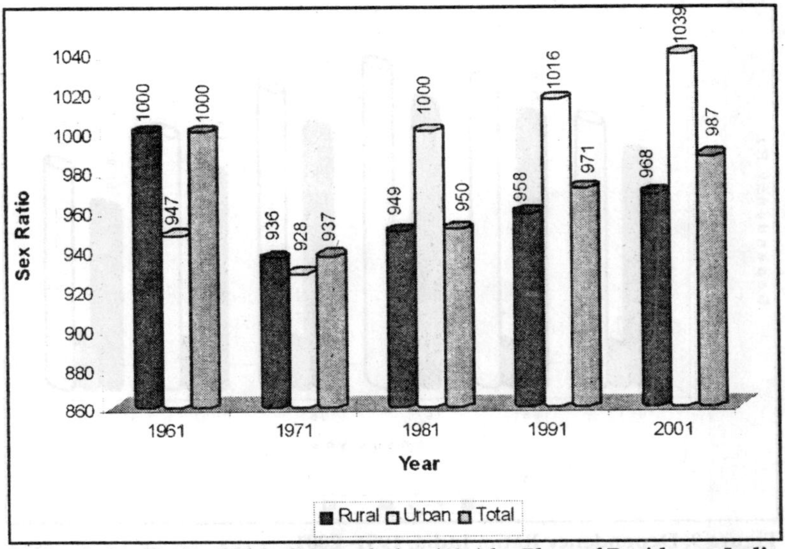

Figure 8: Sex Ratio of Elderly Population (60+) by Place of Residence, India 1961-2001

compared to only 947 females per 1000 males in the general population. The sex ratio of elderly was substantially higher in urban (1039) than in rural areas (968).

Dependency Ratio

The old age dependency ratio and index of ageing are presented in Table 10. The ageing index is defined as the number of people aged 60 years and over per 100 children under the age of 15. Changes in this ratio over time indicate the shifting balance of children versus elderly within the society. In the year 2001, there were about 25 elderly persons per 100 children aged 0-14. The elderly support ratio (dependency ratio) is the number of people aged 60 and over per 100 persons aged 15-59, the working age population. The total dependency ratio which provides a rough indication of the number of non-economically active versus economically active persons in a given society is steadily decreasing from 87.39 in 1961 to 63.53 in 2001 (Figure 9). It is also observed that the young dependency ratio is showing a declining trend in

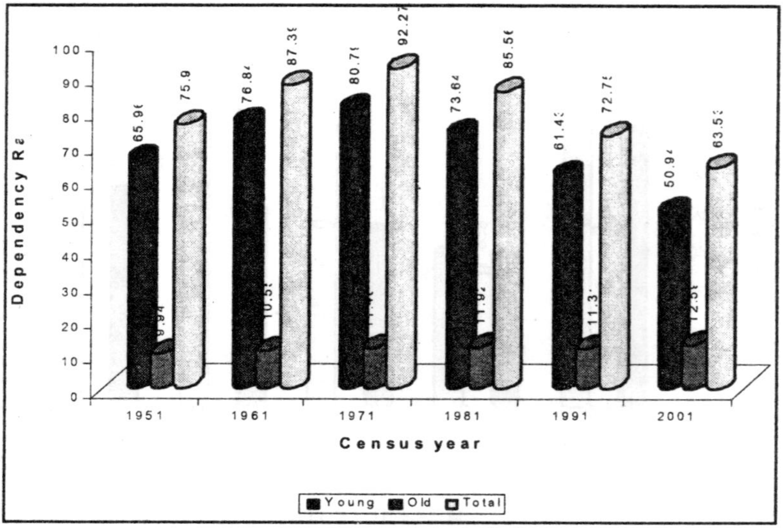

Figure 9: Dependency Ratio, India, 1951- 2001

Table 10
Dependency Ratio and Index of Ageing, India, 1901-2001

Census Year	*Dependency Ratio*			*Index of Ageing*
	Young	*Old*	*Total*	
1901	68.50	8.96	77.46	13.08
1911	68.17	9.13	77.30	13.39
1921	70.57	9.45	80.02	13.39
1931	71.49	7.24	78.73	10.25
1941	67.28	8.62	75.90	12.81
1951	65.96	9.94	75.90	14.31
1961	76.84	10.55	87.39	13.72
1971	80.79	11.48	92.27	14.20
1981	73.64	11.92	85.56	16.18
1991	61.43	11.31	72.75	18.42
2001	50.94	12.59	63.53	24.72

Source: Sharma s.p and peter xenos. "Ageing in India.Demographic background and analysis based on census materials." Occasional paper No.2 of 1992, office of the Registrar General and census commissioner India, New Delhi.1992 and Census of India, 2001.

Young : Number of persons aged 0-14 per 100 aged 15-59

Old : Number of persons aged 60+ per 100 aged 15-59

Total : Number of persons aged 0-14 per 100 aged 15-59 + Number of persons aged 60+ per 100 aged 15-59

Index of ageing : Number of persons aged 60+ per 100 aged 0-14

recent years while the old age dependency ratio is showing an increasing trend. The continued increase in oldage dependency ratio is a major challenge for the government to take care of the growing number of elderly in the coming years.

Projected Population

The projected population of elderly by age and sex presented in Table 11 showed that there will be an estimated 112.96 million elderly in India by the year 2016 which is about 8.94 per cent of the total population of India.

Table 11
Projected Population by Age and Sex, India, 2014–2016

(In '000)

	2014			*2015*			*2016*		
Age-Group	*Male*	*Female*	*Total*	*Male*	*Female*	*Total*	*Male*	*Female*	*Total*
60-64	19143	17798	36941	19783	18412	38195	20496	19108	39604
65-69	14080	13419	27499	14603	13961	28565	15170	14526	29696
70-74	9351	9208	18559	9761	9591	19353	10210	10037	20248
75-79	5612	5975	11587	5774	6116	11890	6024	6321	12345
80+	5098	5138	10236	5276	5368	10644	5461	5609	11069
60+	53284	51538	104822	55197	53448	108645	57361	55601	112962
All-Ages	631395	597111	1228506	640034	605793	1245827	648886	614657	1263543

Source: Population Projections for India and States 1996-2016, Registrar General, Ministry of Home Affairs, Govt. of India

State-Wise Projected Population

The state-wise projected population of elderly by sex and the state-wise percent share of elderly population are presented in Table 12 and Table 13. It is observed that the four southern states (TamilNadu, Kerala, Karnataka and Andhra Pradesh) will have nearly half of the elderly population in India by the year 2016 (about 46 per cent). The results indicate significant shift in the age structure of population in the southern part of India. It is also observed that the population will become ageing in all most all the states of India by the year 2016.

Summary

The analysis of secondary data on the trends in population ageing in India showed that the number of elderly population

Table 12
State-Wise Projected Population Aged 60+ years (in '000) by Sex, 1996-2016

		Year				
States	*Sex*	*1996*	*2001*	*2006*	*2011*	*2016*
Andhra Pradesh	Total	4793	5587	6643	7864	9270
	Male	2395	2768	3272	3881	4599
	Female	2398	2819	3371	3983	4672
Assam	Total	1291	1428	1651	1956	2371
	Male	716	780	892	1051	1271
	Female	575	647	760	905	1100
Bihar	Total	5729	6117	6797	7905	9400
	Male	3123	3281	3679	4293	5077
	Female	2606	2836	3118	3612	4323
Gujarat	Total	2904	3075	3417	3967	4684
	Male	1403	1431	1568	1799	2104
	Female	1501	1644	1849	2168	2580
Haryana	Total	1421	1415	1488	1663	1964
	Male	747	728	760	851	1010
	Female	673	687	728	813	953
Kerala	Total	2726	3162	3604	4101	4741
	Male	1265	1453	1652	1892	2211
	Female	1461	1709	1952	2209	2531
Karnataka	Total	3392	3783	4379	5146	6096
	Male	1689	1884	2179	2570	3046
	Female	1702	1899	2200	2575	3050
Madhya Pradesh	Total	4883	5348	5964	6754	7673
	Male	2478	2688	2986	3345	3769
	Female	2405	2660	2978	3409	3904
Maharashtra	Total	5949	6603	7451	8600	10087
	Male	2949	3217	3581	4089	4771
	Female	3000	3386	3870	4510	5316
Orissa	Total	2431	2651	2934	3277	3677
	Male	1231	1329	1460	1611	1785
	Female	1200	1323	1474	1666	1891
Punjab	Total	1735	1743	1801	1975	2247
	Male	948	893	885	950	1067
	Female	787	851	916	1025	1180
Rajasthan	Total	3051	3458	3986	4640	5434
	Male	1537	1747	2030	2360	2764
	Female	1514	1710	1956	2281	2670
Tamil Nadu	Total	4414	5301	6409	7710	9141
	Male	2304	2727	3249	3867	4540
	Female	2110	2574	3160	3844	4601
Uttar Pradesh	Total	10611	11390	12540	14228	16333

Contd.

States	*Sex*	*Year*				
		1996	*2001*	*2006*	*2011*	*2016*
	Male	5922	6110	6544	7209	8049
	Female	4689	5279	5996	7019	8283
West Bengal	Total	4459	5251	6341	7668	9273
	Male	2296	2699	3265	3959	4811
	Female	2163	2553	3076	3710	4463
India	Total	62317	70571	81811	95921	112962
	Male	32323	36208	41826	48859	57362
	Female	29993	34363	39985	47062	55600

Source: Ageing Population of India, an Analysis of the 1991 Census Data, Registrar General, India.

Table 13
State Wise Percent Share of Population Aged 60+ years by Sex (1996-2016)

States	*Sex*	*Year*				
		1996	*2001*	*2006*	*2011*	*2016*
Andhra Pradesh	Total	6.64	7.31	8.24	9.27	10.46
	Male	6.55	7.15	8.02	9.05	40.27
	Female	6.74	7.48	8.47	9.50	10.66
Assam	Total	5.22	5.39	5.81	6.42	7.29
	Male	5.57	5.68	6.08	6.71	7.63
	Female	4.85	5.07	5.52	6.12	6.94
Bihar	Total	6.16	6.01	6.12	6.52	7.11
	Male	6.41	6.16	6.34	6.77	7.35
	Female	5.88	5.84	5.88	6.24	6.84
Gujarat	Total	6.38	6.28	6.50	7.08	7.89
	Male	5.96	5.67	5.82	6.27	6.95
	Female	6.82	6.92	7.23	7.92	8.87
Haryana	Total	7.66	7.03	6.84	7.09	7.80
	Male	7.51	6.80	6.61	6.90	7.67
	Female	7.82	7.30	7.10	7.30	7.94
Kerala	Total	8.80	9.72	10.55	11.50	12.86
	Male	8.32	9.09	9.82	10.76	12.14
	Female	9.27	10.33	11.25	12.22	13.56
Karnataka	Total	6.87	7.18	7.79	8.63	9.71
	Male	6.71	7.02	7.64	8.51	9.60
	Female	7.04	7.34	7.69	8.76	9.82
Madhya Pradesh	Total	6.58	6.59	6.73	6.99	7.30
	Male	6.45	6.40	6.51	6.70	6.93
	Female	6.72	6.79	6.97	7.31	7.69
Maharashtra	Total	6.87	7.17	7.66	8.38	9.36
	Male	6.59	6.78	7.15	7.77	8.65

Contd.

States	*Sex*	*Year*				
		1996	*2001*	*2006*	*2011*	*2016*
	Female	7.18	7.60	8.19	9.03	10.10
Orissa	Total	7.06	7.33	7.76	8.30	8.96
	Male	7.04	7.24	7.61	8.06	8.60
	Female	7.08	7.42	7.91	8.55	9.33
Punjab	Total	7.76	7.33	7.13	7.39	8.01
	Male	7.98	7.11	6.68	6.80	7.31
	Female	7.50	7.57	7.63	8.04	8.77
Rajasthan	Total	6.14	6.34	6.68	7.11	7.61
	Male	5.90	6.14	6.53	6.95	7.46
	Female	6.39	6.57	6.85	7.27	7.77
Tamil Nadu	Total	7.43	8.51	9.86	11.41	13.08
	Male	7.65	8.66	9.90	11.35	12.91
	Female	7.19	8.36	9.82	11.47	13.26
Uttar Pradesh	Total	6.77	6.53	6.46	6.56	6.73
	Male	7.10	6.62	6.40	6.33	6.35
	Female	6.40	6.44	6.53	6.80	7.14
West Bengal	Total	5.98	6.56	7.43	8.44	9.64
	Male	5.90	6.49	7.39	8.45	9.72
	Female	6.06	6.64	7.47	8.44	9.54
India	Total	6.67	6.97	7.48	8.14	8.94
	Male	6.67	6.91	7.41	8.05	8.84
	Female	6.67	7.03	7.55	8.23	9.05

Source: Ageing Population of India. An Analysis of the 1991 Census Data, Registrar General, India.

aged 60 years or older is steadily increasing. The proportion of elderly has increased from 5.63 per cent in 1961 to 7.44 per cent in 2001. The increase in the proportion of elderly was more in rural than in urban areas. There are more number of females than males in all age groups. Population ageing was highest at 9.9 per cent in Kerala followed by Himachal Pradesh (9.2 per cent), Punjab (8.6 per cent), Tamilnadu (8.5 per cent), Maharastra (8 per cent), Orissa (7.7 per cent), Andhra Pradesh (7.6 per cent), Gujarat and Karnataka (7.4 per cent each) and Haryana (7 per cent). The decadal growth rate of elderly increased from 26 per cent in 1961 to 35.18 per cent in 2001. The per cent decadal growth rate of elderly was substantially higher in urban than in rural areas. The sex ratio increased with age for elderly population aged 60 years or older. The sex ratio of elderly was substantially higher in urban (1039) than in rural areas (968). However for the general population of all ages, it was more in rural than in urban areas. It is also observed that the young dependency ratio is showing a declining trend in recent years while the old age dependency ratio is showing an increasing trend. The elderly in India is projected to reach 112.96 million by the year 2016 which is about 8.94 per cent of the total population of India. Four southern states (TamilNadu, Kerala, Karnataka and Andhra Pradesh) will have nearly half of the elderly population in India by the year 2016.

POPULATION AGEING IN TAMILNADU

Trends in Population Ageing

The percent distribution of elderly population in TamilNadu by age, sex and residence presented in Table 14 and Figure 10 showed that the population became ageing in TamilNadu since 1991. The proportion of elderly people aged 60 and over has increased from 5.59 per cent in 1961 to 8.83 per cent in 2001. The proportion of female elderly was nearly same or little lower than the male until 1991 and has become higher than the male

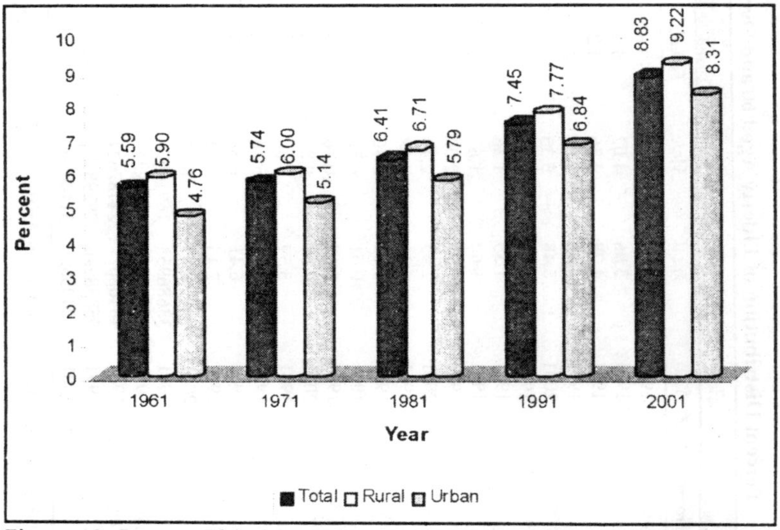

Figure 10: Percent Elderly Aged 60 and Above, TamilNadu, India (1961-2001)

Table 14

Percent Distribution of Elderly Aged 60 and Over by Age, Sex and Residence, TamilNadu, India, 1961-2001

Age Group	Year	Total			Rural			Urban		
		Total	Male	Female	Total	Male	Female	Total	Male	Female
60 - 69	1961	3.85	3.88	3.82	4.07	4.12	3.97	3.29	3.21	3.38
	1971	3.96	4.02	3.90	4.16	4.29	4.04	3.50	3.44	3.57
	1981	4.28	4.36	4.21	4.52	4.67	4.37	3.80	3.72	3.89
	1991	4.83	4.93	4.74	5.07	5.23	5.64	4.37	4.35	4.40
	2001	5.48	5.35	5.62	5.78	5.66	5.90	5.11	4.97	5.24
70 - 79	1961	1.34	1.34	1.34	1.43	1.45	1.41	1.10	1.04	1.17
	1971	1.35	1.36	1.34	1.41	1.45	1.37	1.48	1.67	1.29
	1981	1.60	1.65	1.56	1.66	1.76	1.57	1.49	1.43	1.55
	1991	1.92	2.00	1.84	1.99	2.12	1.86	1.79	1.77	1.80
	2001	2.45	2.49	2.41	2.55	2.64	2.45	2.32	2.28	2.36
80+	1961	0.41	0.38	0.44	0.43	0.42	0.44	0.36	0.30	0.42
	1971	0.43	0.40	0.46	0.43	0.42	0.44	0.40	0.33	0.48
	1981	0.51	0.50	0.52	0.51	0.53	0.50	0.48	0.42	0.55
	1991	0.68	0.76	0.66	0.70	0.75	0.69	0.70	0.68	0.71
	2001	0.88	0.86	0.90	0.89	0.90	0.88	0.87	0.81	0.94
60+	1961	5.59	5.60	5.59	5.90	5.99	5.82	4.76	4.55	4.98
	1971	5.74	5.78	5.70	6.00	6.15	5.85	5.14	4.94	5.34
	1981	6.41	6.53	6.30	6.71	6.99	6.45	5.79	5.56	6.00
	1991	7.45	7.64	7.25	7.77	8.11	7.41	6.84	6.74	6.93
	2001	8.83	8.71	8.94	9.22	9.21	9.24	8.31	8.07	8.55
Total population of all ages	1961	33686953	16910978	16775975	24696425	12331586	12364839	8990528	4579392	4411136
	1971	41199168	20828021	20371147	28734334	14438727	14295607	12464834	6389294	6075540
	1981	48408077	24487624	23920453	32456202	16334231	16121971	15951875	8153393	7798482
	1991	55858946	28298975	27559971	36781354	18567717	18213637	19077592	9731258	9346334
	2001	62405679	31400909	31004770	34921681	17531494	17390187	27483998	13869415	13614583

Source: Ageing Population of India, An Analysis of the 1991 census data and 2001 census data, Registrar General, India.

elderly in 2001. It is also observed that the proportion of elderly was much higher in rural than in urban areas. It was 9.22 per cent in rural and 8.31 per cent in urban areas during the year 2001.

Sex Ratio

The sex ratio of elderly population presented in Table 15 and Figure 11 for the year 2001, showed that there were more number of female than male elderly in TamilNadu. The overall sex ratio of elderly in TamilNadu was 1013 females per 1000 males. It was 995 in rural and 1039 in urban areas. Among the scheduled caste elderly, the number of female was lower than the male. It was 981 females per 1000 males. While the number of female was less in rural, it was comparatively higher in urban areas. It was 958 in rural and 1059 in urban areas. In the case of schedule tribe population, the sex ratio of elderly was 936 females per 1000 males. The number of females per 1000 males was substantially lower both in rural and urban areas. The sex ratio of elderly aged 80 years or more in rural areas of TamilNadu showed a typical figure of substantially lower number of females per 1000 males while it is expected that there will be more number of females than males at this age group.

Table 15
Sex Ratio of Elderly by Age and Scheduled Caste and Scheduled Tribe, TamilNadu, India 2001

Population	*Area*	*Age Group*					
		60-64	*65-69*	*70-74*	*75-79*	*80+*	*All*
All	Total	1011	1072	982	905	1040	1013
	Rural	1016	1065	946	860	965	995
	Urban	1005	1082	1036	967	1146	1039
SC	Total	995	1058	926	843	980	981
	Rural	981	1031	890	812	924	958
	Urban	1037	1141	1034	931	1128	1059
ST	Total	948	1065	846	866	818	936
	Rural	943	1065	831	857	792	928
	Urban	980	1061	949	918	959	986

Source: Census of India 2001, Registrar General of India

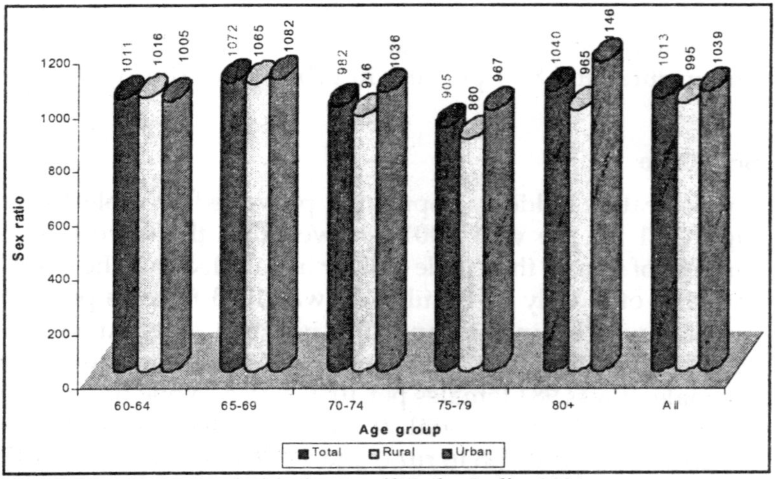

Figure 11: Sex Ratio of Elderly, TamilNadu, India, 2001

Dependency Ratio

The old age dependency ratio presented in Table 16 and Figure 12 showed an increasing trend both in rural and urban

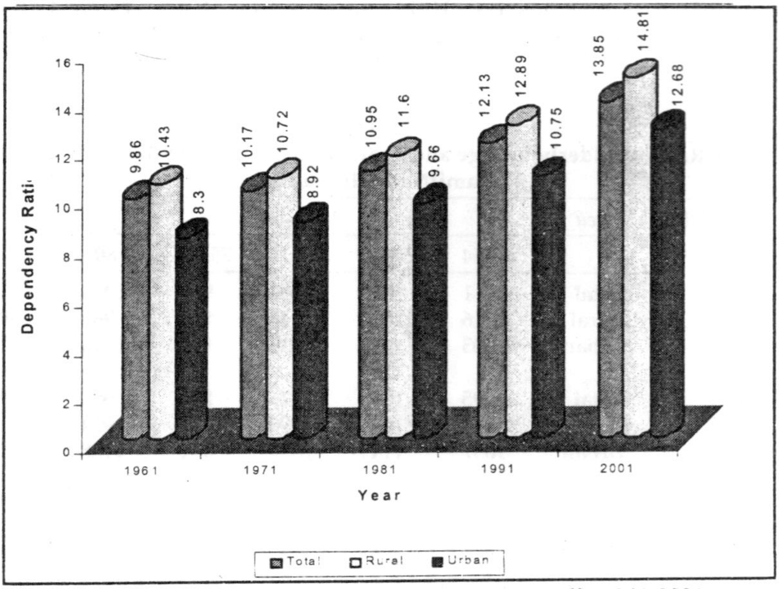

Figure 12: Oldage Dependency Ratio, TamilNadu, India 1961-2001

Table 16
Old Age Dependency Ratio by Sex and Residence, TamilNadu, India, 1961-2001

State	Year	Total			Rural			Urban		
		Total	Male	Female	Total	Male	Female	Total	Male	Female
TamilNadu	1961	9.86	9.89	9.83	10.43	10.66	10.22	8.30	7.88	8.76
	1971	10.17	10.24	10.09	10.72	11.05	10.39	8.92	8.47	9.40
	1981	10.95	11.18	10.72	11.60	12.19	11.03	9.66	9.26	10.09
	1991	12.13	12.55	11.71	12.89	13.65	12.13	10.75	10.58	10.92
	2001	13.85	13.77	13.92	14.81	14.98	14.65	12.68	12.34	13.04
India	1961	10.93	10.91	10.94	11.45	11.64	11.24	8.71	8.10	9.50
	1971	11.47	11.39	11.57	12.18	12.33	12.02	8.89	8.20	9.74
	1981	12.04	11.84	12.24	12.99	13.06	12.93	9.24	8.53	10.08
	1991	12.19	12.16	12.23	13.16	13.34	12.97	9.66	9.21	10.19
	2001	13.09	12.44	13.76	14.60	13.59	14.64	10.74	9.9	11.67

Source: Ageing Population of India, an Analysis of the 1991 and 2001 Census Data, Registrar General, India.

areas. The overall old age dependency ratio for TamilNadu has increased from 9.86 in 1961 to 13.85 in 2001. The old age dependency ratio was much higher in rural than in urban area. It was 14.81 in rural and 12.68 in urban areas in 2001. There was not much gender difference in the oldage dependency ratio both in rural and urban areas.

Index of Ageing

The index of ageing and familial dependency ratio by sex is presented in Table 17. The index of ageing which is intended to measure the structure of dependency showed that there are about 33 elderly aged 60 and above for every 100 population aged 0-14. There was not much difference in the index of ageing between the rural and urban areas. The index of ageing was comparatively less for the scheduled caste and scheduled tribe population than the general population both in rural and urban areas. This shows that the ageing process is much slower among the SC and ST population than the general population in TamilNadu.

Projected Population

The projected population of elderly and their percentage share to the total population for TamilNadu and India presented in Table 18 revealed that there will be 91.41 million elderly in TamilNadu by 2016 and the number of female elderly population will out number male population. The percentage share of elderly population will be 13.08 per cent by the year 2016, which will be a big challenge for the government to initiate programmes for the care and support of elderly particularly in rural areas.

Summary

The analysis of secondary data on the ageing situation in TamilNadu revealed that the proportion of elderly (aged 60 and over) in TamilNadu has increased from 5.59 per cent in 1961 to 8.83 per cent in 2001. It was much higher in rural than in urban areas. There were more number of female than male in TamilNadu. However, in rural areas, there were less number

Table 17

Index of Ageing and Familial Dependency Ratio by Sex, TamilNadu, India 2001

Population		*Index of Ageing*			*0-14/60+ x 100*			*60-74/40-44 x 100*			*80+/60-64x100*		
	Area	*Total*	*Male*	*Female*	*Total*	*Male*	*Female*	*Total*	*Male*	*Female*	*Total*	*Male*	*Female*
All	Total	32.95	31.87	34.09	303.42	313.69	293.28	117.67	111.33	124.61	26.08	26.60	27.36
	Rural	32.01	32.03	33.92	322.27	312.20	294.80	127.66	122.89	132.74	25.66	26.32	25.01
	Urban	32.97	31.66	34.34	303.28	315.84	291.19	105.76	97.93	114.62	28.91	27.00	30.81
SC	Total	23.26	23.01	23.53	429.76	435.55	424.89	104.32	100.35	108.61	20.53	20.69	20.37
	Rural	24.02	24.04	24.00	416.20	415.91	416.51	110.51	181.96	113.07	19.59	20.17	19.00
	Urban	21.37	20.42	22.36	46.77	489.50	447.21	89.88	82.58	98.03	23.18	22.19	24.19
ST	Total	19.93	19.88	19.99	501.56	502.91	500.11	90.49	86.93	94.54	20.72	22.19	19.16
	Rural	17.00	20.20	20.22	586.36	494.96	494.38	92.30	89.05	96.02	19.82	21.48	18.05
	Urban	18.37	18.06	18.69	544.23	553.46	534.88	80.27	75.19	86.11	26.67	26.95	26.38

Source: Census of India 2001, Registrar General of India

Note:

Index of Ageing: The proportion of the population aged 60+ to the population aged 0-14. It is intended to measure the structure of dependency.

Index of children: The population aged 0-14 per 100 to population aged 60 years and above.

Index of parents to children: The population aged 60-74 per 100 to population aged 40-44.100

Index of oldest old to young old: The population aged 80 years above per 100 to population aged 60-64.4.3.5

Table 18
Projected Population of Persons 60+ years and their Percentage Share to the Total Population by Sex, TamilNadu, India, 1996–2016

States	*Number/Percent*	*Sex*	*Year*				
			1996	*2001*	*2006*	*2011*	*2016*
Tamil Nadu	No. of Elderly (in ' 000)	Total	4414	5301	6409	7710	9141
		Male	2304	2727	3249	3867	4540
		Female	2110	2574	3160	3844	4601
	Percentage to total Population	Total	7.43	8.51	9.86	11.41	13.08
		Male	7.65	8.66	9.90	11.35	12.91
		Female	7.19	8.36	9.82	11.47	13.26
India	No. of Elderly (in ' 000)	Total	62317	70571	81811	95921	112962
		Male	32323	36208	41826	48859	57362
		Female	29993	34363	39985	47062	55600
	Percentage to total Population	Total	6.67	6.97	7.48	8.14	8.94
		Male	6.67	6.91	7.41	8.05	8.84
		Female	6.67	7.03	7.55	8.23	9.05

Source: Ageing Population of India. An Analysis of the 1991, Census Data, Registrar General, India.

of female per 1000 male. The overall old age dependency ratio for TamilNadu has increased from 9.86 in 1961 to 13.85 in 2001. The old age dependency ratio was much higher in rural than in urban areas. There was not much difference in the index of ageing between the rural and urban areas. The ageing process is much slower among the Scheduled Caste and Scheduled Tribe population than the general population in TamilNadu. There will be 91.41 million elderly in Tamilnadu by 2016 and the number of female elderly will out number male population. The percentage share of elderly population will be 13.08 per cent by the year 2016. The increase in the oldest old population (80+) will be a greatest challenge for the government to provide adequate health care services to this vulnerable elderly population.

5

SURVEY RESULTS

The informations on the living conditions of elderly in rural areas were collected through personal interview using structured interview schedule. The results of the analysis of data are presented in the following sections.

BACKGROUND CHARACTERISTICS OF THE RESPONDENTS (ELDERLY)

Age and Social Status

About half of the elderly (50.8 per cent) interviewed were in the age group of 60-69 years; about one third (33.9 per cent) were aged 70-79 years; and just 15.3 per cent were aged 80 years or more. Among the 900 elderly interviewed in the study, 42 per cent were male and 58 per cent were female. Among the male, 45.5 per cent were in the age group of 60-69 years, 38.1 per cent were in the age group of 70-79 years and the remaining 16.4 per cent were aged 80 years or more. Among the female, 54.8 per cent were aged 60-69 years, 30.8 per cent were aged 70-79 years and the remaining 14.4 per cent were aged 80 years or more.

The proportion of literates was more among male than female. Among the male, 37.8 per cent of elderly were illiterates, 38.4 per cent were primary, 16.4 per cent were middle and the remaining 7.4 per cent were secondary and above. Among the female, 79.1 per cent were illiterates, 14.9

per cent were primary, 5.2 per cent were middle and just 0.8 per cent were secondary and above.

Table 1
Percent Distribution of Elderly by Sex and Selected Background Characteristics

Background Characteristics	*Male N=378*	*Female N=522*	*Total N=900*
Age (Years)			
60-64	18.3	22.0	20.4
65-69	27.2	32.8	30.4
70-74	22.0	20.5	21.1
75-79	16.1	10.3	12.8
80+	16.4	14.4	15.3
Education			
Illiterate	37.8	79.1	61.8
Primary(5th)	38.4	14.9	24.8
Middle(up to 8th)	16.4	5.2	9.9
Secondary+	7.4	0.8	3.6
Religion			
Hindu	91.0	91.8	91.5
Muslim	4.8	5.7	5.3
Christian	4.2	2.5	3.2
Caste			
SC/ST	30.4	23.4	26.3
Others	69.6	76.6	73.7
Marital Status			
Married	82.5	20.9	46.8
Single	17.5	79.1	53.2

Majority of the elderly (91.5 per cent) were Hindus. Christians and Muslims constituted only 5.3 and 3.2 per cent of the total sample respectively. Among the male, 91 per cent were Hindus, 4.8 per cent were Muslims and 4.2 per cent were Christians. Among the female, 91.8 per cent were Hindus, 5.7 per cent were Muslims and 2.5 per cent were Christians. SC/ST constituted only 26.3 per cent of the total sample. Among the male, 30.4 per cent were SC/ST and the remaining 69.6 per cent were other than SC/ST. Among the female, 23.4 per cent belonged to SC/ST and the remaining 76.6 per cent belonged to other than SC/ST group. Proportion of married was more among male than female it was 82.5 per cent among male and only 20.9 per cent among female.

Occupation and Economic Status

The results of the analysis of data on the past and present occupation and income level presented in Table 2 showed that a majority of male elderly had involved in coolie work (65.3 per cent) in the past. Agriculture was the next major occupation as reported by 18.8 per cent of male respondents. Among the female also, majority of them reported to have worked as coolie (65.5 per cent) followed by agriculture (9 per cent). At the time of interview only 33.3 per cent of male and 21.3 per cent of female had involved in some sort of income earning activities.

Among those who had involved in money earning activities, 46.8 per cent of male and 78.4 per cent of female were working as coolies; 27 per cent of male and 7.2 per cent of female involved in agriculture activities and 21.4 per cent of male and 10.8 per cent of female had involved in some sort of business activities.

The analysis of data on the income earned through their current occupation showed that a majority of the male elderly (69.3 per cent) were earning more than Rs.1000 per month. About 11.2 per cent were reported to have earned between Rs.501-1000 per month and 19.5 per cent reported to have earned less than Rs.500 per month. Among the female, 78.9 per cent were earning more than Rs.1000 per month, just 1.9 per cent were earning between Rs.501-1000 per month and 19.2 per cent were earning less than Rs.500/- per month.

Table 2
Percent Distribution of Elderly by their Past and Present Occupation, Income and Sex

Occupation and Income	*Male* N=378	*Female* N=522	*Total* N=900
Past occupation			
No work	1.1	21.5	12.9
Coolie	65.3	65.5	65.4
Agriculture	18.8	9.0	13.2
Government employee	7.1	0.7	3.4
Others	7.7	3.3	5.1

Contd.

Occupation and Income	*Male* N=378	*Female* N=522	*Total* N=900
Currently involved in any income earning work			
Yes	33.3	21.3	26.3
No	66.7	78.7	73.7
*If yes, Type of work**			
Coolie	46.8	78.4	61.6
Business	21.4	10.8	16.5
Agriculture	27.0	7.2	17.7
Others	4.8	3.6	4.2
Income through current occupation (rupees)			
≤500	19.5	19.2	19.3
501-1000	11.2	1.9	5.8
1001+	69.3	78.9	74.9
Any other sources of income			
Yes	21.7	31.4	27.4
No	78.3	68.6	72.6
*Monthly income from other sources** (rupees)*			
≤1500	13.8	27.4	21.7
1501+	86.2	72.6	78.3
Total monthly individual income (rupees)			
≤1000	39.7	42.9	41.6
1001-2000	5.0	2.9	3.8
2001+	55.3	54.2	54.7
Total monthly family income (rupees)			
≤1000	24.6	33.1	29.5
1001-2000	18.7	12.1	14.9
2001-3000	14.6	13.4	13.9
3001+	42.1	41.4	41.7

* Applicable only for those who had involved in work
** Applicable only for those who had other sources of income

The respondents were also asked whether they had any other sources of income. In response to this question, only 21.7 per cent of male and 31.4 per cent of female had reported to have income from other sources like pension, interest, etc. The monthly income from other sources was more than Rs.1500/- for 86.2 per cent of male and 72.6 per cent of female elderly. The overall total individual income was more than Rs.2000 per month for 55.3 per cent of male and 54.2 per cent of female respondents.

The total monthly family income was less than Rs.1000/- per month for 24.6 per cent of male and 33.1 per cent of female respondents. It was in the range of Rs.1001 – 2000 for 18.7 per cent of male and 12.1 per cent of female respondents. About 14.6 per cent of male and 13.4 per cent of female respondents had reported to have a monthly income in the range of Rs.2001-3000 and the remaining 42.1 per cent of male and 41.4 per cent of female had a monthly family income of more than Rs.3000 per month.

Housing Characteristics

The percent distribution of elderly by sex and housing characteristics are presented in Table 3. It is observed that 37.6 per cent of male and 38.3 per cent of female were living in huts; 27.2 per cent of male and 27.4 per cent of female were living in katcha houses; and 35.2 per cent of male and 34.3 per cent of female were living in pucca houses.

Table 3
Percent Distribution of Elderly by Sex and Housing Characteristics

Housing Characteristics	*Male* N=378	*Female* N=522	*Total* N=900
Type of house			
Hut	37.6	38.3	38.0
Katcha	27.2	27.4	27.3
Pucca	35.2	34.3	34.7
Ownership of house			
Respondent's house	54.5	54.4	54.4
Son's house	19.3	17.4	18.2
Brother's/Sister's house	12.7	14.2	13.6
Others	13.5	14.0	13.8
Electrification			
Yes	89.4	81.4	84.8
No	10.6	18.6	15.2
Toilet facilities			
Yes	24.6	25.7	25.2
No	75.4	74.3	74.8
No. of rooms			
≤2	59.5	60.9	60.3
3-4	28.0	31.2	29.9
5+	12.5	7.9	9.8

Majority of both male and female respondents were living in their own house. It was 54.5 per cent for male and 54.4 per cent for female. It is also observed that 19.3 per cent of male and 17.4 per cent of female respondents were living in their son's house and 12.7 per cent of male and 14.2 per cent of female were living in their brother/sister's house. Most of the respondent's houses were electrified. It was 89.4 per cent for male and 81.4 per cent for female. Importantly, only 24.6 per cent of male and 25.7 per cent of female respondents' households were having toilet facilities. About three fifth of households were having only one or two rooms indicating the poor living conditions of elderly in rural areas.

Facilities Amenable to Household

The percent distribution of elderly by sex and facilities amenable to household are presented in Table 4. It is observed that main road was available within two kilometers (Kms) from the household for 91 per cent of male and 86.6 per cent of female. Hospital was available at a distance of less than two Kms for 46.8 per cent of male and 48.7 per cent of female and it was available at a distance of 2-4 Kms away from their household for 35.2 per cent of male and 29.5 per cent of female respondents. Market was available within two Kms for 51.9 per cent of male and 49.8 per cent of female respondents and it was available at a distance of 2-4 Kms away from the household for 27.2 per cent of male and 25.7 per cent of female elderly. School facilities were very nearer (<2 Kms) to 86.2 per cent of male and 84.5 per cent of female households and public transport facilities were available within two Kms distance for 88.9 per cent of male and 84.3 per cent of female elderly. Post office was available within two Kms for 81.5 per cent of male and 79.9 per cent of female elderly. Bank facilities were reported to be available within two Kms for 49.2 per cent of male and 52.3 per cent of female elderly. Temples were available to most of the elderly with in two Kms distance. About 94.2 per cent of male and 92 per cent of female elderly had reported to have temple facilities within the reachable distance (<2Kms).

Library facilities were reported to be available within the reachable distance (<2 Kms) for 55.3 per cent of male and 54.2 per cent of female and recreation facilities were reported to be

Table 4
Percent Distribution of Elderly by Sex and Facilities Amenable to the Household

Facilities	*Male*					*Female*					*Total*				
	N	<2 Km	2-4 Km	5-7 Km	8+ Km	N	<2 Km	2-4 Km	5-7 Km	8+ Km	N	<2 Km	2-4 Km	5-7 Km	8+ Km
Main road	378	91.0	7.1	0.8	1.1	522	86.6	8.4	1.7	3.3	900	88.4	7.9	1.3	2.4
Hospital	378	46.8	35.2	7.7	10.3	522	48.7	29.5	10.0	11.8	900	47.9	31.9	9.0	11.2
Market	378	51.9	27.2	6.3	14.6	522	49.8	25.7	9.3	15.2	900	50.7	26.3	8.1	14.9
School	378	86.2	10.6	2.6	0.6	522	84.5	7.7	5.3	2.5	900	85.2	8.9	4.2	1.7
Public transport	378	88.9	7.9	1.3	1.8	522	84.3	9.6	2.9	3.2	900	86.2	8.9	2.2	2.7
Post office	378	81.5	14.6	2.6	1.3	522	79.9	12.8	3.7	3.6	900	80.6	13.6	3.2	2.6
Bank	378	49.2	33.9	7.1	9.8	522	52.3	30.1	6.9	10.7	900	51.0	31.7	7.0	10.3
Temple	378	94.2	1.9	1.6	2.3	522	92.0	3.3	1.5	3.2	900	92.9	2.7	1.6	2.8
Library	378	55.3	18.8	4.8	21.1	522	54.2	17.2	5.9	22.7	900	54.7	17.9	5.4	22.0
Recreation club	378	48.4	15.1	3.2	33.3	522	49.4	11.3	3.6	35.7	900	49.0	12.9	3.4	34.7

available within two Kms for 48.4 per cent of male and 49.4 per cent of female elderly. The results indicate that except for hospital, bank, library and recreation facilities, all other important facilities were available to a majority of elderly at a reachable distance of within two Kms from their households.

Summary

The analysis of data on the background characteristics of elderly showed that about half of the elderly (50.8 per cent) interviewed in the survey were in the age group of 60-69 years. Among the 900 respondents interviewed in the survey 42 per cent were male and 58 per cent were female. Majority of elderly (61.8 per cent) were illiterates. The proportion of illiterates was more among female (79.1 per cent) than male (37.8 per cent). Most of the elderly (91.5 per cent) were Hindus. About three fourth (76.6 per cent) belonged to other than SC/ST group. Agriculture coolie was the main past occupation for nearly two third of elderly (65.4 per cent). Only one third of male (33.3 per cent) and 21.3 per cent of female were currently involved in income earning activities. About 42.1 per cent of male and 41.4 per cent of female had a monthly family income of more than Rs.3000/-. It is observed that 37.6 per cent of male and 38.3 per cent of female were living in huts. Majority of both male and female respondents were living in their own house. Most of the respondent's houses were electrified. Only 24.6 per cent of male and 25.7 per cent of female respondent's households were having toilet facilities. About three fifth of households were having only one or two rooms. The results indicate that except for hospital, bank, library and recreation facilities, all other important facilities were available to the elderly at a reachable distance of within two Kms from their households.

LIVING ARRANGEMENTS

Place of Living

The percent distribution of elderly by sex and living arrangements presented in Table 5 and Figure 1 showed that about one fourth of the total respondents (25.2 per cent) were living alone. Proportion of elderly living alone was more among female (31 per cent) than male (17.2 per cent). Nearly one fifth (19.3 per cent) of elderly were living with spouse. Proportion of elderly living with spouse was substantially higher among male (36 per cent) than female (7.5 per cent). Nearly two fifth (38.6 per cent) of respondents were living with sons. Proportion of elderly living with son was higher among female (40.2 per cent) than male (36.2 per cent). About 8.7 per cent of respondents were living with their daughters. Proportion of elderly living with their daughters was more among female (11.5 per cent) than male (4.8 per cent). It is also to be noted that 8.2 per cent of elderly were living with their distant relatives or friends.

Table 5

Percent Distribution of Elderly by Sex and Living Arrangements

Living Arrangements	*Male N=378*	*Female N=522*	*Total N=900*
Alone	17.2	31.0	25.2
Living with spouse	36.0	7.5	19.3
Living with son's family	36.2	40.2	38.6
Living with daughters family	4.8	11.5	8.7
Others	5.8	9.8	8.2

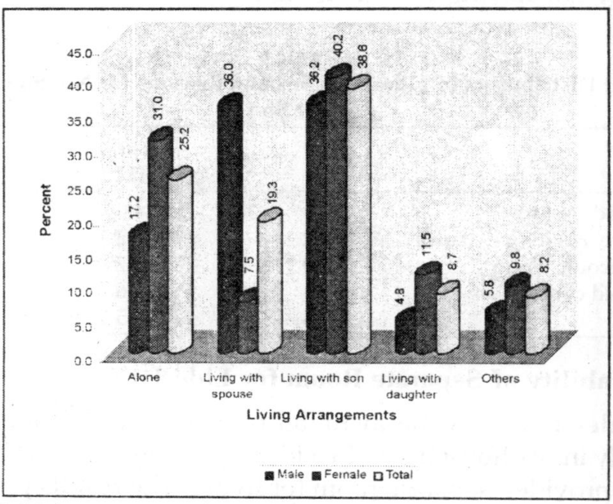

Figure 1: Living Arrangements of Elderly

Reasons for Not Staying with their Son

Traditionally elders used to live with their son's family. Hence the respondents who were not staying with their son were asked why they were not staying with their son's family. The results presented in Table 6 and Figure 2 revealed that 28.7 per cent of elderly were not having son at the time of interview. Higher proportion of female (34 per cent) were not having son as compared to male (22 per cent). About one third of elderly (32 per cent) reported that their sons were living at a long distance. Substantially higher proportion of male (38.2 per cent) reported that their sons were living at a long distance as compared to female elderly (27.2 per cent). About 17.6 per cent of elderly reported that they were not living with their son because of their poor living conditions. Higher proportion of male elderly (19.9 per cent) had reported 'low income' as the reason for not staying with their son compared to female elderly (15.7 per cent). The other major reason reported by the respondents was 'avoiding conflict' as reported by 16.6 per cent of male and 19.6 per cent of female respondents. The results indicated that migration of youngsters to long distance for employment and poverty were the major reasons for the elderly not staying with their son.

Table 6
Percent Distribution of Elderly by Sex and Reasons for Not Staying with their Son

Reasons	*Male* N=241	*Female* N=312	*Total* N=553
Son died/No son	22.0	34.0	28.7
Son live at a long distance	38.2	27.2	32.0
Low income status	19.9	15.7	17.6
To avoid conflict	16.6	19.6	18.3
Others	3.3	3.5	3.4

Availability of Separate Room for Elderly

In order to assess the availability of separate room for the elderly in the household, the elderly were asked whether they were provided separate room for living. The results presented in Table 7 revealed that 43.2 per cent of elderly were having

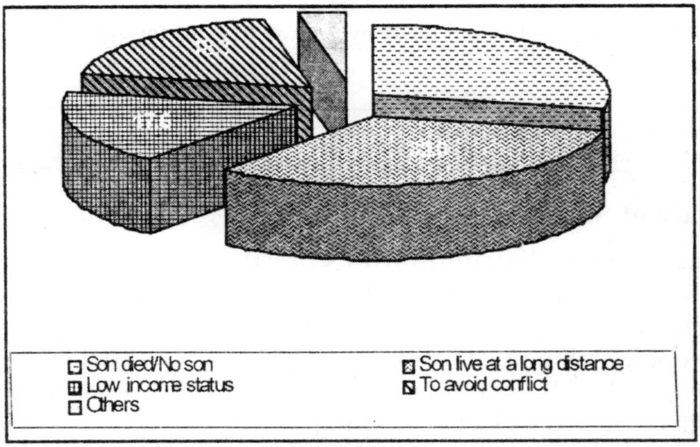

Figure 2: Reasons for Not Staying with Son

separate room in the household which includes 25.2 per cent of elderly who were living alone. Higher proportion of female elderly (47.9 per cent) were reported to have separate room in the household compared to male elderly (36.8 per cent).

Table 7
Percent Distribution of Elderly by Sex and Availability of Separate Room

Separate Room	*Male N=378*	*Female N=522*	*Total N=900*
Available	36.8	47.9	43.2
Not available	63.2	52.1	56.8

Reasons for Separate Room

The elderly who were provided separate room were asked about the reasons for the provision of separate room. The results presented in Table 8 revealed that most of the elderly (84.6 per cent) were given separate room for their comfortability. However 15.4 per cent reported that they were given separate room in order to prevent them being mingle with other family members and household activities. Slightly higher proportion of female elderly (16 per cent) were given separate room for isolation compared to male elderly (14.3 per cent).

Table 8
Percent Distribution of Elderly by Sex and Reasons for Separate Room

Reasons	*Male* N=42	*Female* N=75	*Total* N=117
Isolation	14.3	16.0	15.4
Facilitation	85.7	84.0	84.6

Place of Sleeping

The percent distribution of elderly by sex and place of sleeping/taking rest in the household is presented in Table 9. It is observed that most of the elderly (89.2 per cent) were sleeping/taking rest inside the house. Only 9.8 per cent were sleeping in the veranda of the house. There was not much difference in the place of sleeping/taking rest between the male and female elderly.

Table 9
Percent Distribution of Elderly by Sex and Place of Sleeping/Talking Rest

Place of Sleeping	*Male* N=239	*Female* N=272	*Total* N=511
Inside the house	88.3	90.1	89.2
Veranda of the house	10.0	9.6	9.8
Common place in the village	1.3	-	0.6
Friends/neighbour house	0.4	0.3	0.4

Reasons for Not Sleeping Inside the House

The elderly who were not sleeping inside the house were asked about the reasons for not sleeping inside the house. The results presented in Table 10 revealed that the main reason for not sleeping inside the house was 'inadequate space' (45.5 per cent), followed by 'not allowed' (29 per cent) and 'preferred to

Table 10
Percent Distribution of Elderly by Sex and Reasons for Not Sleeping Inside the House

Reasons	*Male* N=28	*Female* N=27	*Total* N=55
Inadequate space	42.9	48.1	45.5
Not allowed	28.6	29.6	29.0
Preferred to go outside	28.5	22.3	25.5

go outside' (25.5 per cent). The reasons stated for not sleeping inside the house did not vary much between male and female respondents.

Living Arrangements and Background Characteristics

The percent distribution of elderly by living arrangements and selected background characteristics presented in Table 11 showed that the proportion of elderly living alone was lowest at 21.2 per cent among elderly aged 80 years or more. The proportion of elderly living with spouse was also lowest at 10.9 per cent for elderly aged 80 years or more. Living with daughter increased with the age of elderly. It has increased from 7.2 per cent for elderly aged 60-69 years to 12.4 per cent for elderly aged 80 years or more. The c^2 test of significance showed significant association between age and living arrangements.

Significantly higher proportion of female elderly (31 per cent) were living alone compared to only 17.2 per cent of male elderly. This may be due to the fact that more number of female became widowed at older ages as they marry to persons aged several years more than themselves. Higher proportion of male elderly (36 per cent) were living with spouse, compared to only 7.5 per cent of female elderly. Proportion of elderly living with daughter was substantially higher among female (11.5 per cent) than male (4.8 per cent). The c^2 test of significance showed significant association between the sex of the elderly and living arrangements.

Proportion of elderly living alone was significantly lowest at 12.5 per cent among the elderly studied up to secondary and above. At the same time the proportion of elderly living with son decreased with the higher level of education (secondary and above). Education did not make much difference in the proportion of elderly living with daughter.

Earlier occupation of the elderly did not make much difference in the proportion of elderly living alone. Proportion of elderly living with spouse is observed to be high among those who had worked in government service (29 per cent) which was followed by those involved in agriculture work

Table 11
Percent Distribution of Elderly According to their Living Arrangements by Selected Background Characteristics

Back ground Characteristics	*N*	*Alone*	*Living with Spouse*	*Living with Son*	*Living with Daughter*	*Others*	*Chi-square*	*DF*	*P-value*
Age (Years)									
60 - 69	458	23.4	21.2	41.9	7.2	6.3			
70 - 79	305	29.8	20.7	32.8	9.2	7.5	28.330	8	0.000*
80+	137	21.2	10.9	40.2	12.4	15.3			
Sex									
Male	378	17.2	36.0	36.2	4.8	5.8	124.865	4	0.000*
Female	522	31.0	7.5	40.2	11.5	9.8			
Education									
Illiterate	556	27.3	14.9	38.7	9.7	9.4			
Primary (5th)	223	22.0	22.4	41.2	7.2	7.2	@	@	@
Middle (upto 8th)	89	24.7	29.2	33.8	6.7	5.6			
Secondary +	32	12.5	50.0	31.2	6.3	-			
Earlier occupation									
No work	116	24.1	7.8	44.8	11.2	12.1			
Coolie	589	26.0	19.7	38.0	7.8	8.5			
Agriculture	118	22.0	25.4	40.8	7.6	4.2	@	@	@
Government	31	25.8	29.0	35.5	3.2	6.5			
Others	46	26.1	23.9	26.1	19.6	4.3			

Contd.

Back ground Characteristics	N	Alone	Living with Spouse	Living with Son	Living with Daughter	Others	Chi-square	DF	P-value
Religion									
Hindu	823	25.1	19.6	39.1	8.1	8.1			
Muslim	48	31.3	16.6	31.2	14.6	6.3	@	@	@
Christian	29	20.7	20.7	34.5	13.8	10.3			
Caste									
SC / ST	237	19.0	24.9	37.1	7.2	11.8			
Other than SC/ST	663	27.5	17.5	39.0	9.2	6.8	10.310	4	0.003*
Monthly individual income (rupees)									
≤ 1000	226	32.7	29.2	29.3	4.4	4.4	@	@	@
1001 +	674	22.7	16.2	41.7	10.1	9.3			
Monthly family income (rupees)									
≤ 1000	266	61.3	22.9	7.5	3.4	4.9			
1001 - 2000	134	14.9	32.8	30.6	12.7	9.0			
2001 - 3000	125	6.4	20.0	52.8	12.0	8.8	354.203	12	0.000*
3001+	375	9.6	12.0	58.7	9.9	9.9			

* P<0.01 ** P<0.05 *** P<0.10

@ χ^2 not calculated as some of the cell frequencies are less than 5.

(25.4 per cent). Proportion of elderly living with son was highest at 44.8 per cent among those who had no work compared to those involved in agriculture work (40.8 per cent) and coolie (38 per cent).

Proportion of elderly living alone was more among Muslims (31.3 per cent) compared to Hindus (25.1 per cent) and Christians (20.7 per cent). Proportion of elderly living with spouse was nearly same around 20 per cent for both Hindus and Christians where as it was 16.6 per cent for Muslims.

Proportion of elderly living with son was highest among Hindus (39.1 per cent) compared to Christians (34.5 per cent) and Muslims (31.2 per cent). Proportion of elderly living with daughter was highest among Muslims (14.6 per cent) compared to Christians (13.8 per cent) and Hindus (8.1 per cent).

Higher proportion of elderly among other than SC/ST group (27.5 per cent) were living alone compared to SC/ST group (19 per cent). On the other hand, proportion living with spouse was more among SC/ST (24.9 per cent) compared to other than SC/ST group (17.5 per cent). There was not much difference between the proportion of elderly living with son (or) daughter between the SC/ST and non SC/ST groups. The χ^2 test of significance showed significant association between caste and living arrangements.

Significantly higher proportion of elderly from low income family (≤Rs.1000) were living alone compared to those who had higher monthly family income (>Rs.1000). Proportion of elderly living with son increased with monthly family income. It has increased from 7.5 per cent for those who had a monthly family income of Rs.1000 or less to 58.7 per cent for those who had a monthly family income of Rs.3000 or more. The χ^2 test of significance showed significant association between monthly family income and living arrangements of elderly.

Logistic Regression Analysis of Living Arrangements

The logistic regression analysis of the data on living arrangements by selected background characteristics of the respondents presented in Table 12 showed that the chances of living alone was 1.6 times higher for elderly aged 70-79 years

Table 12

Logistic Regression Analysis of Living Arrangements of Elderly by Selected Background Characteristics

		Alone		*Living with spouse*		*Living with son*		*Living with daughter*		*Others*	
Characteristic	*Reference*	*Yes=227 Odds ratio*	*No=673 Signi-ficant*	*Yes=175 Odds ratio*	*No=725 Signi-ficant*	*Yes=347 Odds ratio*	*No=553 Signi-ficant*	*Yes=78 Odds ratio*	*No=822 Signi-ficant*	*Yes=73 Odds ratio*	*No=827 Signi-ficant*
Age (years)											
	60 - 69										
70 – 79		1.630	0.006*	0.864	0.474	0.645	0.006*	1.297	0.349	1.184	0.570
80+		1.048	0.851	0.406	0.006*	0.823	0.343	1.661	0.125	2.828	0.001*
Sex											
	Male										
Female		2.547	0.000*	0.160	0.000*	1.018	0.918	2.740	0.002*	1.415	0.274
Education											
	Illiterate										
Primary (5th)		1.011	0.957	0.923	0.730	1.170	0.383	0.944	0.862	0.878	0.693
Middle (upto 8th)		1.259	0.432	1.172	0.598	0.878	0.620	0.904	0.836	0.639	0.397
Secondary+ (+2)		0.450	0.216	3.602	0.008*	0.772	0.574	0.779	0.780	0.003	0.572
Earlier occupation											
	No work										
Coolie		1.321	0.273	1.012	0.977	0.895	0.617	1.053	0.884	0.767	0.451
Agriculture		1.193	0.596	1.025	0.958	1.044	0.880	1.196	0.708	0.427	0.135
Government		3.012	0.046**	0.525	0.310	0.841	0.719	0.661	0.717	1.476	0.652
Others		1.548	0.313	0.764	0.635	0.578	0.177	3.690	0.013**	0.493	0.383

Contd.

		Alone		Living with spouse		Living with son		Living with daughter		Others	
Characteristic	*Reference*	*Yes=227 Odds ratio*	*No=673 Signi-ficant*	*Yes=175 Odds ratio*	*No=725 Signi-ficant*	*Yes=347 Odds ratio*	*No=553 Signi-ficant*	*Yes=78 Odds ratio*	*No=822 Signi-ficant*	*Yes=73 Odds ratio*	*No=827 Signi-ficant*
Religion											
	Hindu										
Muslim		1.296	0.440	0.948	0.903	0.661	0.203	1.842	0.170	0.861	0.810
Christian		0.946	0.910	0.659	0.438	0.894	0.784	2.073	0.219	1.256	0.729
Caste											
	SC/ST										
Other than SC/ST		1.586	0.019**	0.699	0.083***	1.066	0.696	1.181	0.582	0.504	0.011**
Monthly individual income (rupees)											
	≤ 500										
501 - 1000		0.667	0.300	2.759	0.005*	0.495	0.076***	1.199	0.827	0.464	0.478
1001 +		0.481	0.000*	0.766	0.259	1.582	0.014**	2.208	0.046**	1.594	0.220

*P<0.01 **P<0.05 ***P<0.10

compared to elderly aged 60-69 years. The chances of living alone were 2.5 times higher for female compared to male elderly. Elderly who had served in government had three times more chances of living alone compared to those who had no work. Similarly, elderly belonged to other than SC/ST group were having significantly higher chances of living alone compared to SC/ST group. Increase in the individual income significantly increases the chances of elderly living alone.

The chances of living with spouse was significantly less for elderly aged 80 years or more compared to elderly aged 60-69 years. The chances of living with spouse significantly less for female compared to male. Elderly who had higher education (higher secondary and above) were having more chances of living with spouse compared to illiterates. Elderly belonged to other than SC/ST group were having significantly less chances of living with spouse compared to SC/ST group. It is observed that elderly who had a monthly income in the range of Rs.501 to 1000 were having nearly three times higher chances of living with spouse compared to those who had an income of less than Rs.500/- per month.

The chances of elderly living with son was significantly less for those aged 70-79 years compared to those aged 60-69 years. Increase in the individual income significantly increases the chances of elderly living with son's family. Elderly who had an income of more than Rs.1000 per month had 1.6 times more chances of living with their son compared to those who had an income of Rs.500 or less per month.

The chances of living with daughter were 2.7 times higher for female compared to male. Elderly who had a monthly income of more than Rs.1000/- per month had 2.2 times more chances of living with daughter compared to those who had a monthly income of Rs.500 or less per month.

Summary

The analysis of data on the living arrangements of elderly revealed that about one fourth of elderly were living alone (25.2 per cent), nearly one fifth (19.3 per cent) were living with their spouse and nearly two fifth (38.6 per cent) were living with son. It is also observed that 8.7 per cent of elderly were living with their daughter. Substantially higher proportion of female elderly (31 per cent) were living alone compared to male elderly (17.2 per cent). The main reasons for not staying with son was 'son live at a long distance' (32 per cent) followed by 'no son' (28.7 per cent), 'to avoid conflict' (18 per cent) and 'poverty' (17.6 per cent). Only 43.2 per cent of elderly had reported to have separate room in the household. Higher proportion of female elderly (47.9 per cent) were having separate room in the household compared to male elderly (36.8 per cent). Most of the elderly (89.2 per cent) were sleeping/ taking rest inside the house. The main reasons for not sleeping inside the house were 'inadequate space' (45.5 per cent). Elderly living with daughter increased with the age. Proportion of elderly living with daughter was significantly higher among female than male. Proportion of elderly living with son was lowest among those who had studied up to higher secondary and above than others. Proportion of elderly living alone was more among Muslims than among Hindus and Christians. Proportion of elderly living with daughter's family was also more among Muslims than Hindus and Christians. The logistic regression analysis showed that elderly aged 70-79 years, female elderly, those who served in government, those who had higher income (more than Rs.1000/- per month) were having significantly higher chances of living alone.

FAMILIAL RELATIONSHIP

In order to assess the extent of cordial relationship maintained by elderly with other family members, informations were collected on various aspects of familial relationship from the elderly and the results are presented in this section.

Freedom to Avail Household Facilities

The percent distribution of elderly by sex and their level of freedom to use household facilities in their daily life are presented in Table 13. It is observed that most of the elderly were accessible to use the available household amenities such as TV/Radio, sofa set/furniture and sharing of bathroom/

toilet. Overall, 82.5 per cent of elderly reported to have freedom to use television/radio at home. There was not much gender difference in the proportion of elderly having freedom to use television/radio at home. Freedom to use sofa/furniture was reported by more than three fourth of elderly (76.7 per cent). Substantially higher proportion of male elderly (82.3 per cent) were having freedom to use sofa/furniture compared to female elderly (71.9 per cent). Freedom to share bathroom/toilet was reported by 86.5 per cent of elderly. There was not much gender difference in the freedom to use bath room/toilet at home.

Table 13
Percent Distribution of Elderly by Sex and Freedom to Avail Facilities at Home

Facilities	*Male* N=378	*Female* N=522	*Total* N=900
Using TV/Radio	83.2	81.9	82.5
Using sofa/Furniture	82.3	71.9	76.7
Sharing bath room/Toilet	88.2	85.0	86.5

Cordial Relationship

The percent distribution of elderly having cordial relationship with family members by sex is presented in Table 14. It is observed that most of the respondents were having cordial relationship with family members. Substantially higher proportion (91.2 per cent) of elderly were having cordial relationship with spouse, 74.3 per cent were having cordial relationship with their son, 72.4 were having cordial relationship with their daughters, 70.5 per cent were having cordial relationship with daughter-in-law, 73.1 per cent were having cordial relationship with their son-in-law and 85 per cent were having cordial relationship with other family members. There was not much gender difference in the proportion of elderly having cordial relationship with all family members except for daughter-in-law and son-in-law where the proportion of elderly having cordial relationship was comparatively lower among female than male.

Table 14
Percent Distribution of Elderly having Cordial Relationship with Family Members by Sex

Family Members	*Male* N=378	*Female* N=522	*Total* N=900
Spouse	92.3	88.1	91.2
Son	78.0	71.4	74.3
Daughter	81.4	74.5	72.4
Daughter-in-law	74.7	67.3	70.5
Son-in-law	77.5	69.7.	73.1
Other family members	85.6	84.5	85.0

Participation in Family Ceremonies

The percent distribution of elderly by sex and their participation in family ceremonies is presented in Table 15. It is observed that only 58.2 per cent of male and 46.3 per cent of female elderly had been participating in all family ceremonies. It is seen that the proportion elderly participating in all family ceremonies was substantially higher among male than female.

Table 15
Percent Distribution of Elderly by Sex and their Participation in Family Ceremonies

Participation	*Male* N=368	*Female* N=492	*Total* N=860*
Yes	58.2	46.3	51.4
No	41.8	53.7	48.6

* 40 respondents did not have child

Reasons for Not Participating in Family Ceremonies

The percent distribution of elderly by sex and reasons for not participating in family ceremonies is presented in Table 16. The major reasons reported by male elderly were 'no interest' and 'physical condition not good' (44.8 per cent each). Among the female, the major reasons were 'not interested' (43.6 per cent) and 'physical condition not good' (41.7 per cent). 'No respect' was reported by 5.8 per cent of male and 9.1 per cent of female elderly. The reasons reported for non-participation in family ceremonies did not vary much between the male and female elderly.

Table 16
Percent Distribution of Elderly by Sex and Reasons for Not Participating in Family Ceremonies

Reasons	*Male* N=154	*Female* N=264	*Total* N=425
Not Permitted	3.9	4.2	4.1
No interest·	44.8	43.6	44.0
No respect	5.8	9.1	7.9
Physical condition not good	44.8	41.7	42.8
No money	0.7	1.4	1.2

Consultation on Important Family Matters

The percent distribution of elderly by sex and consultation on important family matters is presented in Table 17. It is observed that only 55.4 per cent of male and 38.6 per cent of female elderly were consulted by family members on important family matters. The results showed that higher proportion of male were consulted on important family matters than female.

Table 17
Percent Distribution of Elderly by Sex and Consultation on Important Family Matters

Consultation on Important Family Matters	*Male* N=368	*Female* N=492	*Total* N=860
Yes	55.4	38.6	45.8
No	44.6	61.4	54.2

*40 respondents did not have child

Reasons for Not Consulted on Important Family Matters

The percent distribution of elderly by sex and reasons for not consulting them on important family matters is presented in

Table 18
Percent Distribution of Elderly by Sex and Reasons for Not Consulting them on Important Family Matters

Reasons	*Male* N=164	*Female* N=302	*Total* N=466
Not permitted	9.8	9.2	9.4
No interest	60.4	65.9	63.9
No respect / No money	26.2	21.9	23.5
Physical condition not good	3.6	3.0	3.2

Table 18. The main reasons reported by the elderly were 'no interest' (60.4 per cent of male and 65.9 per cent of female), 'no respect/no money' (26.2 per cent of male and 21.9 per cent of female) and 'not permitted' (9.8 per cent of male and 9.2 per cent of female). The reasons reported for not consulting them on important family matters did not vary much between the male and female elderly.

Role in Solving Family Disputes

The per cent distribution of elderly by sex and their role in solving family disputes presented in Table 19 showed that only 55.4 per cent of male and 40.4 per cent of female elderly had involved in solving family disputes. The results showed that the proportion of elderly who had role in solving family dispute was more among male than female.

Table 19
Percent Distribution of Elderly by Sex and their Role in Solving Family Disputes

Role in Solving Family Disputes	*Male N=368*	*Female N=492*	*Total N=860*
Yes	55.4	40.4	46.9
No	44.6	59.6	53.1

* 40 respondents had no child

Reasons for Not having Any Role in Family Disputes

The percent distribution of elderly by sex and reasons for not having any role in family disputes is presented in Table 20. The major reasons reported by the elderly were 'no interest' (65.2 per cent of male and 73 per cent of female) and 'not

Table 20
Percent Distribution of Elderly by Sex and Reasons for Non Involvement in Solving Family Disputes

Reasons	*Male N=164*	*Female N=299*	*Total N=463*
No interest	65.2	73.0	70.2
Not permitted / No respect	33.0	25.3	28.0
Physical condition not good	1.8	1.7	1.8

permitted/no respect' (33 per cent of male and 25.3 per cent of female). The reasons cited for non involvement in solving family disputes did not vary much between male and female elderly.

Abuse Behaviour of Family Members

The percent distribution of elderly who had experienced abusive behaviour from their family members by sex is presented in Table 21. It is observed that only 20.1 per cent of male and 15.9 per cent of female elderly had experienced abusive behaviour from family members. The results indicated that the proportion of elderly who had experienced abusive behaviour from family members was higher among male than female.

Table 21
Percent Distribution of Elderly who had Experienced Abusive Behaviour from Family Members by Sex

Experience of Abusive Behaviour	*Male N=368*	*Female N=492*	*Total N=860*
Yes	20.1	15.9	17.1
No	79.9	84.1	82.9

*40 respondents had no child

Type of Abuse

The percent distribution of elderly by sex and type of abusive behaviour of family members is presented in Table 22. The main type of abuse reported by the elderly was 'not given food' (43.2 per cent of male and 34.5 per cent of female) followed by

Table 22
Percent Distribution of Elderly by Sex and Type of Abusive Behaviour of Family Members

Type of Abuse	*Male N=74*	*Female N=78*	*Total N=152*
Verbal abuse	18.9	20.5	19.7
Beating and verbal abuse	17.6	16.6	17.2
Lack of care / Neglect	12.2	11.8	11.8
Not given food	43.2	34.5	38.8
Verbal abuse and not given food	8.1	16.6	12.5

'verbal abuse' (18.9 per cent of male and 20.5 per cent of female) and 'both beating and verbal abuse' (17.6 per cent of male and 16.6 per cent of female).

Frequency of Taking Food

The percent distribution of elderly by sex and frequency of taking food daily is presented in Table 23. It is observed that 54.5 per cent of male and 51.3 per cent of female were taking food thrice a day and 39.9 per cent of male and 42.6 per cent of female were taking food twice a day. There was not much gender difference in the frequency of food taken by the elderly. The results indicated that nearly half of the elderly in rural areas were not getting food three times a day.

Table 23
Percent Distribution of Elderly by Sex and Frequency of Taking Food Daily

Frequency of food	*Male* *N=378*	*Female* *N=522*	*Total* *N=900*
Three times	54.5	51.3	52.8
Two times	39.9	42.6	41.4
One time	3.2	3.6	3.4
As many times as need	2.4	2.5	2.4

Adequacy of Daily in Take of Food

The percent distribution of elderly by sex and adequacy of daily intake of food presented in Table 24 showed that 75.4 per cent of male and 78 per cent of female elderly had adequate food daily. About one forth of male (24.6 per cent) and 22 per cent of female elderly did not have adequate food daily. There was not much gender difference in the adequacy of daily intake of food.

Table 24
Percent Distribution of Elderly by Sex and Adequacy of Daily Intake of Food

Adequacy of Food	*Male* *N=378*	*Female* *N=522*	*Total* *N=900*
Yes	75.4	78.0	76.9
No	24.6	22.0	23.1

Requirement of Special Food

The percent distribution of elderly by sex and requirement of special food to be prepared for them at home is presented in Table 25. It is observed that 30.4 per cent of male and 27 per cent of female elderly were in need of special food to be prepared for them. Majority of elderly (69.6 per cent of male and 73 per cent of female) were not required any special food. It is found that the proportion elderly requiring special food to be prepared for them was higher among male than female.

Table 25
Percent Distribution of Elderly by Sex and Requirement of Special Food to be Prepared for them

Requirement of special food	*Male* N=378	*Female* N=522	*Total* N=900
Yes	30.4	27.0	28.4
No	69.6	73.0	71.6

Availability of Special Food at Home

The percent distribution of elderly by sex and availability of required special food at home is presented in Table 26. It is found that among those who were in need of special food, only 58.3 per cent of male and 55.3 per cent of female elderly were getting their required special food at home. The results showed that the proportion elderly getting special food at home was slightly higher among male than female.

Table 26
Percent Distribution of Elderly by Sex and Availability of Special Food at Home

Getting special food at home	*Male* N=115	*Female* N=141	*Total* N=256
Yes	58.3	55.3	56.6
No	41.7	44.7	43.4

Reasons for Not Getting Special Food

The percent distribution of elderly by sex and reasons for not getting the required special food at home is presented in

Table 27. The major reasons reported by the elderly were poverty (70.9 per cent male and 74.6 per cent female), no affection (18.8 per cent male and 17.5 per cent female) and no one to care (10.3 per cent male and 7.9 per cent female). The reasons reported for not getting special food at home did not vary much between the male and female elderly.

Table 27
Percent Distribution of Elderly by Sex and Reasons for Not Getting Special Food at Home

Reasons	*Male* N=48	*Female* N=63	*Total* N=111
No one to care	10.3	7.9	9.0
No affection	18.8	17.5	18.0
Poverty	70.9	74.6	73.0

Need of Money

The percent distribution of elderly by sex and need of money to meet their personal needs is presented in Table 28. It is observed that most of the elderly (95.8 per cent of male and 96.2 per cent of female) were in need of money to meet their personal needs. The proportion of elderly who were need of money to meet their personal needs did not vary much between male and female.

Table 28
Percent Distribution of Elderly by Sex and Need of Money to Meet their Personal Needs

Need of Money	*Male* N=378	*Female* N=522	*Total* N=900
Yes	95.8	96.2	96.0
No	4.2	3.8	4.0

Personal Needs

The percent distribution of elderly by sex and main personal needs that required money is presented in Table 29. The main personal needs which required money for elderly were 'tea/ coffee/ tobacco' (56.4 per cent of male and 49.6 per cent of female). 'Medicine' (31 per cent of male and 34.2 per cent of female) and 'going to hospital/temple' (6 per cent of male and 10 per cent of female). The main personal needs reported by the elderly did not vary much between the male and female.

Table 29
Percent Distribution of Elderly by Sex and Main Personal Needs that Required Money

Main personal needs	*Male* N=362	*Female* N=502	*Total* N=864
Medicines	31.0	34.2	32.8
Tea/Coffee/Tobacco	56.4	49.6	52.2
Going to hospital / Temple	6.0	10.0	8.0
Others	6.6	6.2	7.0

Availability of Finance

The percent distribution of elderly by sex and availability of sufficient finance of their own to meet their personal needs presented in Table 30 showed that only 34.3 per cent of male and 28.3 per cent of female elderly were having adequate finance of their own to meet their personal needs. Majority of elderly (65.7 per cent of male and 71.7 per cent of female) were not having adequate finance of their own. The results showed that higher proportion of male elderly were having adequate finance of their own to meet their personal needs than female.

Table 30
Percent Distribution of Elderly by Sex and Availability of Sufficient Finance of their Own to Meet their Personal Needs

Availability of finance	*Male* N=362	*Female* N=502	*Total* N=864
Yes	34.3	28.3	30.8
No	65.7	71.7	69.2

Sources of Finance

The percent distribution of elderly by sex and main sources of money to meet their personal needs is presented in Table 31. The main sources of money for the elderly were son (55.5 per cent of male and 51.7 per cent of female), daughter (13 per cent of male and 21.4 per cent of female) and grandchildren

(20.2 per cent of male and 17.5 per cent of female). The reported sources of money to meet their personal needs did not vary much between the male and female elderly.

Table 31
Percent Distribution of Elderly by Sex and Main Sources of Money for their Personal Needs

Sources of money	*Male* N=238	*Female* N=360	*Total* N=598
Son	55.5	51.7	53.2
Daughter	13.0	21.4	18.1
Grand children	20.2	17.5	18.6
Spouse	2.5	1.4	1.7
Others (brothers and sisters, son-in-law, daughter-in-law)	8.8	8.0	8.4

Sufficiency of Money to Meet their Personal Needs

The percent distribution of elderly by sex and sufficiency of money to meet their personal needs is presented in Table 32. Only 20.2 per cent of male and 31.7 per cent of female elderly had reported to have sufficient money to meet their personal needs. Most of the elderly (79.8 per cent of male and 68.3 per cent of female) were not getting sufficient money to meet their personal needs. The results showed that higher proportion of female elderly were having sufficient money to meet their personal needs than male.

Table 32
Percent Distribution of Elderly by Sex and Sufficiency of Money to Meet their Personal Needs

Sufficiency of money	*Male* N=238	*Female* N=360	*Total* N=598
Sufficient	20.2	31.7	27.1
Not sufficient	79.8	68.3	72.9

Summary

The results of the analysis of data on the status of relationship with other family members showed that most of the elderly were having freedom to use household facilities and were maintaining cordial relationship with their spouse. About 70-

74 per cent of elderly were maintaining cordial relationship with their son, daughter, daughter-in-law and son-in-law and 85 per cent were maintaining cordial relationship with other family members. Only half of the elderly had reported to have attended all family ceremonies. The main reasons for not attending the family ceremonies were 'not interested' (44 per cent) and 'poor health condition' (42.8 per cent). Less than half of the elderly (45.8 per cent) were consulted on important family matters. Comparatively higher proportion of male were consulted on important family matters than female elderly. Only 46.9 per cent of elderly had reported to have role in solving family disputes. Higher proportion of male (55.4 per cent) had involved in solving family disputes compared to only 40.4 per cent of female elderly. Only 17.1 per cent of elderly had reported to have experienced abuse behaviour from the family members. About half of the elderly (52.7 per cent) reported to have food thrice a day and 41.9 per cent had two times a day. About 28.4 per cent of elderly were in need of special food to be prepared for them. Only 58.3 per cent of male and 55.3 per cent of female elderly were getting their required special food at home. Most of the elderly (95.8 per cent of male and 96.2 per cent of female) were in need of money to meet their personal needs. The main personal needs which required money were tea/coffee/tobacco (56.4 per cent of male and 49.6 per cent of female). Majority of elderly (65.7 per cent of male and 71.7 per cent of female) were not having adequate finance of their own. Their main sources of money were son (55.5 per cent of male and 51.7 per cent of female). Most of the elderly (79.8 per cent of male and 68.3 per cent of female) were not getting sufficient money to meet their personal needs.

PERSONAL LIFE STYLE BEHAVIOUR OF ELDERLY

Life Style Behaviour

In order to assess the personal life style behaviour of elderly, they were asked whether they had the practice of doing prayer, walking, gardening, meditation, yoga, exercise, going to religious centres, social service activities and going to

Table 33
Percent Distribution of Elderly by Sex and Daily Life Style Behaviour

Daily life style	*N*	*Male*			*Female*			*Total*		
		N	*O*	*R*	*N*	*O*	*R*	*N*	*O*	*R*
Prayer	900	21.5	42.3	36.2	17.0	48.3	34.7	18.9	45.8	35.3
Walking	900	30.5	39.9	29.6	33.1	37.4	29.5	32.0	38.4	29.6
Gardening	900	51.0	15.9	33.1	60.1	9.2	30.7	56.3	12.0	31.7
Meditation	900	66.4	3.7	29.9	68.6	1.7	29.7	67.6	2.6	29.8
Yoga	900	68.3	2.1	29.6	69.3	1.2	29.5	68.8	1.6	29.6
Exercise	900	64.8	7.1	28.1	65.5	5.6	28.9	65.2	6.2	28.6
Going to religious centre	900	37.6	43.1	19.3	39.5	44.6	15.9	38.7	44.0	17.3
Social activities	900	64.3	7.4	28.3	67.8	2.7	29.5	66.3	4.7	29.0
Going to recreation center	900	59.3	14.2	26.5	64.0	8.6	27.4	62.0	11.0	27.0

*N=Never
O=Occasional
R=Regular

recreation centre. The results of the analysis of data presented in Table 33 revealed that only 35.3 per cent of elderly were having the regular practice of prayer, 29.6 per cent were having the regular practice of walking, 31.7 per cent were having the regular practice of gardening, 29.8 per cent were having the regular practice of meditation, 29.6 per cent were having the regular practice of yoga, 28.6 per cent were having the regular practice doing exercise, just 17.3 per cent were having the regular practice of going to religious centres, 29 per cent had involved in social service activities and 27 per cent were having the practice of going to recreation centre regularly. There was not much gender difference in the daily life style behaviour of elderly. Overall, the results indicated that the practice of healthy life style behaviour was very poor among the elderly in rural areas.

Life Style Behaviour by Age and Sex

The life style behaviour of elderly by age and sex presented in Table 34 showed that the practice of prayer was more at ages 80 or more compared to those aged 60-69 and 70-79 years. It was 41.6 per cent among those aged 80 or over compared to 35.2 per cent observed for 60-69 years and 32.8 per cent observed for 70-79 years. The practice of prayer did not vary much between male and female at different age groups of elderly. The practice of walking has declined significantly with the increase in age. The proportion of elderly having the practice of walking was 36.5 per cent at ages 60-69 years, 25.2 per cent at ages 70-79 years and 16.1 per cent at ages 80 years or more.

The practice of gardening was lowest at 24.8 per cent at ages 80 or more compared to 34.5 per cent at ages 60-69 years and 30.5 per cent at ages 70-79 years. The practice of meditation, yoga, exercise, going to religious centre, involving in social service activities and going to recreation centres had decreased with advancement of age. At the terminal ages of 80 or more, most of the elderly could not do any of the physical activities.

Table 34

Percent Distribution of Elderly by their Daily Life Style Behaviour, Age and Sex

Daily life style behaviour	*Male*				*Female*				*Total*			
	60-69 N=172	*70-79* N=144	*80+* N=62	*All* N=378	*60-69* N=286	*70-79* N=161	*80+* N=75	*All* N=522	*60-69* N=458	*70-79* N=305	*80+* N=137	*All* N=900
Prayer	36.6	34.0	40.3	36.2	34.3	31.7	42.7	34.7	35.2	32.8	41.6	35.3
Walking	37.8	25.7	16.1	29.6	35.7	24.8	16.0	29.5	36.5	25.2	16.1	29.6
Gardening	38.4	27.8	30.6	33.1	32.2	32.9	20.0	30.7	34.5	30.5	24.8	31.3
Meditation	29.1	30.6	30.6	29.9	31.1	32.9	17.3	29.7	30.0	31.8	23.4	29.8
Yoga	29.1	30.6	29.0	29.6	30.4	32.9	18.7	29.5	29.9	31.8	23.4	29.6
Exercise	26.7	29.2	29.0	28.0	30.1	31.7	18.7	28.9	28.8	30.5	23.4	28.6
Going to religious centre	18.6	22.9	12.9	19.3	13.3	20.5	16.0	15.9	15.3	21.6	14.6	17.3
Social activities	28.5	28.5	27.4	28.3	30.8	32.3	18.7	29.5	29.9	30.5	22.6	29.0
Going to recreation centre	27.3	25.0	27.4	26.5	28.7	29.2	18.7	27.4	28.2	27.2	22.6	27.0

Support to Household Activities

In order to assess the elder's contribution/support to household chores, the elders were asked whether they had ever involved in the household domestic activities such as cooking, shopping, fetching water, schooling children, cleaning household and disposal of waste. The results of the analysis of data presented in Table 35 showed that comparatively higher proportion of female elderly were supporting/contributing to household chores compared to male elderly. It is observed that 64.8 per cent of female elderly had helped the family in cooking where as it was only 20.4 per cent for male elderly. Nearly two third of female (64.8 per cent) and nearly half of the male (47.9 per cent) respondents had helped the family for shopping. More than half of the female (55.4 per cent) and one fourth of male (25.1 per cent) had helped the family in fetching water. Schooling of children was reported by 17.6 per cent of female and 13.2 per cent of male elderly. Only 22.6 per cent of female and 16.4 per cent of male elderly had reported to have involved in engaging children at home. More than half of the female (53.6 per cent) and just 18.5 per cent of male elderly had involved in the maintenance of household and 51.9 per cent of female and 15.1 per cent of male elderly had involved in the cleaning of house and surroundings. About 47.7 per cent of female and 13.5 per cent of male elderly had involved in disposal of household waste. The results showed that the support to household work decreased with increase in age of the elderly. It is also observed that substantially higher proportion of female had involved in household work than male.

Leisure Time Activities

The percent distribution of elderly by their leisure time activities and living arrangements is presented in Table 36. It is seen that the major leisure time activities was watching television (39.2 per cent) followed by visiting friends (36.1 per cent); visiting temple (35 per cent); listening to radio (23.3 per cent); spending time at local tea shops (20.2 per cent); and reading news papers (18.9 per cent). Elderly living alone mostly

Table 35

Percent Distribution of Elderly by Sex, Age and Involvement in Household Work

Household Work	Male				Female				Total			
	All N=378	60-69 N=172	70-79 N=144	80+ N=62	All N=522	60-69 N=286	70-79 N=161	80+ N=75	All N=900	60-69 N=458	70-79 N=305	80+ N=137
Cooking	20.4	21.5	21.5	14.5	64.8	75.9	55.9	41.3	6.1	55.5	39.7	29.1
Shopping	47.9	57.0	48.6	21.0	64.8	75.2	57.8	40.0	57.7	68.3	53.4	31.4
Fetching water	25.1	29.7	25.0	12.9	55.4	68.2	46.6	25.3	42.7	53.7	36.4	19.7
Schooling of children	13.2	17.4	10.4	8.1	17.6	19.9	16.8	10.7	15.8	19.0	13.8	9.5
Engaging children	16.4	20.9	14.6	8.1	22.6	24.1	21.1	20.0	20.0	22.9	18.0	14.6
Maintain the household	18.5	22.7	18.8	6.5	53.6	64.0	42.9	37.3	38.9	48.5	31.5	23.4
Cleaning the house and the surroundings	15.1	16.3	18.1	4.8	51.9	60.5	42.9	38.7	36.4	43.9	31.1	23.4
Disposal of household waste	13.5	15.1	15.3	4.8	47.7	57.3	40.4	26.7	33.3	41.5	28.5	16.8

spend their leisure time by visiting temple (27.8 per cent), visiting friends (27.3 per cent), watching television (22 per cent), listening to radio (15.9 per cent) and reading news papers (15.4 per cent). Elderly living with spouse spend their leisure times mainly on visiting friends (46.3 per cent), watching television (41.1 per cent), visiting temple (38.9 per cent), spending time in local tea shop (36.6 per cent), listening to radio (36 per cent) and reading newspapers (30.9 per cent). Elderly living with son's family spend their leisure times mainly on watching television (49.9 per cent); visiting friends (39.8 per cent); visiting temple (39.5 per cent); Playing with grandchildren (23.9 per cent); Listening to radio (23.3 per cent) and reading news papers (18.7 per cent). Elderly living with daughter's family spend their leisure times mainly on watching television (41 per cent), visiting temple (32.1 per cent), visiting friends (28.2 per cent), playing with grandchildren (24.4 per cent) and listening to radio (16.7 per cent).

Table 36
Percent Distribution of Elderly by their Leisure Time Activities and Living Arrangements

Leisure Time Activities	*Living Arrangements*					
	Alone N=227	*Living with Spouse N=175*	*Living with Son N=347*	*Living with Daughter N=78*	*Others N=73*	*Total N=900*
Reading newspapers	15.4	30.9	18.7	10.3	11.0	18.9
Listening to radio	15.9	36.0	23.3	16.7	23.3	23.3
Watching T.V	22.0	41.1	49.9	41.0	35.6	39.2
Playing with grand children	6.6	14.3	23.9	24.4	21.9	17.6
Visiting temple	27.8	38.9	39.5	32.1	30.1	35.0
Engage in social activities	4.8	10.3	6.3	5.1	5.5	6.6
Visiting friends	27.3	46.3	39.8	28.2	30.1	36.1
Going to cinema house	0.4	2.3	2.9	1.3	1.4	1.9
Playing cards	1.8	2.9	2.3	0	2.7	2.1
Spending time at local tea shop	12.8	36.6	19.6	12.8	15.1	20.2

Leisure Time Activities by Age and Sex

The percent distribution of elderly by their leisure time activities according to age and sex is presented in Table 37. It

Table 37
Percent Distribution of Elderly by their Leisure Time Activities, Age and Sex

Leisure time activities	*Male*				*Female*				*Total*			
	All N=378	*60-69* N=172	*70-79* N=144	*80+* N=62	*All* N=522	*60-69* N=286	*70-79* N=161	*80+* N=75	*All* N=900	*60-69* N=458	*70-79* N=305	*80+* N=137
Reading news paper	34.9	38.4	26.4	45.2	7.3	7.0	8.1	6.7	18.9	18.8	16.7	24.1
Listening to radio	36.8	38.4	31.9	43.5	13.6	14.3	9.9	18.7	23.3	23.4	20.3	29.9
Watching T.V	43.9	54.7	31.3	43.5	35.8	39.5	32.3	29.3	39.2	45.2	31.8	35.8
Playing with grand children	18.0	22.1	12.5	19.4	17.2	17.5	16.8	17.3	17.6	19.2	14.8	18.2
Visiting temple	37.3	41.3	36.8	27.4	33.3	39.9	31.1	13.3	35.0	40.4	33.8	19.7
Engage in social activities	9.0	49.7	6.3	19.4	4.8	2.8	3.7	14.7	6.6	4.6	4.9	16.8
Visiting friends	45.2	49.4	47.2	29.0	29.5	31.8	32.9	13.3	36.1	38.4	39.7	20.4
Going to cinema	1.9	1.7	1.4	3.2	1.9	2.4	0.6	2.7	1.9	2.2	1.0	2.9
Playing cards	3.2	2.3	2.8	6.5	-	-	-	-	2.1	1.1	2.3	5.1
Spending time at local tea shop	42.9	50.6	40.3	27.4	-	-	-	-	20.2	20.7	21.6	15.3

is observed that the proportion of male elderly involved in physical movement such as visiting temple, visiting friends and spending time in local tea shop has decreased with the increase in age. At the same time, indoor activities such as reading newspapers, listening to radio, playing with grandchildren has increased with age as they could not move freely with the advancement of age. In the case of female also, the proportion of elderly going to temple and visiting friends have decreased significantly with the increase in age. The results indicated that the types of leisure time activities of elderly have changed with the increase in age and most of them have resorted to indoor activities at the ages of 80 and over.

Personal Habits

The percent distribution of elderly by their personal habits and sex is presented in Table 38. The personal habits of elderly were classified into four types as past, present, always and never. Among the male elderly, the use of betel nuts was the main personal habit (30.7 per cent) followed by smoking (22.5 per cent), tobacco (20.9 per cent) and drinking (11.1 per cent). It is also observed that 62.7 per cent of elderly had never used to smoke in their life, 76.5 per cent had never used alcohol, 91 per cent had never used drugs, 76.5 per cent had never used tobacco, 93.6 per cent had never used snuff powder and 64.3 per cent had never used betel nuts in their life. None of the female elderly had ever smoke, drink alcohol or used drugs in their life. Only 12.6 per cent of female elderly were reported to have the habit of tobacco chewing, 36.4 per cent were using betel nuts and just 4.9 per cent were using snuff powder. The personal habits which are injurious to health were observed to be more among male than female. Even among the male, only very small proportion (less than one third) of elderly had reported to have one or the other personal habits which are injurious to health.

Summary

The results of the analysis of data on the life style behaviour of elderly revealed that the practice of healthy life style behaviour was poor among the elderly. The practice of

Table 38
Percent Distribution of Elderly by their Personal Habits and Sex

Personal habits	Male (N=378)				Female(N=522)				Total (N=900)			
	Past	Present	Always	Never	Past	Present	Always	Never	Past	Present	Always	Never
Smoking	14.3	0.5	22.5	62.7	-	-	-	100.0	6.0	0.2	9.4	84.4
Drinking	11.9	0.5	11.1	76.5	-	-	-	100.0	5.0	0.2	4.7	90.1
Drug use	2.1	0.3	6.6	91.0	-	-	-	100.0	0.8	0.1	2.8	96.3
Tobacco	2.1	0.5	20.9	76.5	2.3	1.3	12.6	83.8	2.2	1.0	16.1	80.7
Snuff powder	1.1	1.1	4.2	93.6	1.5	1.7	4.9	91.7	1.3	1.5	4.7	92.5
Betel nuts	4.2	0.8	30.7	64.3	4.6	2.1	36.4	56.9	4.4	1.6	34.0	60.0

walking, gardening, meditation, yoga, social service activities and going to recreation centres had decreased with increase in age. Higher proportion of female elderly had involved in household activities compared to male elderly. The involvement of elderly in household activities decreased with the increase in age. At the ages of 80 and over, comparatively small proportion of elderly had involved in household activities. The main leisure time activities of elderly were watching television, visiting friends, visiting temple, listening to radio and reading newspapers. The leisure time activities of elderly have changed with the increase in age. The personal habits which are injurious to health were observed to be more among male than female. Even among the male, very small proportion (less than one third of elderly) had reported to have one or the other personal habits which are injurious to health.

PHYSICAL DISABILITY

Difficulties in Daily Living Activities

Informations on the physical difficulties faced by the elderly in eating, dressing, bathing, indoor walk, outdoor walk, climbing stairs, combing hair, getting up, going to toilet and boarding train/bus were collected from the elderly and the results of the analysis of data are presented in Table 39. The main difficulty reported by the male elderly was boarding train/bus (32 per cent) which was followed by climbing stairs (31.2 per cent), getting up (29.6 per cent); out door walk (26.7 per cent) and going to toilet (20.6 per cent). Most of the elderly who had difficulties were in need of help. The availability of help ranged from 38.5 per cent for going to toilet to 92.3 per cent for dressing. In the case of female elderly, the main difficulties reported were boarding train/ bus (42.3 per cent), climbing stairs (33.3 per cent), getting up (29.3 per cent), out door walk (22.8 per cent) and going to toilet (14.9 per cent). Most of the female elderly had reported that they were in need of help to meet their difficulties. Substantially higher proportion of elderly who were in need of help were not getting the required help. The availability of help ranged from 41.4 per cent for climbing stairs to 66.7 per cent for eating and

Table 39
Percent Distribution of Elderly by Physical Disabilities, Availability of Help and Sex

Physical activities	Male							Female							Total						
		Difficulties		Need help		Availability of help			Difficulties		Need help		Availability of help			Difficulties		Need help		Availability of help	
	N	No.	%	No.	%	No.	%	N	No.	%	No.	%	No.	%	N	No.	%	No.	%	No.	%
Eating	378	13	3.4	9	69.2	8	88.9	522	16	3.1	15	93.8	10	66.7	900	29	3.2	24	82.5	18	75.0
Dressing	378	16	4.2	13	81.3	12	92.3	522	14	2.7	12	85.7	8	66.7	900	30	3.3	25	83.3	20	80.0
Bathing	378	48	12.7	45	93.3	35	77.8	522	43	8.2	41	95.3	24	58.5	900	91	10.1	86	94.5	59	68.6
Indoor walk	378	29	7.7	26	89.7	19	70.4	522	44	8.4	42	95.5	21	48.8	900	73	8.1	68	93.2	40	54.8
Outdoor walk	378	101	26.7	94	93.1	49	52.1	522	119	22.8	105	88.2	44	41.9	900	220	24.4	199	90.5	93	10.3
Climbing stairs	378	118	31.2	109	92.4	62	56.9	522	174	33.3	145	83.3	60	41.4	900	292	32.4	254	87.0	122	48.0
Combing hair	378	16	4.2	14	87.5	10	71.4	522	24	4.6	21	87.5	12	57.1	900	40	4.4	35	87.5	12	62.9
Getting up	378	112	29.6	97	86.6	45	46.4	522	153	29.3	126	82.4	57	45.2	900	265	29.4	223	84.2	102	45.7
Toilet	378	78	20.6	65	83.3	25	38.5	522	78	14.9	70	89.7	25	35.7	900	156	17.3	135	86.5	50	37.0
Boarding train/bus	378	121	32.0	112	92.6	75	67.0	522	221	42.3	178	80.5	96	53.9	900	342	38.0	290	84.8	171	59.0

dressing. Higher proportion of female were not getting the required help compared to male elderly.

Physical Mobility Status

The percent distribution of elderly by their physical mobility status is presented in Table 40 and Figure 3. It is observed that only 28.6 per cent of male and 19.3 per cent of female elderly were able to move freely every where. The free movement of elderly decreased significantly with the increase in age. Among the male, it has decreased from 40.1 per cent for those aged 60-69 years to 12.9 per cent for those aged 80 years or more. Among the female, the proportion of elderly able to move freely every where declined significantly from 25.5 per cent for those aged 60-69 years to 6.7 per cent for those aged 80 years or more. About three fifth of elderly (59.5 per cent of male and 57.1 per cent of female) were able to move freely to neighbourhood. It is also observed that 10.8 per cent of male and 22.8 per cent of female were able to move inside the house only. Just 1.1 per cent of male and 0.8 per cent of female were bed ridden. Most of the bed ridden elderly were in the age group of 70 years or more.

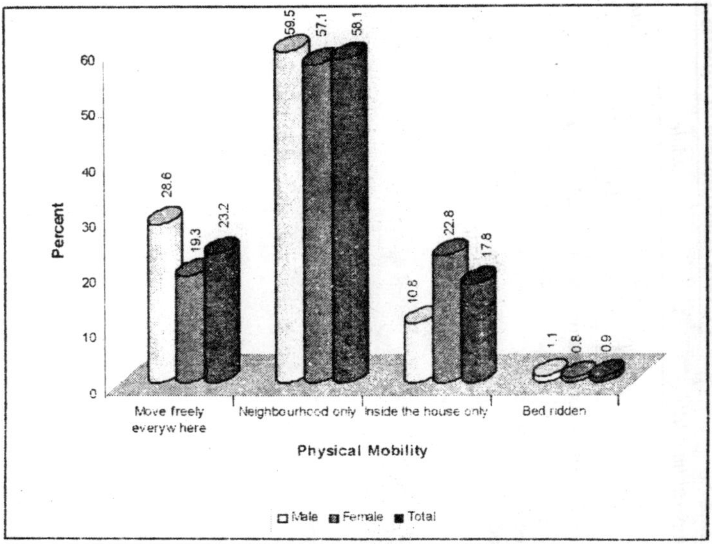

Figure 3: Physical Mobility Status of Elderly Aged 60+

Table 40

Percent Distribution of Elderly by their Physical Mobility Status, Age and Sex

Physical mobility	*Male*				*Female*				*Total*			
	60-69 N=172	*70-79* N=144	*80*+ N=62	*Total* N=378	*60-69* N=286	*70-79* N=161	*80*+ N=75	*Total* N=522	*60-69* N=458	*70-79* N=305	*80*+ N=137	*Total* N=900
Move freely everywhere	40.1	21.5	12.9	28.6	25.5	14.3	6.7	19.3	31.1	17.7	9.5	23.2
Neighbourhood only	52.3	65.3	66.1	59.5	60.8	56.5	44.0	57.1	57.6	60.7	54.0	58.1
Inside the house only	7.6	11.1	19.4	10.8	12.9	28.6	48.0	22.8	10.9	20.3	35.0	17.8
Bed ridden	-	2.1	1.6	1.1	0.8	0.6	1.3	0.8	0.4	1.3	1.5	0.9

Logistic Regression Analysis of Physical Mobility

The logistic regression analysis of physical mobility of elderly by selected background characteristics is presented in Table 41. The chances of moving freely everywhere was significantly less for those aged 70-79 years and 80 years or more compared to those aged 60-69 years. Literates are having significantly more chances of moving freely everywhere compared to illiterates. The chances of elderly moving freely everywhere were 1.8 times higher for primary and 2.8 times higher for middle and secondary compared to illiterates. Elderly who had involved in some sort of work earlier had significantly more chances of moving freely everywhere compared to those who had no work. It is observed that elderly who had monthly income in the range of Rs.501–1000 per month were having nearly two times higher chances of moving freely everywhere compared to those who had an income of less than Rs.500/- per month.

The results showed that increase in age had negative effect and education and involvement in any form of work earlier had positive effect on the elderly's free movement everywhere.

Physical Mobility and Psychological Status

The percent distribution of elderly by physical mobility and psychological status presented in Table 42 showed strong association between the physical mobility and psychological status of elderly. Proportion of elderly having good psychological status was significantly more among elderly who were able to move freely everywhere (51.2 per cent). The proportion of elderly having good psychological status decreased with the decrease in the physical mobility of elderly. It has decreased from 51.2 per cent for those who move freely everywhere to 25 per cent for those who were bedridden. The results indicated that the mobility status of the elderly is having significant influence on their psychological status.

Physiological Status by Age and Sex

The percent distribution of elderly by their physiological status according to their age and sex is presented in Table 43. The

Table 41
Logistic Regression Analysis of Physical Mobility of Elderly by Selected Background Characteristics

		Move freely everywhere		*Neighbourhood only*		*Inside the house only*		*Bed ridden*	
Background characteristics	*Reference*	*Yes=209 Odds ratio*	*No=691 Signifi cant*	*Yes=523 Odds ratio*	*No=377 Signifi cant*	*Yes=106 Odds ratio*	*No=794 Signifi cant*	*Yes=8 Odds ratio*	*No=892 Signifi cant*
Age (years)									
	60–69								
70–79		0.470	0.000*	1.056	0.730	2.276	0.000*	2.429	0.333
80+		0.227	0.000*	0.811	0.312	4.761	0.000*	3.413	0.292
Sex									
	Male								
Female		1.001	0.997	0.693	0.066***	1.918	0.020**	0.817	0.829
Education									
	Illiterate								
Primary (5th)		1.810	0.006*	0.872	0.446	0.701	0.165	0.074	0.045**
Middle (upto 8th)		2.767	0.000*	0.551	0.018**	0.850	0.664	0.000	0.996
Secondary+		2.763	0.027**	0.668	0.376	0.419	0.272	0.000	0.997
Earlier occupation									
	No work								
Coolie		1.860	0.053***	1.285	0.256	0.421	0.001*	0.887	0.996
Agriculture		1.942	0.088***	0.814	0.467	0.883	0.715	0.000	0.996
Government		5.789	0.001*	0.270	0.010**	1.297	0.680	0.036	1.000
Others		2.139	0.115	1.047	0.902	0.410	0.088***	0.001	0.995

Contd.

		Move freely everywhere		Neighbourhood only		Inside the house only		Bed ridden	
Background characteristics	*Reference*	*Yes=209 Odds ratio*	*No=691 Signifi cant*	*Yes=523 Odds ratio*	*No=377 Signifi cant*	*Yes=106 Odds ratio*	*No=794 Signifi cant*	*Yes=8 Odds ratio*	*No=892 Signifi cant*
Marital status	Married								
Single		1.011	0.960	0.989	0.950	1.135	0.600	0.128	0.036**
Religion									
	Hindu								
Muslim		0.628	0.269	1.244	0.490	1.321	0.474	0.000	0.997
Christian		0.495	0.192	2.678	0.033**	0.313	0.135	0.000	0.998
Caste									
	SC/ ST								
Others		1.137	0.516	0.980	0.902	0.827	0.393	00007	0.994
Individual income (rupees)									
	≤ 500								
501 - 1000		1.818	0.082***	0.786	0.466	0.200	0.128	0.000	0.997
1001		0.490	0.000*	1.344	0.103	1.688	0.070***	4.183	0.232

*P<0.01
** P<0.05
*** P<0.10

Table 42
Percent Distribution of Elderly by Physical Mobility and Psychological Status

Physical Mobility	*N=900*	*Psychological Status*		
		Good N=352	*Medium* N=370	*Poor* N=178
Move freely everywhere	209	51.2	36.8	12.0
Neighbourhood only	523	38.2	40.0	21.8
Inside the house only	160	26.9	50.0	23.1
Bed ridden	8	25.0	50.0	25.0

Table 43
Percent distribution of elderly by their physiological status, age and sex

Physiological status	*Male*				*Female*				*Total*			
	60-69 N=172	*70-79* N=144	*80+* N=62	*Total* N=378	*60-69* N=286	*70-79* N=161	*80+* N=75	*Total* N=522	*60-69* N=458	*70-79* N=305	*80+* N=137	*Total* N=900
Recall memory												
Good	61.6	42.4	45.2	51.6	61.2	38.5	36.0	50.6	61.4	40.3	40.1	51.0
Fair	30..8	43.1	41.9	37.3	31.5	47.8	50.7	39.3	31.2	45.6	46.7	38.4
Poor	7.6	14.6	12.9	11.1	7.3	13.7	13.3	10.2	7.4	14.1	13.1	10.6
Recognition												
Good	64.3	45.1	41.9	53.2	62.6	40.4	34.7	51.7	63.1	42.6	38.0	52.3
Fair	27.3	43.1	45.2	36.2	30.1	46.6	50.7	38.1	29.0	44.9	48.2	37.3
Poor	8.7	11.8	12.9	10.6	7.3	13.0	14.7	10.2	7.9	12.5	13.9	10.3
Vision												
Good	38.4	22.9	27.4	30.7	38.1	16.8	17.3	28.5	38.2	19.7	21.9	29.4
Fair	51.7	59.7	56.5	55.6	52.8	67.1	66.7	59.2	52.4	63.6	62.0	57.7
Poor	9.9	17.4	16.1	13.8	9.1	16.1	16.0	12.3	9.4	16.7	16.1	12.9
Speech												
Good	78.5	68.1	71.0	73.3	85.3	72.7	65.3	78.5	82.8	70.5	67.9	76.3
Fair	15.7	21.5	22.6	19.0	9.1	18.0	28.0	14.6	11.6	19.7	25.5	16.4
Poor	5.8	10.4	6.5	7.7	5.6	9.3	6.7	6.9	5.7	9.8	6.6	7.2
Audible range												
Good	68.0	49.3	50.0	57.9	65.0	46.6	37.3	55.4	66.2	47.9	43.1	56.4
Fair	24.4	38.2	40.3	32.3	26.2	41.0	48.0	33.9	25.5	39.7	44.5	33.2
Poor	7.6	12.5	9.7	9.8	8.7	12.4	14.7	10.7	8.3	12.5	12.4	10.3

physiological factors considered in the study are recall memory; recognition; vision; speech; and audible range. It is observed that about half of the elderly (51.6 per cent of male and 50.6 per cent of female) were having good recall memory. The proportion of elderly having good recall memory decreased with increase in age both among male and female elderly. Only half of the elderly (53.2 per cent of male and 51.7 per cent of female) were having good recognition capacity. Proportion of elderly having good recognition decreased with increase in age both among male and female. Only 30.7 per cent of male and 28.5 per cent of female had good vision. However, substantially higher proportion of both male (73.3 per cent) and female (78.5 per cent) elderly were having good speech. The audible range was good for 57.9 per cent of male and 55.4 per cent of female elderly.

The proportion of elderly having good audible range decreased significantly with the increase in age. Overall, the results indicate that the physiological status of elderly became poor with the increase in age of the elderly. Vision was the most affected physiological status among the elderly compared to recall memory, recognition, speech and audible range. Hence eye care is the most of important area of intervention needed to care the elderly in rural areas.

Physiological Status and Background Characteristics

The percent distribution of elderly by their physiological status and selected background characteristics is presented in Table 44. It is found that age, education, earlier occupation, marital status, caste, individual income and family income were having significant association with the physiological status of elderly. While age has significantly negative effect, education has significantly positive effect on the physiological status of the elderly. Significantly higher proportion of married elderly were having good physiological status than single. Comparatively higher proportion of SC/ST elderly were having poor physiological status than others. The proportion of elderly having good physiological status was highest at 53.8 per cent among those who had an individual income between

Rs.501/- – Rs.1000/- per month. Proportion of elderly with good physiological status was significantly more among those living in high income families (more than Rs.2001/- per month) than those who are living in low income families.

In all, it is observed that elderly who were young, literate, married, belonged to other than SC/ST group and living in high income families were having good physiological status than others.

Table 44

Percent distribution of elderly by their physiological status and selected background characteristics

Background characteristics	N=900	Physiological status: Good N=353	Moderate N=230	Poor N=317	χ^2	DF	P- value
Age (Years)							
60 – 69	458	52.0	22.7	25.3			
70 – 79	305	27.5	27.5	44.9	68.519	4	0.000*
80+	137	22.6	30.7	46.7			
Sex							
Male	378	40.7	25.4	33.9	0.732	2	0.694
Female	522	38.1	25.7	36.2			
Education							
Illiterate	556	36.9	23.0	40.1			
Primary (5th)	223	39.5	29.1	31.4	21.016	6	0.002*
Middle (upto 8th)	89	48.3	30.3	21.3			
Secondary+	32	53.1	31.3	15.6			
Earlier Occupation							
No work	116	37.1	25.0	37.9			
Coolie	589	37.7	24.1	38.2			
Agriculture	118	47.5	29.7	22.9	14.634	8	0.067***
Government	31	48.4	32.3	19.4			
Others	46	37.0	30.4	32.6			
Marital Status							
Married	421	43.0	26.1	30.9	7.206	2	0.027**
Single	479	35.9	25.1	39.0			
Religion							
Hindu	823	40.2	25.0	34.8			
Muslim	48	25.0	31.3	43.8	4.936	4	2.294
Christian	29	34.5	31.0	34.5			
Caste							
SC/ST	237	32.1	27.4	40.5	7.190	2	0.027**
Others	663	41.8	24.9	33.3			

Contd.

Background characteristics	N=900	Physiological status Good N=353	Moderate N=230	Poor N=317	χ^2	DF	P- value
Individual Income (rupees)							
≤500	174	46.6	23.0	30.5			
501–1000	52	53.8	25.0	21.2	12.440	4	0.014**
1000 +	674	36.2	26.3	37.5			
Family Income (rupees)							
≤1000	266	32.3	31.6	36.1			
1001–2000	134	32.1	26.1	41.8	18.178	6	0.006*
2001–3000	125	47.2	23.2	29.6			
3001+	375	44.0	21.9	34.1			

*P<0.00
** P<0.05
*** P<0.10

Logistic Regression Analysis of Physiological Status

The logistic regression analysis of the data on the physiological status of elderly by selected background characteristics is presented in Table 45. Elderly aged 70-79 years and 80 years or more were having significantly less chances of keeping good physiological status compared to those aged 60-69 years. Female elderly were having nearly two times higher chances of maintaining good speech compared to male. Literates were having significantly more chances of maintaining good physiological status compared to illiterates. Elderly who had involved in agriculture occupation had 3.8 times more chances of having good speech compared to those who had not involved in any work.

Muslims were having less chances of keeping good physiological status compared to elderly belonged to Hindu. Similarly elderly belonged to other than SC/ST group were having significantly more chances of keeping good physiological status compared to SC/ST. Surprisingly, elderly who had more income (more than Rs.1000/- per month) were having significantly less chances of keeping good physiological status in recognition and vision compared to low income elderly (Rs.d"500 per month). In all, it is observed that younger

Table 45

Logistic regression analysis of physiological status by selected background characteristics

Background characteristics	Reference	Recall memory Yes N=459 Odds ratio	Recall memory No N=441 Significant	Recognition Yes N=471 Odds ratio	Recognition No N=378 Significant	Vision Yes N=265 Odds ratio	Vision No N=635 Significant	Speech Yes N=687 Odds ratio	Speech No N=522 Significant	Audible range Yes N=508 Odds ratio	Audible range No N=392 Significant
Age (Years)											
	60-69										
70 - 79		0.438	0.000*	0.452	0.000*	0.392	0.000*	0.512	0.000*	0.476	0.000*
80+		0.417	0.000*	0.362	0.000*	0.439	0.001*	0.393	0.000*	0.376	0.000*
Sex											
	Male										
Female		1.205	0.349	1.189	0.388	0.925	0.720	1.928	0.005*	1.155	0.471
Education											
	Illiterate										
Primary (5th)		1.338	0.105	1.284	0.165	1.060	0.766	1.216	0.354	1.243	0.229
Middle (upto 8th)		1.906	0.013**	1.816	0.022**	1.226	0.451	2.811	0.004*	1.480	0.131
Secondary+		2.252	0.079***	3.660	0.009*	2.533	0.038**	1.167	0.776	1.712	0.260
Earlier occupation											
	No work										
Coolie		1.133	0.579	1.039	0.864	0.854	0.525	1.153	0.586	1.033	0.885
Agriculture		1.272	0.406	1.200	0.532	1.200	0.559	3.819	0.001*	1.433	0.220
Government		0.715	0.485	0.942	0.903	1.011	0.982	1.518	0.472	1.965	0.192
Others		1.177	0.667	1.026	0.946	1.423	0.384	2.804	0.039**	0.892	0.761

Contd.

Background characteristics	Reference	Recall memory		Recognition		Vision		Speech		Audible range	
		Yes N=459 Odds ratio	No N=441 Significant	Yes N=471 Odds ratio	No N=378 Significant	Yes N=265 Odds ratio	No N=635 Significant	Yes N=687 Odds ratio	No N=522 Significant	Yes N=508 Odds ratio	No N=392 Significant
Marital status											
	Married										
Single		0.887	0.504	0.859	0.398	1.085	0.678	0.887	0.574	0.794	0.201
Religion											
	Hindu										
Muslim		0.643	0.157	0.593	0.096***	0.349	0.014**	0.452	0.018**	0.567	0.068***
Christian		1.039	0.924	0.682	0.353	1.368	0.459	1.023	0.962	0.807	0.593
Caste											
	SC/ST										
Others		1.522	0.010**	1.596	0.004*	1.196	0.320	1.443	0.046**	1.355	0.060***
Individual income (rupees)											
	≤ 500										
501 - 1000		1.590	0.185	1.032	0.928	0.742	0.391	1.456	0.405	1.088	0.806
1001+		0.851	0.377	0.687	0.043**	0.615	0.011**	0.984	0.941	0.964	0.843

*P<0.01
**P<0.05
*** P<0.10

old, literates, Hindu, Christian and other than SC/ST group were having significantly more chances of keeping good physiological status than others.

Logistic Regression Analysis on Activities of Daily Living (ADL)

The logistic regression analysis of the data on disability by selected background characteristics of elderly is presented in Table 46. The results showed that the chances of bathing disability was two times higher for elderly aged 70-79 years and 2.5 times higher for elderly aged 80 years or more compared to elderly aged 60-69 years. The chances of getting disability in indoor walking was 3.3 times higher for elderly aged 70-79 years and 4.1 times higher for elderly aged 80 years or more compared to elderly aged 60-69 years.

The chances of disability in out door walking was two times higher for elderly aged 70-79 years and three times higher for elderly aged 80 years or more compared to elderly aged 60-69 years. Disability in climbing stairs was 2.2 times higher for those aged 70 years or more compared to elderly aged 60-69 years. While the disability in combing hair was two times higher for elderly aged 70-79 years, it was 3.2 times higher for elderly aged 80 years or more compared to elderly aged 60-69 years. Elderly aged 70-79 years had 1.9 times higher chances of becoming disabled in getting up and elderly aged 80 years or more had 2.7 times higher chances of becoming disabled in getting up compared to elderly aged 60-69 years.

Disability in boarding bus/train was 2.2 times higher for elderly aged 70-79 years and it was 2.7 times higher for elderly aged 80 years or more compared to elderly aged 60-69 years. Disability in going to toilet was 1.7 times higher for elderly aged 70-79 years and 2.5 times higher for elderly aged 80 years or more compared to elderly aged 60-69 years.

Female elderly were having significantly less chances of getting disability in bathing, out door walking, climbing stairs, getting up and going to toilet. The chances of getting disability were significantly lower for literates compared to illiterates. It is observed that literates were having significantly less chances

Table 46

Logistic regression analysis of data on Activities of Daily Living (ADL) by selected background characteristics

Background Characteristics	Reference	Eating Yes N=29	Eating No N=871	Dressing Yes N=30	Dressing No N=870	Bathing Yes N=91	Bathing No N=809	Indoor walking Yes N=73	Indoor walking No N=827	Outdoor walk Yes N=220	Outdoor walk No N=680	Climbing stairs Yes N=292	Climbing stairs No N=608	Combing hair Yes N=40	Combing hair No N=860	Getting up Yes N=265	Getting up No N=635	Boarding train Yes N=342	Boarding train No N=558	Toilet Yes N=156	Toilet No N=744
		Odds ratio	Signi-ficant	Odds ratio	Signi-ficant	Odds ratio	Signi-ficant	Odds ratio	Signi-ficant	Odds ratio	Signi-ficant	Odds ratio	Signi-ficant	Odds ratio	Signi-ficant	Odds ratio	Signi-ficant	Odds ratio	Signi-ficant	Odds ratio	Signi-ficant
Age (Years)																					
	60j 69																				
70j 79		1.669	0.244	1.219	0.657	2.074	0.006*	3.356	0.000*	2.080	0.000*	2.184	0.000*	2.020	0.076***	1.977	0.000*	2.250	0.000*	1.756	0.007*
80+		1.621	0.379	1.988	0.175	2.552	0.004*	4.183	0.000*	3.074	0.000*	2.188	0.000*	3.276	0.009*	2.714	0.000*	2.768	0.000*	2.512	0.000*
Sex																					
	Male																				
Female		0.905	0.856	0.781	0.656	0.344	0.001*	0.641	0.227	0.443	0.001*	0.690	0.084***	0.863	0.747	0.463	0.001*	1.219	0.344	0.376	0.000*
Education																					
	Illiterate																				
Primary (5th)		1.096	0.848	1.142	0.780	0.377	0.002*	0.429	0.018**	0.619	0.026**	0.879	0.498	0.255	0.011**	0.702	0.077***	0.872	0.470	0.499	0.006*
Middle (upto 8th)		0.000	0.771	0.741	0.678	0.170	0.003*	0.085	0.018**	0.455	0.019**	0.511	0.026**	0.304	0.123	0.348	0.002*	0.647	0.124	0.411	0.020**
Secondary (+2)		0.000	0.857	0.000	0.849	0.071	0.019**	0.267	0.275	0.675	0.483	0.597	0.329	0.002	0.697	0.698	0.502	0.316	0.050***	0.447	0.219
Earlier Occupation																					
	No work																				
Coolie		2.601	0.218	1.490	0.552	0.739	0.415	0.653	0.249	0.802	0.389	0.635	0.048**	1.260	0.689	0.518	0.005*	0.674	0.083***	0.998	0.993
Agriculture		0.512	0.595	0.259	0.262	0.301	0.034**	0.247	0.025**	0.353	0.004*	0.458	0.012**	1.985	0.315	0.366	0.002*	0.783	0.407	0.345	0.017**
Government		0.003	0.892	1.788	0.655	1.327	0.724	0.427	0.491	0.387	0.131	0.526	0.231	0.010	0.775	0.290	0.038**	0.703	0.508	0.634	0.512
Others		5.304	0.093***	3.915	0.112	1.158	0.802	0.736	0.639	0.530	0.158	0.486	0.077***	2.722	0.229	0.400	0.029**	0.657	0.292	0.803	0.662
Marital Status																					
	Married																				
single		0.925	0.879	0.683	0.447	0.946	0.855	1.009	0.980	1.435	0.095***	1.405	0.079***	0.753	0.505	1.639	0.016**	1.047	0.808	1.270	0.326
Religion																					
	Hindu																				
Muslim		1.281	0.750	1.138	0.867	0.946	0.310	1.065	0.910	0.561	0.801	0.672	0.261	1.642	0.437	0.661	0.260	1.665	0.106	1.221	0.607
Christian		1.503	0.705	2.685	0.231	0.528	0.030**	1.812	0.381	0.365	1.488	0.844	0.701	0.830	0.861	0.693	0.451	0.369	0.056***	1.057	0.917

Contd.

Background Characteristics	Reference	Eating Yes N=29	Eating No N=871	Dressing Yes N=30	Dressing No N=870	Bathing Yes N=91	Bathing No N=809	Indoor walking Yes N=73	Indoor walking No N=827	Outdoor walk Yes N=220	Outdoor walk No N=680	Climbing stairs Yes N=292	Climbing stairs No N=608	Combing hair Yes N=40	Combing hair No N=860	Getting up Yes N=265	Getting up No N=635	Boarding train Yes N=342	Boarding train No N=558	Toilet Yes N=156	Toilet No N=744
		Odds ratio	*Significant*	*Odds ratio*	*Significant*	*Odds ratio*	*Significant*	*Odds ratio*	*Significant*	*Odds ratio*	*Significant*	*Odds ratio*	*Significant*	*Odds ratio*	*Significant*	*Odds ratio*	*Significant*	*Odds ratio*	*Significant*	*Odds ratio*	*Significant*
Caste																					
	SC/ST																				
others		0.962	0.931	1.359	0.506	1.439	0.191	1.280	0.421	1.077	0.693	1.021	0.904	0.907	0.797	1.215	0.287	1.213	0.266	1.273	0.267
Individual income (rupees)																					
	≤500																				
501j 1000		8.158	0.097***	2686.925	0.692	1.657	0.444	1.839	0.411	0.872	0.753	0.835	0.649	1.634	0.592	0.649	0.310	0.763	0.524	1.669	0.289
1001 +		7.863	0.045**	3281.529	0.684	2.728	0.012**	2.042	0.093***	1.285	0.267	1.373	0.121	2.171	0.161	1.237	0.314	2.196	0.000*	2.078	0.010

*P<0.01
**P<0.05
***P<0.10

of getting disability in eating, bathing, indoor walking, out door walking, climbing stairs, getting up, boarding train and going to toilet compared to illiterates.

Single elderly were having significantly more chances of getting disability in out door walking, climbing stairs and getting up compared to married elderly. In the case of religion, Christians were having less chances of getting disability in bathing and boarding train/bus compared to elderly belonging to Hindu. Individual income of elderly seemed to have significant influence on disability. It is observed that higher income (Rs.1000 or more) elderly had 7.8 times higher chances of getting disability in eating, 2.7 times higher chance of getting disability in bathing, two times higher chances of getting disability in indoor walking and 2.1 times higher chances of getting disability in boarding bus/train compared to low income elderly (Rs. 500 or less per month).

Summary

The results of the analysis of data on the physical disability status of elderly showed that boarding train/bus (32 per cent) was the most important difficulty in performing the activities of daily living which was followed by climbing stairs (31.2 per cent), getting up (9.6 per cent), out door walk (6.7 per cent) and bathing (12.6 per cent).

It is found that only 28.6 per cent of male and 19.3 per cent of female elderly were able to move freely every where. The free movement of elderly decreased significantly with the increase in age. About three fifth of elderly (59.5 per cent of male and 57.1 per cent of female) were able to move to neighbourhood only. Mobility within the house was reported by 10.8 per cent of male and 22.8 per cent of female elderly. Just 1.1 per cent of male and 0.8 per cent of female elderly were bed ridden. Most of the bed ridden elderly were aged 70 years or more. The physical mobility status of elderly significantly influenced their psychological status. Increase in age had negative effect and education and involvement in any form of work earlier had positive effect on the elderly's free movement everywhere.

The physiological status of elderly became poor with the increase in age. Among the various physiological factors, vision problem was the major problem reported by a significantly higher proportion of elderly followed by difficulty in recall memory, recognition and audible range.

Elderly who were young, literates, married, belonging to other than SC/ST group and belonging to high income families were having good physiological status than others.

The chances of getting disability in bathing, indoor walking, out door walking, climbing stairs, combing hair, getting up, boarding train/bus and going to toilet were significantly more for elderly aged 70-79 years and 80 years or more compared to elderly aged 60-69 years. The female elderly were having significantly less chances of getting disability in bathing, out door walking, climbing stairs, getting up and going to toilet compared to male. The chances of getting disability were significantly lower for literates compared to illiterates. Single elderly were having significantly more chances of getting disability on out door walking, climbing stairs and getting up compared to married elderly. In the case of religion, Christians were having less chances of getting disability in bathing and boarding train compared to elderly belonging to Hindu. Individual income of elderly seemed to have significant influence on disability.

Younger old, literates, Hindu and Christian and other than SC/ST group were having significantly more chances of keeping good physiological status than others.

PSYCHOLOGICAL PROBLEMS

Psychological Problems by Age

The percent distribution of elderly who had different psychological problems by age is presented in Table 47 and Figure 4. It is observed that, irrespective of age, all elderly were having at least one or the other psychological problem at the time of interview. The major psychological problems reported by the elderly were anxiety (87.4 per cent), unnecessary worry (66.4 per cent), angry (62.8 per cent), isolation (61 per cent), easily upset (55.3 per cent), tension (53.3 per cent), loneliness (52.9 per cent), irritation (51.9 per cent), depression (51.4 per cent), stress (51.2 per cent), fear of dependence (44.1 per cent), inabilities to adjust the changed health condition (42.7 per cent) and behavioural adjustment (42.3 per cent). The overall psychological status obtained by combining and scoring all the 24 psychological variables showed that 39.1 per cent of elderly were in good psychological status, 41.1 per cent were in moderate psychological status and 19.8 per cent were in poor psychological status. The proportion of elderly with good psychological status decreased with age. However the differences are not statistically significant. (The details of scoring is given in Annexure-III)

Table 47
Percent distribution of elderly who had different psychological Problems by Age

Psychological problems	*Age(years)*				χ^2	*DF*	*P-value*
	60 – 69 N=458	*70-79 N=305*	*80+ N=137*	*Total N=900*			
Anxiety	87.3	89.5	83.2	87.4	3.424	2	0.181
Isolation	58.3	65.6	59.9	61.0	4.164	2	0.125
Feeling of guilty	29.0	36.4	29.2	31.6	5.001	2	0.082***
Behavioural adjustment	37.8	48.5	43.8	42.3	8.811	2	0.012**
Easily upset	51.1	58.4	62.8	55.3	7.534	2	0.023**
Angry	64.2	61.0	62.0	62.8	0.844	2	0.656
Tension	55.0	51.8	51.1	53.3	1.087	2	0.581
Fear of dependence	41.5	45.6	49.6	44.1	3.242	2	0.198
Depression	51.1	51.5	52.6	51.4	0.091	2	0.956
Loneliness	51.1	55.1	54.0	52.9	1.252	2	0.535
Irritation	50.7	50.5	59.1	51.9	3.391	2	0.184
Inabilities to adjust with changed health condition	36.7	49.2	48.2	42.7	13.697	2	0.001*
Unnecessary worry	64.8	68.9	66.4	66.4	1.317	2	0.518
Fear	46.3	51.5	47.4	48.2	2.012	2	0.366
Stress	52.2	51.5	47.4	51.2	0.959	2	0.619
Feeling of lack of affection	29.0	35.7	36.5	32.4	4.958	2	0.084***
Fear of uselessness	24.7	35.1	35.0	29.8	11.624	2	0.003*
Feeling of neglect by family members	21.2	27.2	27.0	24.1	4.384	2	0.112

Contd.

Psychological problems	*Age(years)*				χ^2	*DF*	*P-value*
	60 - 69 *N=458*	*70-79* *N=305*	*80⁺* *N=137*	*Total* *N=900*			
Dementia	17.5	21.0	19.7	19.0	1.524	2	0.467
Difficulty in coping with loss of job	19.2	24.3	19.7	21.0	2.975	2	0.226
Loss of social relationship	10.0	14.4	15.3	12.3	4.593	2	0.101
Loss of social security	8.7	12.5	20.4	11.8	14.109	2	0.001*
Loss of self confidence	10.3	14.8	14.6	12.4	4.079	2	0.130
Feeling of lack of care	12.2	14.4	16.1	13.6	1.619	2	0.445
Overall psychological status							
Poor	16.6	23.9	21.2	19.8			
Moderate	42.1	39.0	42.3	41.1	6.754	4	0.149
Good	41.3	37.0	36.5	39.1			

*P<0.00
** P<0.05
***P<0.10

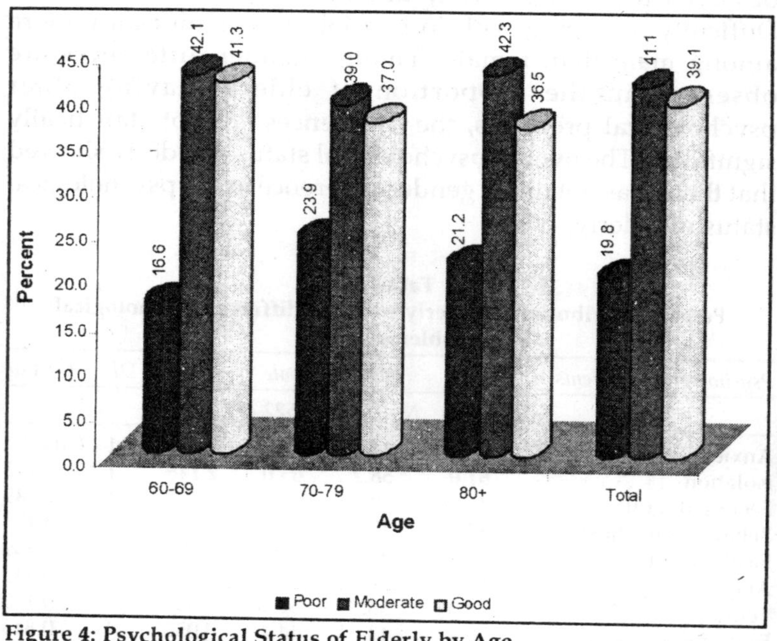

Figure 4: Psychological Status of Elderly by Age

Among the 24 psychological problems examined in the study, feeling of guilty, behavioural adjustment, easily upset, inabilities to adjust with changed health condition, feeling of lack of affection, fear of uselessness and loss of social security were seemed to have significant association with the age of elderly. It is found that the psychological problems such as behavioural adjustment, easily upset, inabilities to adjust with changed health condition, feeling of lack of affection, fear of uselessness and loss of social security increased with increase in age.

Physiological Problems by Sex

The percent distribution of elderly who had different psychological problems by sex presented in Table 48 and Figure 5 revealed that the psychological problems such as anxiety, fear, stress and feeling of lack of affection were observed to be significantly more among female than male. Difficulty in coping with loss of job was significantly more among male than female. Though gender differences are observed in the proportion of elderly having other psychological problems, the differences are not statistically significant. The overall psychological status of elderly showed that there was not much gender difference in the psychological status of elderly.

Table 48
Percent distribution of elderly who had different psychological Problems by Sex

Psychological problems	*Total*	*Male*	*Female*	χ^2	*DF*	*P- value*
	N=900	*N=378*	*N=522*			
Anxiety	87.4	84.9	89.3	3.871	1	0.052***
Isolation	61.0	58.2	63.0	2.146	1	0.143
Feeling of guilty	31.6	32.5	30.8	0.292	1	0.589
Behavioural adjustment	42.3	45.0	40.4	1.861	1	0.173
Easily upset	55.3	54.8	55.7	0.086	1	0.769
Angry	62.8	64.5	61.5	0.876	1	0.349
Tension	53.3	56.3	51.1	2.382	1	0.123
Fear of dependence	44.1	43.7	44.4	0.056	1	0.813
Depression	51.4	51.6	51.4	0.005	1	0.942
Loneliness	52.9	50.5	54.6	1.457	1	0.227
Irritation	51.9	53.2	51.0	0.432	1	0.511

Contd.

Psychological problems	*Total*	*Male*	*Female*	χ^2	*DF*	*P- value*
	N=900	*N=378*	*N=522*			
Inabilities to adjust with changed health condition	42.7	45.2	40.8	1.762	1	0.184
Unnecessary worry	66.4	68.0	65.3	0.698	1	0.404
Fear	48.2	44.4	51.0	3.725	1	0.054***
Stress	51.2	47.4	54.0	3.902	1	0.048**
Feeling of lack of affection	32.4	29.4	34.7	2.820	1	0.093***
Fear of uselessness	29.8	30.2	29.5	0.045	1	0.832
Feeling of neglect by family members	24.1	24.7	24.1	0.246	1	0.620
Dementia	19.0	19.0	19.0	0.001	1	0.975
Difficulty in coping with loss of job	21.0	26.7	16.9	12.851	1	0.000*
Loss of social relationship	12.3	14.3	10.9	2.298	1	0.130
Loss of social security	11.8	12.2	11.5	0.096	1	0.756
Loss of self confidence	12.4	12.7	12.3	0.039	1	0.844
Feeling of lack of care	13.6	15.3	12.3	1.779	1	0.182
Overall psychological status						
Poor	19.8	20.9	19.0			
Moderate	41.1	38.9	42.7	1.399	2	0.497
Good	39.1	40.2	38.3			

*P<0.00
** P<0.05
**P<0.10

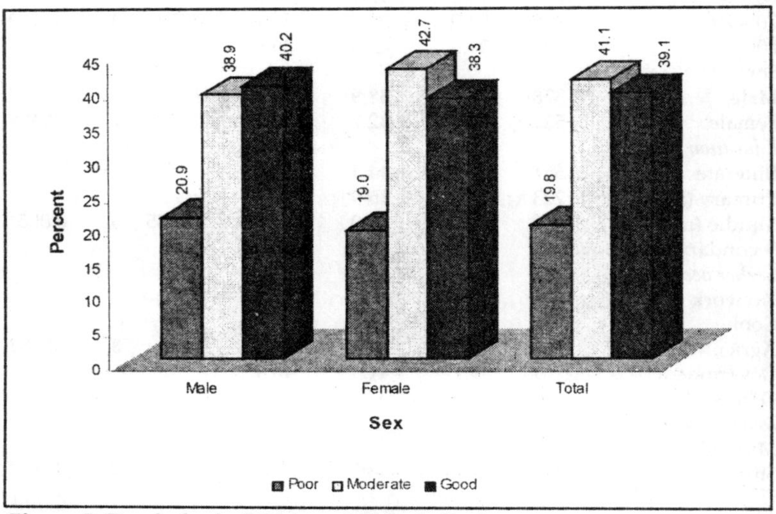

Figure 5: Psychological Status of Elderly by Sex

Psychological Status by Selected Background Characteristics

The psychological status of elderly by selected background characteristics are presented in Table 49. It is observed that education, marital status and total family income were having significant association with the psychological status of elderly. The proportion of elderly with good psychological status significantly improved with the increase in education. Significantly higher proportion of married elderly were having good psychological status than single. Proportion of elderly with good psychological status was significantly more among those living in high income families (more than Rs.3000/- per month) than others.

Table 49
Percent distribution of elderly by their psychological status and Selected Background Characteristics

Background characteristics	N=900	Psychological status: Poor N=178	Moderate N=370	Good N=352	χ^2	DF	P- value
Age (years)							
60 - 69	458	16.6	42.1	41.3			
70 - 79	305	23.9	39.0	37.1	6.754	4	0.149
80+	137	21.2	42.3	36.5			
Sex							
Male	378	20.9	38.9	40.2			
Female	522	19.0	42.7	38.3	1.399	2	0.497
Education							
Illiterate	556	21.4	44.4	34.2			
Primary (5th)	223	18.8	35.9	45.3			
Middle (upto 8th)	89	16.9	36.0	47.1	18.585	6	0.005*
Secondary and above	32	6.2	34.4	59.4			
Earlier occupation							
No work	116	19.8	39.7	40.5			
Coolie	589	20.5	41.5	38.0			
Agriculture	118	16.1	44.1	39.8	5.633	8	0.688
Government	31	9.7	41.9	48.4			
Others	46	26.1	32.6	41.3			
Marital status							
Married	421	20.6	37.1	42.3			
Single	479	19.0	44.7	36.3	5.512	2	0.064***

Contd.

Background characteristics	N=900	Psychological status Poor N=178	Moderate N=370	Good N=352	χ^2	DF	P-value
Religion							
Hindu	823	19.3	41.7	39.0			
Muslim	48	25.0	33.3	41.7	1.963	4	0.743
Christian	29	24.2	37.9	37.9			
Caste							
SC/ST	237	21.5	36.7	41.8			
Others	663	19.2	42.7	38.2	2.592	2	0.274
Individual income (rupees)							
≤ 500	174	19.0	41.3	39.7			
501 - 1000	52	13.5	40.3	46.2	2.035	4	0.729
1000 +	674	20.5	41.1	38.4			
Family income (rupees)							
≤ 1000	266	34.8	45.5	29.7			
1001 - 2000	134	23.9	39.5	36.6			
2001 - 3000	125	20.8	49.6	29.6	36.476	6	0.000*
3001+	375	14.4	35.7	49.9			

*P<0.00
** P<0.05
***P<0.10

Psychological Status and Living Arrangements

The percent distribution of elderly by their level of psychological status and living arrangements presented in Table 50 showed that the proportion of elderly having good psychological status was highest at 45.8 per cent among those

Table 50
Percent Distribution of elderly by their level of psychological status and Living Arrangements

Living arrangements	*N=900*	*Psychological status* Poor	Moderate	Good
Living alone	227	23.8	48.0	28.2
Living with spouse	175	25.7	34.3	40.0
Living with son's family	345	14.1	40.1	45.8
Living with daughter's family	78	17.9	44.9	37.2
Others	73	21.9	37.0	41.1

χ^2 = 27.256, DF = 8, P <0.001*

who were living with son's family which was followed by those living with spouse (40 per cent). The χ^2 test of significance indicate a significant association between living arrangements and psychological status of elderly.

Suggestions to Overcome the Psychological Problems

The percent distribution of elderly by their suggestions to overcome the psychological problems is presented in Table 51. The major suggestions made by the elderly were 'financial support' (65.9 per cent of male and 71.5 per cent of female); 'Family support' (58.2 per cent of male and 62.1 per cent of female); 'recreation facilities' (38.1 per cent of male and 34.9 per cent of female); and 'counselling' (16.9 per cent of male and 15.1 per cent of female). Overall, the results indicate that lack of financial and family support, absence of interaction with family members and non availability of recreational facilities made the elderly get in to deeper psychological problems.

Table 51
Percent distribution of elderly by their suggestions to overcome their psychological problems and sex

Suggestions	*Male N=378*	*Female N=522*	*Total N=900*
Financial support	65.9	71.5	69.1
Family support	58.2	62.1	60.4
Counselling	16.9	15.1	15.9
Frequent interaction with family members	13.5	13.4	13.4
Interacting with friends	12.4	7.5	9.6
Recreation facilities	38.1	34.9	36.2

Summary

Almost all elderly had reported to have one or the other psychological problem. The major psychological problems reported by the elderly were 'anxiety' (87.4 per cent), 'unnecessary worry' (66.4 per cent), 'angry' (62.8 per cent), 'isolation' (61 per cent), 'easily upset' (55.3 per cent), 'tension' (53.3 per cent), 'loneliness' (52.9 per cent), 'irritation' (51.9 per cent), 'depression' (51.4 per cent), 'stress' (51.2 per cent), 'fear of dependence' (44.1 per cent), 'inability to adjust the changed health condition' (42.7 per cent) and 'behavioural adjustment'

(42.3 per cent). The over all psychological status showed that 39.1 per cent of elderly were in good psychological status, 41.1 per cent were in moderate psychological status and 19.8 per cent were in poor psychological status.

The proportion of elderly with good psychological status decreased with age. The over all psychological status of elderly significantly associated with education, marital status and family income. Proportion of elderly with good psychological status significantly improved with the increase in education. Significantly higher proportion of married elderly were having good psychological status than single. Proportion of elderly with good psychological status was significantly more among those living in high income families (more than Rs.3000 per month) than others. The proportion of elderly having good psychological status was highest among those living with son compared to those living with spouse, daughter and living alone. Financial support, family support and recreation facilities were the major suggestions made by the elderly to overcome their psychological problems.

HEALTH STATUS OF ELDERLY

Health Status of Elderly by Sex

The self reported health problems of elderly by sex presented in Table 52 showed that the major health problems of elderly are poor vision/ cataract/other eye impairment (59.9 per cent), arthritis/rheumatic joint pain (59.7 per cent), back pain/ slipped disc (32.4 per cent), high blood pressure (17.2 per cent), lung/respiratory problems/asthma (14.4 per cent) and frailty/ general weakness/run down condition (12.9 per cent). The type of health problems did not vary much between male and female except for lung/respiratory problems/asthma, arthritis/rheumatic joint pain and back pain/slipped disc which are observed to be more among female than male elderly. Though differences are observed in the proportion of elderly having different diseases by sex, the differences are significant only for lung problems and neurological problems. The lung problems were reported to be significantly more

Table 52
Percent Distribution of Elderly by Health Problems and Sex

Health Problems	Male No.	Male %	Female No.	Female %	Total No.	Total %	χ^2	DF	P-value
Poor vision / cataract / other eye impairment	228	60.3	311	59.6	539	59.9	0.050	1	0.823
Lung problems / respiratory problems/asthma.	74	19.6	56	10.7	130	14.4	13.891	1	**0.000***
Tuberculosis/other chronic fever	14	3.7	4	0.8	18	2.0	@	@	@
Diarrhoea/gastro enteritis stomach ulcer	36	9.5	40	7.7	76	8.4	0.982	1	0.322
Skin disease	9	2.4	12	2.3	21	2.3	0.006	1	0.936
Angina/ chest pain/cardiac problem	31	8.2	43	8.2	74	8.2	0.000	1	0.984
High blood pressure	60	15.9	95	18.2	155	17.2	0.832	1	0.362
Arthritis/rheumatic joint pain	218	57.7	319	61.1	537	59.7	1.078	1	0.299
Back pain/slipped disc	112	29.6	180	34.5	292	32.4	2.356	1	0.125
Neurological or mental problems	35	9.3	26	5.0	61	6.8	6.352	1	**0.012****
Cancer	–	–	6	1.1	6	0.7	@	@	@
Dementia/memory loss	2	0.5	8	1.0	10	1.1	@	@	@
Frailty/general weakness/run down condition	51	13.5	65	12.5	116	12.9	0.211	1	0.646
Injury and related disabilities	9	2.4	11	2.1	20	2.2	0.076	1	0.783
Burn and related disabilities	–	–	3	0.6	3	0.3	@	@	@
Diabetes and other problems like prostate/dental etc.	47	12.4	49	9.4	96	10.7	2.136	1	0.144

* $P<0.01$
** $P<0.05$
*** $P<0.10$
@ χ^2 not calculated as some of the cell frequencies are less than 5.

among male where as the neurological problems were significantly more among female. In general, the proportion of elderly suffering with different chronic diseases was significantly more among male than female.

Health Status of Elderly by Age

The percent distribution of elderly by health problems and age is presented in Table 53. It is observed that most of the health problems increased with the age of elderly. Though the proportion of elderly suffering with health problems differ by age, the differences are significant only for poor vision/ cataract/other eye impairment, arthritis/rheumatic pain, frailty/ general weakness and diabetes/other problems.

Need for Treatment

The percent distribution of elderly who are in need of treatment for their health problems and percent availed treatment are presented in Table 54a and 54b. It is seen that almost all elderly (both male and female) who had health problems were in need of treatment. More than 80 per cent of elderly had availed treatment for all health problems except for the eye problem and dementia. In the case of eye problem, only 70.4 per cent had availed treatment and in the case of dementia only 55.6 per cent had availed treatment. Among the male, more than 70 per cent of elderly availed the required treatment for all health problems except for dementia/memory loss for which only 50 per cent had availed treatment. In the case of female also, more than 70 per cent of the elderly had availed treatment except for the dementia/memory loss for which only 57.1 per cent had availed treatment.

Sources of Treatment

The percent distribution of elderly by health problems and sources of treatment is presented in Table 55. It is observed that the main source of treatment was government hospital followed by private hospital. Utilization of services from government hospital was ranging from 60 per cent for dementia and tuberculosis to 100 per cent for cancer. The

Table 53
Percent distribution of elderly by health problems and age

Health Problems	*60-69* N=458	*70-79* N=305	*80+* N=137	*Total* N=900	χ^2	*DF*	*P- value*
Poor vision/cataract/other eye impairment	54.4	66.6	63.5	59.9	12.205	2	**0.002***
Lung problems/respiratory problems/asthma	12.7	15.7	17.5	14.4	2.635	2	0.268
Tuberculosis/other chronic fever	1.5	2.3	2.9	2.0	@	@	@
Diarrhoea/gastro enteritis/stomach ulcer	8.5	7.5	10.2	8.4	0.883	2	0.643
Skin disease	2.0	2.6	2.9	2.3	@	@	@
Angina/ chest pain/cardiac problem	9.0	7.9	6.6	8.2	0.870	2	0.647
High blood pressure	16.8	17.0	19.0	17.2	0.357	2	0.837
Arthritis/rheumatic joint pain	53.7	66.9	63.5	59.7	14.191	2	**0.001***
Back pain/slipped disc	32.3	32.5	32.8	32.4	0.014	2	0.993
Neurological or mental problems	6.6	6.9	7.3	6.8	0.102	2	0.950
Cancer	0.4	0.7	1.5	0.7	@	@	@
Dementia/memory loss	0.9	1.3	1.5	1.1	@	@	@
Frailty/general weakness/run down condition	7.6	16.7	21.9	12.9	25.123	2	**0.000***
Injury and related disabilities	1.7	2.3	3.6	2.2	1.769	2	0.413
Burn and related disabilities	0.2	0.3	0.7	0.3	@	@	@
Diabetes and other problems like prostate/dental etc.	7.9	13.8	13.1	10.7	7.748	2	**0.027****

* P< 0.01

**P<0.05

*** P<0.10

@ χ^2 not calculated as some of the cell frequencies are less than 5.

Table 54a

Percent distribution of elderly by sex and need for treatment

	Male		*Female*		*Total*	
Health Problems	*Number with problem*	*% Need treatment*	*Number with problem*	*% need treatment*	*Number with problem*	*% need treatment*
Poor vision/cataract/other eye impairment	228	93.9	311	96.5	539	95.4
Lung problems/respiratory problems/asthma	74	98.6	56	98.2	130	98.5
Tuberculosis/other chronic fever	14	100.0	4	100.0	18	100.0
Diarrhoea/gastro enteritis stomach ulcer	36	100.0	40	100.0	76	100.0
Skin disease	9	100.0	12	91.7	21	95.2
Angina/ chest pain/cardiac problem	31	96.8	43	90.7	74	93.2
High blood pressure	60	100.0	95	95.8	155	97.4
Arthritis/rheumatic joint pain	218	97.7	319	95.0	537	96.1
Back pain/slipped disc	112	98.2	180	98.3	292	98.3
Neurological or mental problems	35	94.3	26	96.2	61	95.1
Cancer	–	–	6	100.0	6	100.0
Dementia/memory loss	2	100.0	8	87.5	10	90.0
Frailty/general weakness/run down condition	51	92.2	65	89.2	116	90.5
Injury and related disabilities	9	100.0	11	90.9	20	95.0
Burn and related disabilities	–	–	3	100.0	3	100.0
Diabetes and other problems like prostate/dental etc.	47	97.9	49	95.9	96	96.9

Table 54b

Percent distribution of elderly by sex and treatment for illness

Health Problems	Male		Female		Total	
	Need treatment No.	% Availed treatment	Need treatment No.	% Availed treatment	Need treatment No.	% Availed treatment
Poor vision/cataract/other eye impairment	214	71.0	300	70.0	514	70.4
Lung problems/respiratory problems/asthma	73	86.3	55	85.5	128	85.9
Tuberculosis/other chronic fever	14	78.6	4	100.0	18	83.3
Diarrhoea/gastro enteritis stomach ulcer	36	94.4	40	82.5	76	88.2
Skin disease	9	88.9	11	81.8	20	85.0
Angina/ chest pain/cardiac problem	30	90.0	39	84.6	69	87.0
High blood pressure	60	95.0	91	94.5	151	94.7
Arthritis/rheumatic joint pain	213	90.1	303	85.5	516	87.4
Back pain/slipped disc	110	90.0	177	85.3	287	87.1
Neurological or mental problems	33	87.9	25	80.0	58	84.5
Cancer	–	–	6	83.3	6	83.3
Dementia/memory loss	2	50.0	7	57.1	9	55.6
Frailty/general weakness/run down condition	47	80.9	58	86.2	105	83.8
Injury and related disabilities	9	88.9	10	80.0	19	84.2
Burn and related disabilities	–	–	3	100.0	3	100.0
Diabetes and other problems like prostate/dental etc.	46	97.8	47	95.7	93	96.8

Table 55
Percent Distribution of Elderly by their Health Problems and Sources of Treatment

Health Problems	Male					Female					Total				
	N	1	2	3	4	N	1	2	3	4	N	1	2	3	4
Poor vision/cataract and other eye impairment	152	75.0	74.3	1.3	3.9	210	74.3	22.4	0.5	2.9	362	74.6	21.3	0.8	3.4
Lung problems/respiratory problems/asthma	63	74.6	17.5	3.2	4.8	47	83.0	17.0	-	-	110	78.2	17.3	1.8	2.7
Tuberculosis/other chronic fever	11	63.6	36.4	-	-	4	50.0	50.0	-	-	15	60.0	40.0	-	-
Diarrhoea/gastro enteritis/stomach ulcer	34	64.7	23.5	5.9	5.8	33	66.7	33.3	-	-	67	65.7	28.4	3.0	3.0
Skin disease	8	87.5	12.5	-	-	9	66.7	33.3	-	-	17	76.5	23.5	-	-
Angina/ chest pain/cardiac problem	27	66.7	29.6	-	3.7	33	60.6	36.4	-	3.0	60	63.3	33.3	-	3.4
High blood pressure	57	80.7	15.8	3.5	-	86	67.4	32.6	-	-	143	72.7	25.9	1.4	-
Arthritis/rheumatic joint pain	192	79.2	15.6	2.1	3.1	259	76.8	19.1	-	3.5	451	77.8	18.0	0.9	3.4
Back pain/slipped disc	99	71.7	22.2	3.0	3.0	151	72.2	25.2	-	2.8	250	72.0	24.0	1.2	2.8
Neurological or mental problems	29	62.1	31.0	-	6.8	20	60.0	35.0	-	5.0	49	61.2	32.7	-	5.0
Cancer	-	-	-	-	-	5	100.0	-	-	-	5	100.0	-	-	-
Dementia/memory loss	1	-	100.0	-	-	4	75.0	25.0	-	-	5	60.0	40.0	-	-
Frailty/general weakness/run down condition	38	76.3	21.1	2.6	-	50	76.0	20.0	-	4.0	88	76.1	20.5	1.1	2.3
Injury and related disabilities	8	100.0	--	-	-	8	62.5	25.0	-	12.5	16	81.3	12.5	-	6.3
Burn and related disabilities	-	-	--	-	-	3	66.7	33.3	-	-	3	66.7	33.0	-	-
Diabetes and other problems like prostate/dental etc.	46	65.2	30.4	4.3	-	44	59.1	36.4	-	-	90	62.3	33.3	2.2	2.2

1=Government, 2=Private, 3=Government + Private, 4=Others

utilization of the services of private hospital was ranging from 12.5 per cent for injury and related disabilities to 40 per cent for tuberculosis and dementia. The overall pattern of utilization of different sources of health care services did not vary much between male and female elderly.

Reasons for Not Availing Treatment

The percent distribution of elderly by reasons for not getting treatment for their health problems presented in Table 56 showed that the main reasons for not getting treatment were 'poverty' (no money), 'lack of family support' and 'no one helps them to go to hospital'.

Morbidity Pattern

In order to assess the morbidity pattern among the elderly, they were asked whether they had experienced any health problems in the past two weeks prior to the survey. The results of the analysis of data on the self reported symptoms of elderly are presented in Table 57. The major complaints reported by the male elderly were persistence cough (11.9 per cent), body weakness (10.6 per cent), wheezing (8.5 per cent), blocked nose (6.3 per cent) and breathlessness (6.1 per cent). The major complaints reported by female elderly were body weakness (11.7 per cent), persistence cough (8.4 per cent), head ache (6.7 per cent), fever (5.7 per cent) and wheezing (5.2 per cent).

Summary

The health status of elderly assessed based on the self reported health problems revealed that poor vision/cataract/other eye impairment were the major health problems reported by a majority of elderly (59.9 per cent) which was followed by arthritis/rheumatic joint pain (59.7 per cent), back pain/ slipped disc (32.4 per cent), high blood pressure (17.2 per cent), lung/ respiratory problems (14.4 per cent) and frailty/general weakness/rundown condition (12.9 per cent). In general, the proportion of elderly who had suffered with different chronic diseases was significantly more among male than female. Most of the health problems increased with the age of elderly.

Table 56

Percent Distribution of Elderly Who Had Health Problems by Reasons for Not Getting Treatment

	Male					Female					Total				
Health Problems	*N*	*1*	*2*	*3*	*4*	*N*	*1*	*2*	*3*	*4*	*N*	*1*	*2*	*3*	*4*
Poor vision/cataract other eye impairment	62	32.3	16.1	37.1	14.5	90	33.3	21.1	30.0	15.6	152	32.9	19.1	32.9	15.1
Lung problems/respiratory problems/asthma	10	40.0	50.0	10.0	-	8	50.0	-	-	50.0	18	44.4	27.8	5.6	22.2
Tuberculosis/other chronic fever	3	100.0	-	-	-	0	-	-	-	-	3	100.0	-	-	-
Diarrhea/gastro enteritis stomach ulcer	2	50.0	-	50.0	-	7	51.1	14.3	14.3	14.3	9	55.6	11.1	22.2	11.1
Skin disease	1	-	-	100.0	-	2	100.0	-	-	-	3	66.7	-	33.3	-
Angina/ chest pain/cardiac problem	3	33.3	33.3	33.3	-	6	33.3	-	50.0	16.7	9	33.3	11.1	44.4	11.1
High blood pressure	3	33.3	33.3	33.3	-	5	40.0	-	40.0	20.0	8	37.5	12.5	37.5	12.5
Arthritis/rheumatic joint pain	21	42.9	28.6	19.0	9.5	44	34.1	38.6	6.8	20.5	65	36.9	35.4	10.8	16.9
Back pain/slipped disc	11	36.4	18.2	27.3	18.2	26	38.5	34.6	3.8	23.1	37	37.8	29.7	10.8	21.6
Neurological or mental problems	4	50.0	25.0	25.0	-	5	40.0	-	40.0	20.0	9	44.0	11.1	33.3	11.1
Cancer	-	-	-	-	-	-	100.0	-	-	-	1	100.0	-	-	-
Dementia/memory loss	1	100.0	-	-	-	3	33.3	-	33.3	33.4	4	50.0	-	25.0	25.0
Frailty/general weakness/run down condition	9	22.2	-	33.3	44.5	8	62.5	12.5	12.5	12.5	17	41.2	5.9	23.5	29.4
Injury and related disabilities	1	100.0	-	-	-	2	-	-	50.0	50.0	3	33.3	-	33.3	33.4
Burn and related disabilities	-	-	-	-	-	-	-	-	-	-	-	-	-	-	-
Diabetes and other problems like prostate/dental etc.	-	-	-	-	-	4	25.0	25.0	25.0	25.0	4.0	4.0	25.0	25.0	25.0

1=No money, 2=Lack of family support, 3=No help to go to hospital, 4=Not interest to go to hospital

Table 57
Percent Distribution of Elderly by Sex and Health Problems in the Past Two Weeks Prior to the Survey

Diseases	*Male* N=378	*Female* N=522	*Total* N=900
Persistence cough	11.9	8.4	9.9
Wheezing	8.5	5.2	6.6
Blocked nose	6.3	3.6	4.8
Breathlessness	6.1	4.2	5.0
Skin infection	2.1	2.1	2.1
Body weakness	10.6	11.7	11.2
Fever	3.4	5.7	4.8
Malaria	0.8	1.0	0.9
Head ache	4.8	6.7	5.9
Cholera	0.5	1.0	0.8
Diarrhea	2.1	1.1	1.6

Almost all elderly who were having health problems were in need of treatment. More than 80 per cent of elderly had availed treatment for all their health problems except for eye problem and dementia. In the case of eye problem, 70.4 per cent had availed treatment and in the case of dementia only 55.6 per cent had availed treatment. The main source of treatment for the health problems of elderly was government hospital.

EXPECTATIONS OF ELDERLY

In order to assess the expectations of elderly, informations were collected on their expectations from family and government. Their suggestions for the youth and their opinion on the increased longevity and the availability of minimum basic needs for their livelihood were also elicited. The results of the analysis of data are presented in this section.

Expectations from Family Members

The percent distribution of elderly by sex and expectations from family members is presented in Table 58. Love and affection from family members was the main expectation of both male and female elderly (29.1 per cent of male and 30.2 per cent of female) followed by care and support (19.8 per cent of male and 21.7 per cent of female), regular food (14.2 per cent of male and 15.5 per cent of female) and money (13.1 per cent of male and 9.2 per cent of female). Nearly one fourth of both male and female elderly (23.8 per cent of male and 23.4 per cent of female) expected that their children should earn and support the family without depending on the parents.

Table 58
Percent distribution of elderly by sex and expectations from family members

Expectations from family	*Male N=378*	*Female N=522*	*Total N=900*
Money	13.1	9.2	10.8
Love and affection	29.1	30.2	29.8
Care and support	19.8	21.7	20.8
Regular Food	14.2	15.5	15.0
Children should earn and support family	23.8	23.4	23.6

Expectations from Government

The percent distribution of elderly by sex and expectations from government is presented in Table 59. The main expectation from the government as reported by 75.3 per cent of male and 70.5 per cent of female elderly was financial support. Opportunity to work was the next major expectation of elderly from government as reported by 13 per cent of male and 15.7 per cent of female elderly. The other expectations of elderly from government were care and support, housing, medical treatment and food.

Table 59
Percent distribution of elderly by sex and expectations from the government

Expectations from Government	*Male N=378*	*Female N=522*	*Total N=900*
Financial support	75.3	70.5	72.4
Care and support, services	2.7	1.5	2.0
House	2.9	2.1	2.4
Free medical treatment	2.3	5.9	4.3
Food	2.2	3.3	2.9
Opportunity to work	13.0	15.7	14.6
Nothing	1.6	1.0	1.4

Suggestions for the Youth

The percent distribution of elderly by sex and suggestions for the youth and youngsters is presented in Table 60. The main suggestions made by the elderly for the youth and youngsters was 'education' (29.9 per cent of male and 29.1 per cent of

Table 60
Percent distribution of elderly by sex and suggestions for the youth and youngsters

Suggestions	*Male N=378*	*Female N=522*	*Total N=900*
Respect elders	13.8	12.3	12.9
Education	29.9	29.1	29.4
Good understanding	3.4	1.7	2.4
Good character	28.0	28.0	28.0
No suggestion	28.9	27.9	25.3

female) followed by 'good character' (28 per cent each of male and female) and 'respect for elderly' (13.8 per cent of male and 12.3 per cent of female). It is also to be noted that 28.9 per cent of male and 27.9 per cent of female did not make any suggestions.

Opinion on Increased Longevity

The percent distribution of elderly by sex and their opinion on the increased longevity of human life is presented in Table 61. Significantly higher proportion of elderly (66.4 per cent of male and 79.7 per cent of female) were reluctant to give their opinion on the increased longevity of human life. Only 11.4 per cent of male and just 6.7 per cent of female elderly opined that the increase in longevity was good. Surprisingly, 22.2 per cent of male and 13.6 per cent of female elderly opined that the increase in longevity was bad.

Table 61
Percent distribution of elderly by sex and their opinion on the increased longevity of human life

Opinion	*Male* N=378	*Female* N=522	*Total* N=900
Good	11.4	6.7	8.7
Bad	22.2	13.6	17.2
No opinion	66.4	79.7	74.1

Reasons for Considering the Increased Longevity as Bad

The percent distribution of elderly by sex and reasons for feeling bad about increased longevity is presented in Table 62. About one fourth of elderly (23.8 per cent of male and 26.8 per cent of female) reported that the increased longevity was a burden to others and unable to bare the increased health problems. Substantially higher proportion of elderly (41.7 per cent of male and 36.6 per cent of female) felt that the increased longevity made them very difficult to depend on others. More than one third of elderly (34.5 per cent of male and 36.6 per cent of female) reported that they felt bad about increased longevity because no one takes care of them.

Table 62
Percent distribution of elderly by sex and reasons for feeling bad about increased longevity

Reasons	*Male* N=84	*Female* N=71	*Total* N=155
Burden to others/unable to bare the health problems	23.8	26.8	25.1
Difficult to depend on others	41.7	36.6	39.4
No one to take care of them	34.5	36.6	35.5

Opinion on their Living Condition

In order to assess the living conditions of elderly, they were asked whether they were getting the basic needs to lead a healthy life. The results of the analysis of data presented in Table 63 revealed that only 45.8 per cent of male and 51.1 per cent of female elderly were getting the basic needs to lead a healthy life. The proportion of elderly reported to have availed the basic needs to lead a healthy life was higher among female than male.

Table 63
Percent distribution of elderly by sex and whether they get basic needs to lead a healthy life

Getting basic needs	*Male* N=378	*Female* N=522	*Total* N=900
Yes	45.8	51.1	48.9
No	54.2	48.9	51.1

Basic Needs Not Available to Elderly

The percent distribution of elderly by sex and type of basic needs not available to lead a healthy life is presented in Table 64. Money was the major basic need reported to be not

Table 64
Percent distribution of elderly by sex and type of basic needs not available to lead a healthy life

Basic needs not available	*Male* N=197	*Female* N=240	*Total* N=437
Medical care	25.4	22.1	23.6
Money	63.5	64.2	63.8
Food	4.6	4.6	4.6
Care and support from family	6.5	9.1	8.0

available to a majority of elderly (63.8 per cent) followed by medical care (23.6 per cent), care and support from family (8 per cent) and food (4.6 per cent). The basic needs reported as not available to elderly did not vary much between male and female.

Summary

The main expectation of elderly from the family members was love and affection followed by care and support, regular food and money to meet their personal needs. The main expectations of the elderly from the government were financial support and opportunity to work. The elderly were expecting that the youth and youngsters should have good education and good character and give respect to elderly. Significantly higher proportion of elderly (66.4 per cent of male and 79.7 per cent of female) had refused to give their opinion on the increased longevity of human life. Only 45.8 per cent of male and 51.1 per cent of female elderly had reported that they were getting the basic needs to lead a healthy life.

6

FOCUS GROUP DISCUSSION

Focus Group Discussions (FGDs) were organized in the three selected districts to collect qualitative data on the perception of the elderly on their living arrangement, health condition and care and the support available to them. One FGD was organized in each of the selected districts. Thus a total of three FGDs were held in the three districts. The outcome of the FGDs is given in this section.

Each of the FGD was attended by 12–15 elderly people and each session lasted for 1½ to 2 hours. The participants were a mixed group of elderly people, both male and female, in the age group of 60-89 years. Both literates and illiterates were included in the group discussion. Participants were also selected from different caste groups in order to have representation from all sections of the society.

The elderly were unanimous in their desire to stay with their children and they wanted to spend most of their time with the children. But the children did not like their presence in the home, they said. The elderly were of the opinion that youngsters now-a-days didn't like their parents' participation in any decision making process in the family. A few said that they were not willing to stay with their children due to the indifferent attitude of the children. They felt that, after marriage, most of the children were not taking care of their parents.

They said that they are longing for love and affection but they are not getting it because of the fact that the attitude of male children had changed drastically after marriage. The elderly were of the opinion that due to higher educational status, better job and migration from their native place, their children started giving importance to their own family and neglected the parents.

Most of the elderly expected that they should be consulted before taking decisions in all family matters as they were more experienced than the youngsters in family life. Some of them were also of the opinion that they need not be consulted in all aspects because of the fact that the youngsters now-a-days are more educated than the elderly people. In that situation, the expectations of the youngsters will be entirely different from the elderly people's experience.

The elderly felt that their role in solving family disputes was minimal because children now-a-days do not give much importance to the suggestions made by them. Further, as most of the children were living in a nuclear family system, the role of the elderly in solving family disputes was minimal, they said.

Elderly people like to maintain cordial relations with their family members but their in-laws are not interested to maintain cordial relations with them. Due to this unnecessary conflicts arose in the family, they said.

The elderly people felt that they were getting sufficient food but it was not nutritious. They added that they were not in a position to work due to various health problems and chronic diseases. They felt that their children were not taking care of them properly because their income was low. They also added that they were considered a burden to the family members due to various economic problems.

All the elders wanted to have a separate room for taking rest in the house, but they were not able to get it due to inadequate space in the house, which was generally a hut.

The elderly people were very eager to attend all the family ceremonies. They felt that, while attending the functions, they would have a chance to meet their relatives and share their views with them. Some of the elderly stated that they were not in a position to attend the family ceremonies due to their poor health condition as well as inadequate money in hand.

With reference to increased longevity, they said that they were not interested to live long due to their poor health condition and inability to work and earn for themselves. Even for their own personal needs, they had to depend on their children but their children's earnings were not enough to meet their own family needs, they felt. Further, the elderly felt that children now-a-days are not much concerned for the elderly people. The female elderly felt that they were happy to contribute to some extent in the household chores. Elderly people did not possess much knowledge about their rights and they were not aware of the government benefits available to them.

Elderly people were very much concerned about their physical mobility in very old age (say, 70 and above) and they felt that they could not get adequate care and support at the stage when they were not able to move about.

Going to hospital itself was a difficult task for them. They were not satisfied with the services provided by government hospitals for the elderly. They wanted the government to provide minimum health care services at the door step. They also wanted that all elderly people, irrespective of the presence of children, should be given old age pension to take care of their personal needs.

Overall, increased longevity without adequate social security, economic security and health care services was a nightmare for the poor vulnerable elderly in rural areas.

7

SUMMARY AND CONCLUSION

There are about 77 million Indians who are elderly individuals in the age group of 60 years and above and this elderly population is expected to increase to 114 million by 2016, an increase of over 60 per cent in a 15 year period. About one third of elderly in India live below poverty line and an additional one third live just above the poverty line. This means that 66 per cent of elderly in India are vulnerable to shortages of food, clothing and shelter. Most of the elderly are economically depending on others most commonly on their children or other relatives. Some have to depend on charitable and religious institutions. Their most glaring need is proper care and support. While the urban elderly are more accessible to health care and recreational facilities, the elderly in rural areas are completely deprived of all needed care and support. Hence the present study was undertaken to assess the living arrangements and health conditions of elderly in rural TamilNadu and to suggest suitable measures to provide care and support to the vulnerable elderly in rural areas.

The study was carried out on a sample of 900 elderly aged 60+ living in the rural areas of three districts of TamilNadu. The informations collected from the elderly covered a range of subjects which include the living arrangements of elderly, their social and economic status, physiological, psychological and health status and the care and support available to elderly in rural TamilNadu. Besides the primary data collected from the elderly, secondary data on the levels and trends in ageing at global, national and state level were also collected from books, journals and internet. The primary data collected from the elderly were entered in to the computer and analysed using the Statistical Package for Social Sciences (SPSS). The secondary data collected from various sources were compiled and compared at global, national and state level.

LEVELS AND TRENDS IN POPULATION AGEING

The results of the analysis of secondary data revealed that the decline of fertility and increased survival has resulted in the population ageing both in developed and developing countries of the world in the 20th century. During the period from 1990 to 2000, the world elderly population aged 60+ has increased from 8.9 per cent to 10 per cent. The proportion of elderly in the more developed countries of the world was 19.4 per cent in 2000 compared to only 7.7 per cent in the less developed countries of the world. However in terms absolute numbers, there were more number of elderly aged 60+ in developing countries (368,040 million) than those in developed countries (229,182 million). The United Nations projected figures indicate that there will be more number of elderly aged 60+than the younger population aged 0-14 in the developing countries of the world by the year 2050. As the large shifts in age structure are being compressed in to a relatively short period in developing countries, these countries have less time to adapt to the problems posed by the changing age structure.

In India, the number of elderly people aged 60+ is steadily increasing. The significant reduction in the death rates and the improvements in the life expectancy have lead to more number of elderly in the country. Though the percentage of elderly to the total population is estimated around seven per cent, their number increased from 12 million in 1901 to about 77 million in 2001. The 2001 census results indicate that in India, population ageing was highest at 9.9 per cent in Kerala followed by Himachal Pradesh (9.2 per cent), Punjab (8.6 per cent), TamilNadu (8.5 per cent), Maharastra (8 per cent), Orissa (7.7 per cent), Andhra Pradesh (7.6 per cent), Gujarat and

Karnataka (7.4 per cent each) and Haryana (7 per cent). In all these states, the proportion of elderly was comparatively higher in rural and than in urban areas. It is also observed that the proportion of elderly was more among female than male. The index of ageing has increased from 13.08 in 1901 to 24.72 in 2001. The oldage dependency ratio has increased from 8.96 in 1901 to 12.59 in 2001. The continued increase in oldage dependency ratio in India is a major challenge for the government to allocate resources to take care of the growing number of elderly in the coming years.

In TamilNadu, the proportion of elderly people aged 60+ has increased from 5.59 per cent in 1961 to 8.83 per cent in 2001. The 2001 census results indicate that the proportion of elderly was more among female than male. Similarly, the proportion of elderly was more in rural than in urban areas. The oldage dependency ratio in TamilNadu has increased from 9.80 in 1961 to 13.85 in 2001. The oldage dependency ratio was slightly higher among female (13.92) than male (13.77). It is also observed that the oldage dependency ratio was higher in rural (14.81) than in urban areas (12.68). It is estimated that there will be 9.14 million elderly in TamilNadu by 2016 which will be a big challenge for the government to initiate social security and heath care programmes for the vulnerable elderly particularly in the rural areas of TamilNadu.

BACKGROUND CHARACTERISTICS OF ELDERLY

The results of the analysis of survey data on the living conditions of elderly revealed that among the 900 elderly interviewed in the study, 42 per cent were male and 58 per cent were female. A majority of them were aged 60-69 years (50.8 per cent) which was followed by 70-79 years (33.9 per cent) and 80 years and above (15.3 per cent). Most of the elderly interviewed were Hindus (91.5 per cent). Christians and Muslims constituted only 5.3 and 3.2 per cent of the total respondents respectively. More than half of the elderly were single (53.2 per cent) and 46.8 per cent were married. Nearly three fourth of elderly (73.7 per cent) had not involved in any sort income earning activities at the time of interview.

LIVING ARRANGEMENTS

It is observed that about one fourth of elderly were living alone (25.2 per cent), nearly one fifth (19.2 per cent) were living with their spouse and nearly two fifth (38.6 per cent) were living with son's family. It is also observed that 8.7 per cent of elderly were living with their daughter's family. Substantially higher proportion of female elderly (31 per cent) were living alone compared to male (17.2 per cent). The main reason for not staying with son's family was 'son live at a long distance' (32 per cent) followed by 'no son' (28.7 per cent), 'to avoid conflict' (18 per cent) and 'poverty' (17.6 per cent). Proportion of elderly living alone was significantly less among elderly aged 80 years or more. Elders living with daughter's family increased with the age. Proportion of elderly living with daughter's family was significantly higher among female than male. Proportion of elderly living with son was lowest among those who had studied up to higher secondary and above than others. Proportion of elderly living alone was more among Muslim than Hindu and Christian. The Proportion of elderly living with daughter's family was also more among Muslim than Hindu and Christian. The logistic regression analysis showed that female, those who served in government and those who had higher income (more than Rs.1000/- per month) were having significantly higher chances of living alone.

FAMILIAL RELATIONSHIP

Most of the elderly were having freedom to use household facilities and were maintaining cordial relationship with their spouse. About 70–74 per cent of elderly were maintaining cordial relationship with their son, daughter, daughter-in-law and son-in-law and 85 per cent were maintaining cordial relationship with other family members. Only half of the elderly had reported to have attended all family ceremonies. The main reasons for not attending the family ceremonies were 'no interested' (44 per cent) and 'poor health condition' (42.8 per cent). Less than half of the elderly (45.8 per cent) were consulted on important family matters. Comparatively higher proportion of male elderly were consulted on important family matters than female. Only 46.9 per cent of elderly had reported to have role in solving family disputes. Higher proportion of male elderly (55.4 per cent) had involved in solving family disputes compared to female (40.4 per cent). Only 17.1 per cent of elderly had reported to have experienced abuse behaviour from the family members. About half of the elderly (52.7 per cent) had reported to have availed three times food daily and 41.9 per cent had availed two times per day. More than three fourth of elderly were having adequate food daily. About 28.4 per cent of elderly were in need of special food to be prepared for them. However, only 56.6 per cent of them were getting the special food. Most of the elderly were in need of money to meet their personal needs like medicine, tea/coffee and tobacco. Only 30.8 per cent of elderly were able to get the required finance from sources like son and daughter. However, nearly three fourth of them (72.9 per cent) reported that the available money was not sufficient to meet their personal needs.

PERSONAL LIFE STYLE

The personal life style behaviour of elderly was assessed based on their regular practice of prayer, walking, gardening, meditation, yoga, exercise, going to religious centre, social service activities and going to recreation centre. It is observed that only 19 to 36 per cent of male elderly were having regular practice of doing the above said activities. In the case of female, only 16 to 35 per cent were having the regular practices of doing the above said activities. Overall, it is observed that the practice of healthy life style behaviour was poor among the elderly. Higher proportion of female elderly had involved in household activities such as cooking, shopping, fetching water, schooling children, cleaning household and disposal of waste compared to male. The involvement of elderly in household activities decreased with the increase in age. At the ages of 80 and above, comparatively small proportion of elderly were involved in household activities. The main leisure time activities of elderly were watching television, visiting friends, visiting temple, listening to radio, spending time at local tea shop and reading newspaper. Significantly higher proportion of elderly were not having the habit of smoking, drinking, use of drug, tobacco, snuff powder and betel nuts.

PHYSICAL DISABILITIES

The most important difficulty reported by the elderly in doing the activities of daily living was boarding train/bus (32 per cent) followed by climbing stairs (31.2 per cent), getting up (9.6 per cent), outdoor walk (6.7 per cent) and bathing (12.6 per cent).

It is found that only 28.6 per cent of male and 19.3 per cent of female elderly were able to move freely everywhere. About three fifth of elderly (59.5 per cent of male and 57.1 per cent of female) were able to move to neighbourhood only. 10.8 per cent of male and 22.8 per cent of female elderly were able to move inside the house only. Just 1.1 per cent of male and 0.8 per cent of female elderly were bedridden. Most of the bedridden elderly were aged 70 years and above. The physical mobility status of elderly significantly influenced their psychological status. Increase in age had negative effect and education and involvement in any form of work earlier had positive effect on the elderly's free movement everywhere.

The physiological status of elderly became poor with the increase in age. Among the various physiological factors, vision problem was the major problem reported by a significantly higher proportion of elderly followed by difficulty in recall memory, recognition and audible range. Elderly who were young, literates, married, SC/ST and from high income families were having good physiological status than others. The chances of getting disability in bathing, indoor walking, out door walking, climbing stair, combing hair, getting up, boarding train/bus and going to toilet were significantly more for elderly aged 70-79 years and 80 years and above compared to elderly aged 60-69 years. The female elderly were having significantly less chances of getting disability in bathing, out door walking, climbing stairs, getting up and going to toilet compared to male. The chances of getting disability were significantly lower for literates compared to illiterates. Single elderly were having significantly more chances of getting disability in outdoor walking, climbing stairs and getting up compared to married. In the case of religion, Christians were having less chances of getting disability in bathing and boarding train compared to Hindu. Individual income of elderly seemed to have significant influence on disability. Younger old, literates, Hindu, Christian and other than SC/ ST group were having significantly more chances of keeping good physiological status than others.

PSYCHOLOGICAL PROBLEMS

A set of 24 psychological problems were listed and the elderly were asked about the presence or absence of these psychological problems. The psychological status of elderly was assessed based on the response of the elderly to each of these psychological problems. It is found that almost all elderly had one or the other psychological problem. The major psychological problems reported by the elderly were anxiety (87.4 per cent), unnecessary worry (66.4 per cent), angry (62.8 per cent), isolation (61 per cent), easily upset (55.3 per cent), tension (53.3 per cent), loneliness (52.9 per cent), irritation (51.9 per cent), depression (51.4 per cent), stress (51.2 per cent), fear of dependence (44.1 per cent), inability to adjust with the changed health condition (42.7 per cent) and behavioural adjustment (42.3 per cent).

The over all psychological status of elderly showed that 39.1 per cent of elderly were in good psychological status, 41.1 per cent were in moderate psychological status and 19.8 per cent were in poor psychological status. The proportion of elderly with good psychological status decreased with age. The over all psychological status of elderly significantly associated with education, marital status and family income. Proportion of elderly with good psychological status significantly improved with the increase in education. Significantly higher proportion of married elderly were having good psychological status than single. Proportion of elderly with good psychological status was significantly more among those living in high income families (more than Rs.3000 per month) than those who are living in low income families The proportion of elderly having good psychological status was more among those living with son compared to others. Financial support, family support and recreation facilities were the major suggestions made by the elderly to overcome their psychological problems.

HEALTH STATUS OF ELDERLY

The major health problems reported by the elderly were poor vision/cataract/other eye impairments were the major health problems reported by a majority of elderly (59.9 per cent) and by arthritis/rheumatic joint pain (59.7 per cent). Back pain/slipped disc (32.4 per cent), high blood pressure (17.2 per cent), lung/respiratory problems (14.4 per cent) and frailty/general weakness/rundown condition (12.9 per cent) were the other health problems reported by the elderly. Almost all elderly who were having health problems were in need of treatment. More than 80 per cent of elderly had availed treatment for all their health problems except for eye problem and dementia. In the case of eye problem, only 70.4 per cent had reported to have availed treatment and in the case of dementia only 55.6 per cent had availed treatment. The main source of treatment for the health problems of elderly was government hospital.

EXPECTATION OF ELDERLY

The main expectations of elderly from the family members were love and affection, care and support, regular food and money to meet their personal needs. The main expectations of the elderly from the government were financial support and opportunity to work. The elderly were expecting that the youth and youngsters should have good education and good character and give respect to elderly.

About three fourth of elderly were not having any opinion on the increased longevity of human life because they felt it as a burden to others and unable to bare the health problems. About half of the elderly reported that their present living condition was not good as they were not able to get minimum basic needs such as medical care, money, food and care and support from family.

CONCLUSION AND POLICY IMPLICATIONS

The continued increase in the old age dependency ratio is the major challenge for the government to take care of the growing number of elderly in the coming years. The living arrangements of elderly indicate the traditional practice of elderly staying within the family system. However, it is very disturbing to note that about one fourth of elderly were living alone and a majority of them were female. Practice of healthy life style behaviour was poor among elderly. Higher proportion of female elderly had contributed to household chores. The leisure time activities of elderly have changed with the increase in age. Most of the elderly were reported to be healthy until the age of seventy. Many health and psychological problems arose only after the age of seventy. Proportion of elderly suffering with different chronic diseases was significantly more among male than female. Due to poverty, lack of mobility, inadequate and in accessible health care services and lack of familial and societal support, the elderly were vulnerable to many health and psychological problems at older ages.

The emerging issues identified are the decline in the joint family, changing values which emphasize the needs of the immediate family, fewer children as care providers to the elderly, greater female employment demands, migration of the young, limited housing, complex living conditions due to modernization and the economic dependence of the elderly. This changing situation poses a challenge for policy makers in the provision of personal care and financial support for the growing elderly population.

The needs of the elderly were getting changed with age. Self-sufficiency is a major requirement for the elderly regardless of their living arrangements. The chronic health conditions or disabilities of the elderly prevent them to make a long walk to a health centre. Treatment for the elderly is a difficult task particularly for elderly in rural areas. The elderly are in a difficult emotional adjustment from independence to dependence. The available health services are not adequate to meet the unique needs of the elderly. Hence, there is a need for a community based health care services to meet the requirements of vulnerable elderly in rural areas. The existing services of the community health nurses supported by mobile clinics and referral services will certainly be a healing touch for the sufferings of the elderly in rural areas.

The State Governments are having a number of programmes for the welfare of the elderly. But the understanding is that families have the primary responsibility to care for their aged. State programmes appear to be more dependent on the state's predisposition and ability to allocate funds to the elderly than on elderly demand. Housing for low income elderly is a particularly neglected sector. Unemployment of the elderly is expected to emerge as a major public issue in the decades ahead. The healthy elderly should be provided with employment opportunities and strategies should be developed for the elderly people's involvement in community development activities.

Elderly in India needs the protection of an integrated national policy for the aged. Policies should identify needs, recognize rights to the benefits of development, provide the framework for the development of appropriate social security and social services and have sufficient funding. National policy should recognize the potential of the aged to contribute to development. Negative perceptions of the economic burden of the elderly should be abandoned and replaced with a positive image. Policy must be adapted to meet the diverse needs of subgroups based on residence, sex, education and employment or income. There is a need for a high level organization, which would protect and promote the needs of the elderly particularly in rural India. The findings of the study suggests that the existing programmes for the welfare of the aged most focus on three important aspects - social security, economic security and health care services for the vulnerable elderly in rural areas.

REFERENCES

Achir, Y.C. (1998), 'Strategies to Formulate Family Support Systems and Community based Services for the Care of the Old': State Ministry for Population/National Family Planning Coordinating Board [BKKBN], Jakarta, Indonesia. *Technical Report Series Monograph* No. 93.p.26.

Agree, E.M. (1993), 'Effects of Demographic Change on the Living Arrangements of the Elderly in Brazil 1960-1980'. Ann Arbor, Michigan, University Microfilms International, 1993. ix, Order No. 9416893. p.233.

Allain, T.J., A.O. Wilson, Z.A. Gomo, E. Mushangi, B. Senzanje, D.J. Adamchak, J.A. Matenga (1997), 'Morbidity and Disability in Elderly Zimbabweans'. *Age Ageing,* 26:2, pp.115-21.

Amirtha Gowri, R. and Bmitha Sukumran (2003), 'A Comparative Study on the Attitudes of Adolescents and Adults Towards the Care of Elderly'. *Research Highlights Journal of Avinashilingam Institute for Home Science and Higher education for women,* 13:1.

Angra, S.K., G.V.S. Murthy, S.K. Gupta and V. Angra (1997), 'Cataract related Blindness in India and Its Social Implications'. *Indian Journal of Medical Research,* 106, pp.312-324.

Ania Lafuente, B.J. 1985. 'Healthy ageing and functional disability among the elderly inhabitants of the Canary Islands (Spain)'. *Introduction to Demography,* 4:7, pp.1-6.

Asgarali Patel and Aruna Broota (2000), 'Loneliness and Death–Anxiety Among the Elderly– The Role of Family Set up and Religious Belief'. *Research and Development Journal,* HelpAge India, 6:3.

Ashakrishnakumar (2004), 'The Old and the Ignored'. *Frontline,* India's national magazine, September 24, pp.90-95.

Audinarayana, N. and J. Sheela (2002), 'Physical Disability Among the elderly in TamilNadu: Patterns, Differentials and Determinants'. *Health and Population - Perspectives and Issues,* 25:1, pp.26-37.

Bagga, A. and Sakurkar (1999), 'A Recent Study on General Physical Health of Middle Class', Unpublished UGC reported.

Baginda, A.M. (1987), The Emerging Issues of the Ageing of Population: Malaysia, In: Population Ageing: Review of Emerging Issues. Report, Proposed Study Design and Selected Background Papers from the Meeting on Emerging Issues on the Ageing of Population, 22-26 September 1986, Bangkok. Bangkok, Thailand, *Economic and Social Commission for Asia and the Pacific, Asian Population Studies Series,* No. 80; ST/ESCAP/496, pp.33-43.

Bajpai (1998), Generation Gap: Implications on the Aged, in Social Work Perspectives on Health. Rawat Publications, New Delhi.

Bali, A. (1997), 'Socio-economic Status and Its Relationship to Morbidity Among Elderly'. *Indian Journal of Medical Research,* 106, pp.349-360.

Bannerjee Mrinmayi Tyagi and Deepak (2001), 'Role of Adjustment and Status if Aged: A Case Study of Bengali Population of Meghalaya', 15 (3 & 4), 53-362, (IJG).

Barai, D.C. (1997), Impact of Population Change on Older Age Groups in India: Trends and Prospects. In: Demographic Transition: The Third World Scenario, edited by Aijazuddin Ahmad, Daniel Noin, H.N. Sharma. Rawat Publications, Jaipur, India, pp.268-77.

Barry Mirkin and Mary Beth Weinberger (2001), 'The Democracy of Population Ageing'. *Population bulletin of the United Nations,* Nos.42/43, pp.37-53.

Beard, V.A. and Y. Kunharibowo (2001), 'Living Arrangements and Support Relationships Among Elderly Indonesians: Case Studies from Java and Sumatra'. *International Journal of Population Geography,* 7:1, pp.17-33.

Bhamini Mehta and Indira Mallya (2003), 'Self Appraisal of Elderly in Slums of Vadara City'. *Research and Development Journal,* HelpAge India, 7:2.

Bisht, P.S. (2000), 'Population Ageing: Global and Nepalese Perspectives'. *Population and Development in Nepal,* 7:1, pp.167-82.

Blanchet, D. and D. Kessler (1990), 'Forecasting the Economic Effects of the Ageing Population'. [Prevoir les effets economiques du vieillissement.], *Economie Et Statistique,* Jun;(233):9-17, pp.86-88.

Bongaarts, J. and Z. Zimmer (2001), 'Living Arrangements of Older Adults in the Developing World: An Analysis of DHS Household Surveys', Population Council, New York. Policy Research Division Working Papers No. 148, p.30.

Boyd, M. (1988), 'Immigration and Living Arrangements: Elderly Women in Canada'. [Unpublished] Paper presented at the Population Association of America Annual Meeting, New Orleans, Louisiana, April 21-23, 1988, p.9.

Casterline, J.B., L. Williams, A. Hermalin, M.C. Chang, N. Chayovan, P. Cheung, L. Domingo, J. Knodel, M.B. Ofstedal (1991), 'Differences in the Living Arrangements of the Elderly in Four Asian Countries: the Interplay of Constraints and Preferences'. Ann Arbor, Michigan, University of Michigan, Population Studies Center, 1991 Mar. [2], 17, Research Report No. 91-10, p.31.

Chan, A. (1997), 'An Overview of the Living Arrangements and Social Support Exchanges of Older Singaporeans'. *Asia-Pacific Population Journal,* 12:4, pp.35-50.

Chan, A. and J. DaVanzo (1991), 'Living Arrangements of Older Malaysians—Who Coresides with their Adult Children?' [Unpublished]. Presented at the Annual Meeting of the Population Association of America, Washington, D.C., March, 21-23,1991, p.2.

Chandra Paul Singh, Dr. (2005), 'Social-Economic Status and Health Conditions of Handless Rural Aged in Haryana'. *Research and Development Journal,* HelpAge India, 11:1.

Chen, C. (1992), 'Living Arrangements and Economic Support for the Elderly in Taiwan'. Taipei, Taiwan, Academia Sinica, Institute of Economics, Discussion Paper No. 9201.

China Population Today (1999), Population Ageing. Apr;16(1-2):23-5.

Chowdhry, D.P. (1992), Ageing and the Aged– A Source Book Inter-India Publications, New Delhi. Government of India, Ministry of welfare, Annual Report (1992-93).

Crews, D.E. and S. Zavotka (2006), 'Ageing, Disability and Frailty: Implications for Universal Design'. *Journal of Physiological Anthropology,* 25:1, pp.113-118.

Dalal, P.M. (1997), 'Strokes in the Elderly: Prevalence, Risk Factors and the Strategies for Prevention'. *Indian Journal of Medical Research*, 106, pp 332-352.

De Vos S. (1987), 'Living Arrangements of Older People in Six Latin American Countries', Madison, Wisconsin, University of Wisconsin-Madison. Center for Demography and Ecology, CDE Working Paper No. 87-40.

Dey, A.B. and D. Chowdhury (1997), 'Infections in the Elderly'. *Indian Journal of Medical Research*, 106, pp.273-285.

Dhar, H.L. (2001), 'Gender, Ageing, Health and Society'. *Journal of the Association of Physicians of India*, pp.1012-1020.

Dharmalingam, A. (1994), 'Old Age Support: Expectations and Experiences in South Indian Village'. *Population Studies*, 48:1, pp.5-19.

Dharmalingam, B. and K.R. Murugan (2001), 'Elderly Widows and their Place in the Family'. *Social welfare*, 48:1, pp.7-11.

Dillip, T.R. (2001), 'The Burden of Ill Health Among Elderly in Kerala'. *Research and Development Journal*, HelpAge India, 7:2, pp.40-50.

Do-Le, K.D. and Y. Raharjo (2002), Community-based Support for the Elderly in Indonesia: The case of PUSAKA:' [Unpublished] 2002. Presented at the 2002 International Union for the Scientific Study of Population [IUSSP] Conference on Southeast Asia's Population in a Changing Asian Context, Bangkok, Thailand, June 10-13.

Du, P. (1998), 'Changes in Living Arrangements of the Elderly in Beijing'. *Chinese Journal of Population Science*, 10:3, pp.231-40.

El-Bawdry, M.A. (1986), 'Ageing in Developing Countries: One More Population Problem?, Cairo, Egypt', *Cairo Demographic Centre*, 15, CDC Working Paper No. 13, p.2.

Eldermire, D. (1997), 'Ageing, Poverty and Health'. *People*, Aug-Nov; 6(2-3), p.6-7.

Fratczak, E. (1993), 'Population Ageing in Poland – Selected Aspects', Valletta, Malta, *International Institute on Ageing*, p.114.

Goh, V.H. (2005), 'Ageing in Asia: A Cultural, Socio-economical and Historical Perspective'. *The Ageing Male*, 8:2, pp.09-96.

Gokhale, S.D. (1994), 'Towards Productive and Participatory Ageing in India', In: The Ageing of Asian Populations, Proceedings of the United Nations Round Table on the Ageing of Asian Populations,

Bangkok, 4-6 May 1992, [compiled by] United Nations. Department for Economic and Social Information and Policy Analysis. New York, New York, United Nations, 1994, pp.76-87. ST/ESA/SER.R/125.

Goyal, S. (1989), Analysed the Problem of Ageing in India. *Population Education News*, September (15), 6, pp.4-8.

Gutierrez Robledo, L.M. (1989), 'The Ageing Situation in Latin America'. *Impact of Science on Society*, 39:1, pp.65-80.

HelpAge India (2002), 'Active Participation of Older Persons in Economic- Social and Political Life'. *Research and Development Journal*, HelpAge India, 8:3.

Hema Nalini, V. and S. Meera (2002), 'Emerging Trends, Issues and Needs of the Elderly in the Context of Globalization'. *Research Highlights, published by Avinashilingam Deemed University,* 12:2, pp.104-109.

Hermanova, H. (1998), 'Ageing Populations in Rural Areas', In: Ageing and Health: A Global Challenge for the Twenty-first Century. Proceedings of a WHO Symposium, Kobe, 10-13 November 1998, [compiled by] World Health Organization [WHO]. Kobe, Japan, WHO, 1999 :192-7. WHO/WCK/ SYM/99.1

Hernandez, R. (1992), 'Demography of Ageing'. *BOLD*, 1992. Aug:2(4): 8-12.

Higuchi, K. (1996), 'Women in an Ageing Society', In: Added years of life in Asia: current situation and future challenges, [compiled by] United Nations. Economic and Social Commission for Asia and the Pacific [ESCAP]. [Bangkok, Thailand], ESCAP, 1996. :145-65. Asian Population Studies Series No.14; ST.

Hitesh, Dr. Patel (1997), 'Mental problems of Ageing and care of them by their family'. *Research and Development journal, HelpAge India,* 4:1.

Hosmath, S. Revati, V. Gaonkar and P.K. Khadi (1993), 'Life Satisfaction during Later Years'. Man in India, 73:3, pp.229-232.

Ilango Ponnuswami (1987), 'Situation of the Older Persons in India'. *Ageing research foundation of India,* S.India. 151.

Indira Jai Prakash (2001), 'Health Concerns of Older Women in India'. Research and Development Journal, HelpAge India, 10:3.

Indirani Gupta and Deepa Sankar (2003), 'Health of the Elderly in India: A Multivariate Analysis'. *The Journal of Health and Population in developing countries.* ISSN 1095 – 8940.

Irudaya Rajan, S. and S. Sanjay Kumar (2003), 'Living Arrangements Among the Indian Elderly Evidence from National Family Health Survey'. *Economic and political weekly,* 38:1, January 4-10, pp.75-80.

Irudaya Rajan, S., P. Sankara Sarma and U.S. Mishra (2005), 'Demography of Indian Ageing, 2001-2051', Phoebe, S. Liebig and S.Irudaya Rajan, *An Ageing India: Perspectives, Prospects and Policies*: Rawat Publications, New Delhi.

Jayarani Reddy, P. and D.Usharani (1999), 'Perspectives on Elderly in India: Rural– Urban Analysis in Murali Desai and Siva Raju" (eds), *Geronrological social work in India: Some issues and perspectives,* B.R. Publishing Corporation, New Delhi.

Jayashree, Dr. (1999), 'Living Arrangements Enhance Quality of Life'. *Social Welfare,* 46:7.

Jayashree (2004), 'Ageing Men and Health Concerns'. *The Journal of Family Welfare, 50:1*

Jorm, A.F., Henderson, R. Scott, A.J. Mackinnon, A.I. Korten, H.Christensen (2001), 'The Disabled Elderly Living in the Community: Care Received from Family and Formal Services'. *Journal of American Geriatrics Society,* 49:5, pp.549-56.

Kabir, M.H. (1994), Demographic and Socio-economic Aspects of Ageing in Bangladesh,' In: The Ageing of Asian Populations. Proceedings of the United Nations Round Table on the Ageing of Asian Populations, Bangkok, 4-6 May 1992, [compiled by] United Nations. Department for Economic and Social Information and Policy Analysis. New York, New York, United Nations, 52-7., ST/ESA/SER.R/125.

Kacker, S.K. (1997), 'Hearing Impairment in the Aged'. *Indian Journal of Medical Research,* 106, pp.333-339.

Kamo, Y. (1988), 'A Note on Elderly Living Arrangements in Japan and the United States'. *Research on Ageing,* 10:2, pp.279-305.

Karkal and Malini (1999), 'Ageing and Women in India'. *Economic and Political Weakly,* 34:44, pp.54-56.

Kesavan, S. (1998), 'The Problems of the Old in N.Panjampatti Village in Dindigul District', Paper presented at national seminar on Psycho-social characteristics, problems and strategies for the welfare of the aged in Rural India, Department of Applied Research, Gandhigram Rural Institute, March 11-13, 1998.

Ketshukietue DzuvichÜ (2005), 'Health Problems of the Aged Among the Angaminagas'. *Journal of Human Ecology,* 17:2.

Kinsella, K. (2000), 'Demographic Dimensions of Global Ageing'. *Journal of Family Issues.* 21:5, pp.541-58.

Knodel, J. and N. Chayovan (1997), 'Family Support and Living Arrangements of Thai Elderly'. *Asia-Pacific Population Journal,* 12:4,pp.51-68.

Kovar, M.G. (1991), 'Functional Ability and the Need for Care': Issues for Measurement Research'. *Vital and Health Statistics, 5:6,* pp.97-103.

Kuroda, T. (1993), 'Population Ageing in Asia and Its Economic and Social Implications', In: The Fourth Asian and Pacific Population Conference, 19-27 August 1992, Bali, Indonesia. Selected papers, [compiled by] United Nations' Economic and Social Commission for Asia and the Pacific [ESCAP]. New York, New York, United Nations, Asian Population Studies Series No. 12; ST/ESCAP/1299, pp.155-9.

Lakshmi Pathi Raju, M. and V.Venkateswaran (2002), 'The Aged: A Social Development Perspective: Implications for Social Work Practice'. *Social Change,* ISSN:0049-0857, 32:1,2.

Lalitha, N. (1998), 'Most Deprived of the Deprived – The Rural Aged'. *Social Welfare,* 45:10, pp.13-17.

Li, B. and W. Zhang (1998), 'Trend of Population Ageing in China and the Strategy'. *China Population Today,* Apr;15(1-2), pp.2-4.

Majumdar (1985), 'The End of the Rood', *Hindustan Times,* Sunday Magazine, Oct 6,1985.

Martin, L.G. (1998), 'Determinants of Living Arrangements of the Elderly in Fiji, Korea, Malaysia and the Philippines'. [Unpublished] 1988. Presented at the Annual Meeting of the Population Association of America, New Orleans, Louisiana, April 21-23, Also published in: Demography 26(4): 627-43, November 1989.

Mba, C.J. (2002), 'Determinants of Living Arrangements of Lesotho's Elderly Female Population'. *Journal of International Women's Studies,* 3:2, pp.22.

Meena, H.S., A. Kumar, A.N. Malaviya and Muralidhar (1995), 'Spectrum of Inflammatory Joint Disorders in the Elderly and Clinical Profile of Late onset Rheumatoid Arthritis'. *Journal of Indian Rheumatism Association,* 33:1, pp.4-6.

Murphy, M. (1995), 'Assessing the Link Between Household and Family Living Arrangements and Health', In: Morbidity and mortality data: problems of comparability. Proceedings of the European Association for Population Studies and the Hacettepe Institute of Population Studies Workshop, Urgup (Turkey), 18-20 October, 1995, edited by Guillaume Wunsch and Attila Hancioglu. Ankara, Turkey, Hacettepe Universitesi, Nufus Etutleri Enstitusu, 1997 Jul. :157-88. Publication No. IPS-HU.97-01.

Nair, P.S. (1989), The Aged in Rural India: A Study of the Socio-economic and Health Profile, In: Population Transition in India, Vol. 2, edited by S.N. Singh, M.K. Premi, P.S. Bhatia and Ashish Bose. B.R. Publishing, Delhi, India, pp.63-70.

Nath, D.C., D.L.Leonetti and A.K. Deka (2000), Socio-demographic and Ecological Correlates of Health Among Elderly Population in an Indian Society, [Unpublished]. Presented at the Millennium Conference on Population, Development and Environment Nexus, New Delhi, India, February 14-16, 2000, p.19. jhu_ddr

National Sample Survey Organisation (NSSO) (1991), Socio-economic Profile of the Aged Persons. NSSO 42nd round (July 1986–June 1987), Sarveh Shana, 15:2, New Delhi.

Natividad, J.N. and G.T. Cruz (1997), 'Patterns in Living Arrangements and Familial Support for the Elderly in the Philippines'. *Asia-Pacific Population Journal,* 12:4, pp.17-34.

Nayar, P.K.B. (2000), 'The Ageing Senario in Kerala: A Holistic Perspective'. *Research and Development Journal,* HelpAge India, 6:2.

Ng, T.P., M.Niti, P.C. Chiam and E.H., Kua (1988), 'Prevalence and Correlates of Functional Disability in Multiethnic Elderly Singaporeans'. *Population Research,* 5:2, pp.33-9.

Osako, M. (1982), 'Increase of Elderly Poor in Developing Nations—The Implications of Dependency Theory and Modernization Theory for the Ageing of World Population'. *Studies in Third World Societies.* 1982 December, 22, pp.85-113.

Pappathi, K. and M.A. Sudhir (2005), 'Psycho-social Characteristics and Problems of the Rural Aged'. *Research and Development Journal,* HelpAge India, 11:1.

Patil, P.B., Gaonkar and V.S.Yadav (1998), 'Prevalence of Depression Among the Elderly'. *Research Highlights,* 8:1,pp12-15.

Perera, P.D. (1994), 'Ageing of Sri Lankan Population', In: The Ageing of Asian Populations. Proceedings of the United Nations Round Table on the Ageing of Asian Populations, Bangkok, 4-6 May 1992, [compiled by] United Nations. Department for Economic and Social Information and Policy Analysis. New York, New York, United Nations, 1994, ST/ESA/SER.R/ 125, pp.133-44.

Phillips, D.R. (1999), 'An Ageing Society in Hong Kong', In: Ageing and health: A Global Challenge for the Twenty-first Century, Proceedings of a WHO Symposium, Kobe, 10-13 November 1998, [compiled by] World Health Organization [WHO]. Centre for Health Development. Kobe, Japan, WHO, 1999, WHO/WCK/ SYM/99.1, pp.347-52.

Population Ageing: A Public Health Challenge. *Journal of Communicable Diseases,* 1996;28:4, pp.311-4.

Population Briefs (2001), Studying Living Arrangements of Developing-Country Elderly, 7:3, p.6. weblink:http://www.popcouncil.org/ publications/popbriefs/pb7(3)_6.html

Prema, B. Patil (2000), 'Psycho-social Problems of the Retired'. *Social Welfare,* pp.18-25.

Purohit, C.K. and R. Sharma (1974), 'Chronic Bronchitis in Rural Aged Persons 60 Years and Above'. *Indian Journal of Medical Sciences,* 28:11, pp.487-493.

Rafique Alam and M.G. Husain (1997), Psycho Social Problems of Ageing: Indian Perspective, Changing Indian Society and Status of aged. Manak Publication, New Delhi.

Rajkumar, S. Kumar and Shuba (1998), 'Prevalence of Dementia in the Community: A Rural Urban Comparison from Madras, India'. *Australian Journal on Ageing.* 15:2, pp.57-61.

Rao, M.K. (2003), 'Health Status of the Rural Aged in Andhra Pradesh; A Sociological Perspective'. *Research and Development Journal,* HelpAge India, 9:2.

Rao, S.R. and J.W. Townsend (1998), 'Health Needs of Elderly Indian Women: An Emerging Issue', In: Gender, population and development, edited by Maithreyi Krishnaraj, Ratna M. Sudarshan, Abusaleh Shariff. Delhi, India, Oxford University Press, pp.340-63.

Reddy, P.H. (1996), 'The Health of the Aged in India'. *Health Transition Review:6,* pp.233-44.

Restrepo, H.E. and M. Rozental (1994), 'The Social Impact of Ageing Populations: Some Major Issues'. Social Science and Medicine. 39:9(1), pp/323-38.

Richard, E. Pearson (1999), Counseling and Social Support Perspectives in Contemporary Theory, Research and Practice. Sage Publications, New Delhi.

Saad, P.M. (2001), 'Impact of Pension Reform on the Living Arrangements of Older Persons in Latin America'. [Impacto de la reforma jubilatoria en los planes de vida de las personas mayores en América Latina.] *Population Bulletin of the United Nations.* 42-43, pp.13.

Salas, R.M. (1982), 'Ageing a Universal Phenomenon'. *Population,* 9:4, pp.3-7.

Samita manña and Ranchali Chakraborty (1990), 'Aged Widows: A Micro Study in the Urban Setting of West Bengal'. *Journal of social research,* 33:1 and 2.

Selvi (2001), 'Socio-Economic Conditions and Health Profile of the Rural Aged'. M.Sc. dissertation in Home Science Extension, Gandhigram Rural University, Gandhigram.

Shah, B. and A.K. Prabhakar (1997), 'Chronic Morbidity Profile Among Elderly'. *Indian journal of medical research,* 106, pp.265-272.

Shubha Soneja (2000), 'Our Elderly'. *Health Action,* 13:10.

Shuman, T.M. (1986), 'Ageing in the Third World'. *Population,* 13:4, pp.239.

Sibai, A. (1997), 'Ageing in Lebanon'. *World Health.* 50:4, p.36.

Simmom, L. (1945), The Role of the Aged in Primitive Society, New Haven, Connectcut: Archon Books.

Siva Raju, S. (2002), 'Health of the Elderly in India, Issues and Implications. *Research and development journal,* HelpAge India, 8:1.

Sobieszczyk, T., J. Knodel and N. Chayovan (2002), 'Gender and Well-being Among the Elderly: Evidence from Thailand', Ann Arbor, Michigan, University of Michigan, Institute for Social Research. Population Studies Center, PSC Research Report No. 02-531, p.34.

Soldo, B.J. (1978), 'Living Arrangements of the Elderly: Future Trends and Implications', In: United States. Congress. House of Representatives. Select Committee on Ageing. Consequences of changing U.S. population: demographics of ageing. Vol. 1. Hearings, May

24, 1978. Washington, D.C., U.S. Government Printing Office, pp.208-230.

Speare, A. Jr., R. Avery and L. Lawton (1988), 'Disability, residential Mobility and Changes in Living Arrangements'. [Unpublished] 1988. Presented at the Annual Meeting of the Population Association of America, New Orleans, Louisiana, April 21-23, 1988.

Srivatsava, M., U. Kapil, V. Kumar, A.B., Dey, K.M. Nagarkar, and G.Sekaran (1996), 'Knowledge, Attitude and Practices regarding nutrition in patients attending geriatric clinic at the AIIMS, in Kumar, V. (ed) Ageing – Indian perspective and global scenario. New Delhi: *All India Institute of Medical Sciences,* pp.407-409.

Sudha Katyal, Dr. and Banal Sector (1999), 'Old People are Happiest in the Family'. *Social Welfare,* 45:11.

Sundar Lal, Dr., (Brig) S.L. Chadha and Dr. P.C. Bhatta (1999), 'A Study on Senior Citizens in Rural Areas'. *Health for the Million,* 25:5.

Sundar, P. and R. Bakshi (2004), 'Impact of Social Change an Elderly Women of Urban Punjab'. *Research and Development journal,* HelpAge India, 6:3.

Sunil Goyal and Navin Goyal (1999), 'Health Profile of Elderly Tribal of Betel, M.P.' *Social welfare,* 46:7.

Surendra Singh (1997), Psycho-social Problems of the Aged in the Contemporary Indian Society, Changing Indian Society and Status of Aged, Manak Publication, New Delhi.

Suresh, K.N. (2002), 'The Old Age Problems and Care of Senior Citizen'. *Nursing Journal of India.*

Suryanarayana, M. (1998), 'Changing Status in the Family Life of the Rural and Tribal Aged', paper presented at the regional conference of HelpAge India, Madras.

Susuman, A.S. (2005), 'The Health of the Aged in India: Emerging Problems', [Unpublished]. Presented at the 2nd Indian Association of Social Sciences in Health National Conference on "Globalization and Health Equity", Bhabha Atomic Research Center, Training School, Mankhurd, Mumbai, India, February 4-5, 2005, p.20.

Suyono, M. (1999), 'Implications of an Ageing Population in the Asian Context'. *Journal of Development Communication,* 10:2, pp.41-8.

Swain, P. and T.P. Sherin Raj (2004), 'Demography of Ageing in India: State and District Level Analysis', [Unpublished]. Presented at the International Seminar on Demographic Changes and Implications, Department of Demography, University of Kerala, Trivandrum, India, December 7-9, p.12.

Tripathi, R.M. (2001), 'Health and Health Services from Senior Citizens: A Case Study of Allahabad'. *Man and development journal,* 23:3.

Truong S.A., T.C. Bui, D. Goodkind and J. Knodel (1997), 'Living Arrangements, Patrilineality and Sources of Support Among Elderly Vietnamese'. *Asia-Pacific Population Journal,* 12:4, pp.69-88.

United Nations (1994a), Economic and Social Commission for Asia and the Pacific [ESCAP]. Population Division. 'Population Ageing and Socio-economic Development in Asia', In: The Ageing of Asian Populations. Proceedings of the United Nations Round Table on the Ageing of Asian Populations, Bangkok, 4-6 May 1992, [compiled by] United Nations. Department for Economic and Social Information and Policy Analysis. New York, New York, United Nations, 1994, ST/ESA/SER.R/ 125. pp.47-51.

United Nations (1994b), 'Department for Economic and Social Information and Policy Analysis. Population Division, Fertility decline and ageing in the ESCAP region,' In: The ageing of Asian populations. Proceedings of the United Nations Round Table on the Ageing of Asian Populations, Bangkok, 4-6 May 1992, [compiled by] United Nations. Department for Economic and Social Information and Policy Analysis. New York, New York, United Nations, 1994, ST/ESA/SER.R/125, pp.41-6.

United Nations (1998), World Population Prospects, the 1998, Revision, Volume 11: Sex and Age. The Population Division, Department of Economic and Social Affairs, United Nations Secretariat.

United Nations (1999a), Long Range World Populations Projections, based on the 1998 revision, ESA/P/WP/153.

United Nations (1999b), Population Ageing 1999. Sales No. E.99 XIII.II.

United Nations (2001), Living Arrangements of Older Persons: Critical Issues and Policy Responses'. *Population Bulletin of the United Nations,* special issue Nos.42/43, New York, pp.22.

US. Department of State (2007), 'Why Population Ageing Matters, A Global Perspective'. *National Institute on Ageing.*

Vasantha and Premakumar (1998), 'Nutrition and Health Problems of Aged', paper presented at national seminar on psycho-social characteristics, problems and strategies for the welfare of the aged in Rural India, Department of Applied Research, Gandhigram Rural Institute, March 11-13, 1998.

Vaswani, T.G. (1996), 'Dangers of Neglect of the Elderly in the Family'. In the WHO DSIC News Letter, special issue on ageing, 15 March. Baroda, women's household development studies information centre, M.S. University, Baroda.

Verhasselt, Y. (1998), 'Ageing in a New World', In: Ageing and Health: A Global Challenge for the Twenty-first Century. Proceedings of a WHO Symposium, Kobe, 10-13 November 1998, [compiled by] World Health Organization [WHO]. Centre for Health Development. Kobe, Japan, WHO, 1999, WHO/WCK/SYM/99.1, pp.163-72.

Victoria A. Velkoff (2001), 'Living Arrangements and Well Being of the Older Population: Future Research'. *Population Bulletin of the United Nations,* nos. 42/43-2001, pp. 376-392.

Vijayakumar, K. (1994), 'Life and Health of the Elderly in a Community in Transition', Results of a Survey in Thiruvananthapuram city. Health policy and planning, 9:3, pp.331-336.

Vijayakumar, S. (1998), 'Health Services for the Rural Elderly'. *Social Change,* 28:4.

Vukovich, G. (1991), 'Population Ageing in Hungary: Selected Aspects', Valletta, Malta. *International Institute on Ageing,* p.60.

Walker, A. (1992), 'The Care of the Elderly People in Industrial Society: A Conflict between the Family and the State in P.Krishan and KMahadevan (eds)'. *The elderly population in developed and developing world: Polices, problems and perspectives.* B.R. publishing Co., Delhi, pp.3-28.

Weeks, D.J. (1994), 'A Review of Loneliness Concepts with Particular References of Oldage'. *International journal of Geriatric psychiatry,* 9:5, pp.345-355.

WHO (1989), 'Health of the Elderly'. WHO Geneva, Technical Report Series. 779.

Wibowo, A. (1999), 'Ageing in the South-East Asian Region'. *Health for the Millions,* 25:5, pp.8-9.

World Population Data Sheet (2007), Population Reference Bureau.

Yadava, K.N.S., S.S. Yadava and R.E. Roberts (1996), 'Ageing and Health Hazards in Rural Northern India'. *Health and Population,* 19:1, pp.1-18.

Yi, Z. and L. George (2002), 'Extremely Rapid Ageing and the Living Arrangements of the Elderly: The Case of China'. *Population Bulletin of the United Nations.* 42/43, p.28.

Zarit, S.H., B. Johansson and S. Berg (1993), 'Functional Impairment and Co-disability in the Oldest Old'. *Journal of Ageing and Health,* 5:3, pp.291-305.

Zengyi, James, W., et al. (2002), 'Social Demographic and Health Profiles of the Oldest Old in China'. *Population and Development Review,* 28:2.

ANNEXURE

Annexure – I
District-wise Human Development Index (HDI) Values, 2001

Sl. No	*District*	*HDI*
	INDIA	***0.571***
	TAMIL NADU	*0.657*
1	Chennai	0.757
2	Kancheepuram	0.712
3	Kanniyakumari	0.711
4	Thoothukudi	0.703
5	Coimbatore	0.699
6	Nilgiris	0.685
7	Thiruchirapalli*	0.671
8	Madurai	0.661
9	Erode	0.658
10	Thirunelviii	0.658
11	Vellore*	0.658
12	Thiruvallur	0.654
13	Nagapattinam	0.654
14	Virudhunagar	0.651
15	Karur	0.647
16	Cuddalore	0.644
17	Dindigul	0.641
18	Sivagangai	0.640
19	Thiruvarur	0.637
20	Namakkal	0.636
21	Thanjavur	0.630
22	Ramanathapuram	0.629
23	Theni	0.628
24	Salem	0.626
25	Pudukkottai	0.618
26	Thiruvannamalai	0.612
27	Perambalur	0.596
28	Villupuram*	0.587
29	Dharmapuri	0.584

* Districts selected for the study
Source: Human Development Report, TamilNadu, 2001.

Annexure – II
Sample Area

District	*Name of the Primary Health Centre*	*Name of the Sub-Centre*
1. Trichy	1. Anbil	Somarasampettai (N)
	2. Sirugambur	Sirugambur (M)
	3. Inamkulathur	Ariyur (L)
2. Vellore	1. Kammavanpettai	Edayansathu (N)
	2. Kaveripakkam	Kaveripakkam (M)
	3. Ussoor	Konavattam (L)
3. Villupuram	1. Kanai	Kanai (N)
	2. Omandur	Omandur (M)
	3. Radhapuram	Radhapuram (L)

L-Long distance (≥ 10 Kilometers)
M-Medium (6-10 Kilometers)
N-nearer (≤ 5Kilometers)

Annexure – III
Scoring and Measurement Procedure Adopted to Assess the Psychological Status

Sl No	*Psychological Problems*	*Scoring*	
1.	Anxiety	Yes – 0;	No – 1
2.	Isolation	Yes – 0;	No – 1
3.	Feeling of guilty	Yes – 0;	No – 1
4.	Behavioural adjustment	Yes – 0;	No – 1
5.	Easily upset	Yes – 0;	No – 1
6.	Angry	Yes – 0;	No – 1
7.	Tension	Yes – 0;	No – 1
8.	Fear of dependence	Yes – 0;	No – 1
9.	Depression	Yes – 0;	No – 1
10.	Loneliness	Yes – 0;	No – 1
11.	Irritation	Yes – 0;	No – 1
12.	Inability to adjust with changed health condition	Yes – 0;	No – 1
13.	Unnecessary worry	Yes – 0;	No – 1
14.	Fear	Yes – 0;	No – 1
15.	Stress	Yes – 0;	No – 1
16.	Feeling of lack of affection	Yes – 0;	No – 1
17.	Fear of uselessness	Yes – 0;	No – 1
18.	Feeling of neglect	Yes – 0;	No – 1
19.	Dementia	Yes – 0;	No – 1
20.	Difficulty in coping with loss of job	Yes – 0;	No – 1
21.	Loss of social relationship	Yes – 0;	No – 1
22.	Loss of social security	Yes – 0;	No – 1
23.	Loss of self confidence	Yes – 0;	No – 1
24.	Feeling of lack of care	Yes – 0;	No – 1

Maximum expected score – 24

Psychological Status Score

Good	–	17 or more
Moderate	–	9 to 16
Poor	–	8 or less

Annexure - IV

Department of Applied Research Gandhigram Rural Institute -Deemed University

Changing Living Arrangements, Health Condition and Care of Elderly in Rural TamilNadu

Interview Schedule

I. IDENTIFICATION PARTICULARS

1.1 District :

1.2 Block/Primary Health Centre (PHC):

1.3 Sub-Centre (SC) / Village :

1.4 Street name /Door number :

1.5 Name of the household head :

1.6 Name of the respondent :

II. RESPONDENT'S BACKGROUND CHARECTERISTICS

2.1 Age (in completed years) :

2.2 Sex : 1. Male
2. Female

2.3 Religion : 1. Hindu
2. Muslim
3. Christian
4. Others

2.4 Caste : 1. SC/ST
2. OBC
3. Others

2.5 Education : 1. Illiterate
2. Primary (upto5th)
3. Middle (upto8th)
4. Secondary (upto10th)
5. Highersecondary (upto12th)
6. College and above
7. Others

2.6 Marital status : 1. Married
2. Never Married
3. Widow/Widower
4. Divorced
5. Separated

2.7 Number. of children: Male [ ] Female [ ] Total [ ]

2.8 What was your main occupation up to 60 years of age?
1.
2.
3.

2.9 Was your income adequate to run your family?
1. Yes 2. No

2.10 Whether your occupation required to move from one place to another?
1. Yes 2. No

2.11 If yes, did you went alone or with your Family

2.12 Are you currently involved in any money earning work:
1. Yes [ ] 2. No [ ]

2.13 If yes, what type of work :
1. Coolie
2. Business
3. Agriculture
4. Others (Specify)

2.14 Monthly earning : Rs .[ ].

2.15 Do you have any other source of income? 1. Yes [ ] 2. No [ ]

2.16 If yes, Income from other sources

S. No	*Sources*	*Income per month*
1	Pension	
2	Interest (From deposit/lending etc.)	
3	others (Specify)	
	Total	

2.17 Total individual income : Rs .[ ].
(2.14 + 2.16)

III. FAMILY BACKGROUND

3.1 Number of family members in the household including the Respondent

S. No	*Name of person*	*Sex*	*Relation-ship to respondent*	*Age*	*Educa-tion*	*Occu-pation*	*Monthly income(Rs)*
						Total :	

3.2 Other sources of income :

3.3 Total Monthly Family income (3.1 + 3.2) : Rs.[ ]

3.4 Property ownership

S. No	*Property*	*In the name of respondent*	*In the name of other family members*	*Total value (Rs.)*
1.	Land			
2.	House			
3.	Jewels			
4.	Fixed deposit			
5.	Others (Specify)			
	Total			

3.5 whether the property owned by you is in your possession?
1. Yes 2. No

3.6 If No under whose possession it now?
1. Son
2. Daughter
3. Wife/Husband
4. Others (specify)

IV HOUSING CHARACTERISTICS

4.1 Type of house :
1. Hut
2. Katcha
3. Pucca

4.2. Ownership of house :
1. Respondent's house
2. Son's house
3. Daughter's house
4. Rented/Lease
5. Others (specify)

4.3. If rented / Lease house, who pay the amount?
1. Respondent
2. Other family members

4.4 Electrification : 1. Yes 2. No

4.5 Toilet facilities : 1. Yes 2. No

4.6 Number of rooms in the house :

4.7. Facilities amenable to the household

S. No	*Facilities*	*With in 1 km*	*Away distance (kms)*
1.	Main road		
2.	Hospital		

3. Market
4. School
5. Public transport
6. Post office
7. Bank
8. Temple
9. Library
10. Recreation club

V. LIVING ARRANGEMENTS

5.1 Type of living arrangement:

1. Alone
2. Living with spouse
3. Living with son's family
4. Living with daughter's family
5. Living with relatives
6. Living with friend's house
7. Other's (specify)

5.2 Why you are not staying with your son's family?

1. There is no son
2. Son live at a long distance
3. Not willing to live with them
4. To avoid conflict
5. Others (specify)

5.3 Whether any separate room/ place available for you for sleeping/ taking rest?

1. Yes 2. No

5.4 If yes, whether it is for Isolation /Facilitation:

1. Isolated 2. Facilitated

5.5 If no, where do you sleep/ take rest?

1. Sharing with others inside the house
2. Veranda of the house
3. Common place in the village (temple, community hall etc)
4. Friends / neighbour's house
5. Others (Specify)

5.6 If not sleeping inside the house, why?

1. Inadequate place
2. Not allowed
3. Preferred to go outside
4. Others (Specify)

5.7 Freedom to avail facilities at home

S. No	*Facilities*	*Yes*	*No*
1.	Using TV/ Radio	Yes	No
2.	Using sofa /Furniture	Yes	No
3.	Using dining hall	Yes	No
4.	Sharing bath room / Toilets	Yes	No
5.	Others (specify)	Yes	No

VI. FAMILIAL RELATIONSHIP

6.1 Relationship with family members:

S. No	*Family members*	*Whether having cordial relationship*	
		Yes	*No*
1.	Wife		
2.	Son		
3.	Daughter		
4.	Daughter in law		
5.	Son in law		
6.	Other family members		

6.2 Do you participate in all family ceremonies?

1. Yes 2. No

6.3 If No, why?
1. Not permitted
2. No interest
3. No respect
4. Others (specify)

6.4 Consultation on important family matters?

1. Yes 2. No

6.5 If No why?
1. Not permitted
2. No interest
3. No respect
4. Others (specify)

6.6 Role in solving family dispute, if any?

1. Yes 2. No

6.7 If No why?
1. Not permitted
2. No interest
3. No respect
4. Others (specify)

6.8 Do you face any abusive behaviour from family members?

1. Yes 2. No

6.9 If yes, what type of abuse?
1. Verbal abuse
2. Beating
3. Lack of care/neglect
4. Not given food
5. Others (Specify)

6.10 Interaction with your family members

S. No	*Family members*	*Level of Interaction* Frequently	Rarely	Never
1.	Son			
2.	Daughter			
3.	Spouse			
4.	Grand children			
5.	Son in law			
6.	Daughters in law			

6.11 How many times you get food in a day?
1. Three times
2. Two times
3. One time
4. As many times as I need

6.12 Do you get adequate food daily?
1. Yes 2. No

6.13 Do you require any special food to be prepared for you?
1. Yes 2. No

6.14 If yes, do you get it?
1. Yes 2. No

6.15 If No why?
1. No one to care
2. No affection
3. Others (specify)

6.16 Other than food, do you need money /cash to meet your personal needs? 1. Yes 2.No

6.17 If yes what are the main personal needs that require money?
1. Medicines
2. Tea / Coffee/Tobacco
3. Going to hospital / Temple
4. Others (specify)

6.18 How much amount you need for a month Rs:[ ]

6.19 Do you have adequate finance of your own to meet your personal needs?
1. Yes 2. No

6.20 If No, where did you get the money?
1. None to help
2. Son
3. Daughter
4. Daughter-in-law
5. Son-in-law
6. Others (specify)

6.21 The money given by others is sufficient to meet your personal needs?
1. Yes 2. No

6.22 If No one helps you or if you are not getting sufficient money to meet your personal need, how do you meet your personal needs?
1. Borrowing
2. Poor life
3. Others (specify)

VII. PERSONAL LIFE STYLE

7.1 Do you ever have the following habits at any time in your life?

S. No.	*Habits*	*Only in the past not now*	*From which age to which age*	*Only at present not in the past*	*From which age*	*Always*	*Never*
1.	Smoking						
2.	Drinking						
3.	Betel nut						
4.	Tobacco chewing						
5.	Snuff powder						
6.	Drugs (Ganja, Injectable etc)						
7.	Others (Specify)						

7.2 Do you have the following practices in your daily routine?

S. No.	*Practices*	*Regular*	*Occasional*	*Never*
1.	Prayer			
2.	Walking			
3.	Gardening			
4.	Meditation			
5.	Yoga			
6.	Exercise			
7.	Going to religious center			
8.	Social activities			
9.	Going to recreation center			
10.	Others (specify)			

7.3 Contribution/Support to house hold domestic chores

S. No	*Domestic chores*	*Contribution/ Support*	
1.	Cooking	1. Yes	2.No
2.	Shopping	1. Yes	2.No

3.	Fetching water	1. Yes	2.No
4.	Schooling of children	1. Yes	2.No
5.	Engage the children	1. Yes	2.No
6.	Cleaning the house and the surroundings	1. Yes	2.No
7.	Disposal of household waste	1. Yes	2.No
8.	Others (specify)	1. Yes	2.No

7.4 What are your leisure time activities?

S. No	*Activities*	*Yes*	*No*
1.	Reading newspaper and books	1. Yes	2.No
2.	Hearing radio	1. Yes	2.No
3.	Watching T.V	1. Yes	2.No
4.	Playing with grand children	1. Yes	2.No
5.	Visiting Temple	1. Yes	2.No
6.	Engage in social activities	1. Yes	2.No
7.	Visiting friends	1. Yes	2.No
8.	Going to cinema house	1. Yes	2.No
9.	Playing cards	1. Yes	2.No
10.	Spending time at local tea shop	1. Yes	2.No
11.	Others (specify)	1. Yes	2.No

VIII. PHYSICAL DISABILITY

8.1 Do you have any difficulty in any of the following physical activities?

S. No	*Physical activities*	*Difficulties*		*Need help*		*Availability of help*	
		Yes	*No*	*Yes*	*No*	*Yes*	*No*
1.	Eating						
2.	Dressing						
3.	Bathing						
4.	Indoor walk						
5.	Out door walk						
6.	Climbing stairs						
7.	Combing hair						
8.	Getting up						
9.	Toilet						
10.	Boarding train/bus						

8.2 What is the level of your Physical mobility?

1. Move freely every where :
2. Neighbourhood only :
3. Inside the house only :
4. Bed ridden :

8.3 Physiological status :

S. No	Physiological status	Good	Fair	Poor
1.	Recall memory			
2.	Recognition			
3.	Vision			
4.	Speech			
5.	Audible range			

IX. PSYCHOLOGICAL STATUS

9.1 Do you have any of the following psychological problems?

S. No.	Problems	Yes	No
1.	Anxiety	1. Yes	2. No
2.	Isolation	1. Yes	2. No
3.	Feeling of guilty	1. Yes	2. No
4.	Behavioural adjustment	1. Yes	2. No
5.	Easily upset	1. Yes	2. No
6.	Angry	1. Yes	2. No
7.	Tension	1. Yes	2. No
8.	Fear of dependence	1. Yes	2. No
9.	Depression	1. Yes	2. No
10.	Loneliness	1. Yes	2. No
11.	Irritation	1. Yes	2. No
12.	Inability to adjust with changed health condition	1. Yes	2. No
13.	Unnecessary worry	1. Yes	2. No
14.	Fear	1. Yes	2. No
15.	Stress	1. Yes	2. No
16.	Feeling of lack of affection	1. Yes	2. No
17.	Fear of uselessness	1. Yes	2. No
18.	Feeling of neglect by family members	1. Yes	2. No
19.	Dementia	1. Yes	2. No
20.	Difficulty in coping with loss of job	1. Yes	2. No
21.	Loss of social relationship	1. Yes	2. No
22.	Loss of social security	1. Yes	2. No
23.	Lack of self confidence	1. Yes	2. No
24.	Feeling of lack of care	1. Yes	2. No
25.	Others (specify)	1. Yes	2. No

9.2. What sort of support you seek to overcome these problems?

1. Financial support
2. Family support
3. Counselling
4. Frequent interaction with family members

5. Interacting with friends
6. Recreation facilities
7. Others (Specify)

X. HEALTH STATUS

10.1 Do you have any of the following health problems?

Type of Disease	*Yes*	*No*	*Need Treatment*		*Getting Treatment*		*If getting Treatment Source of Treatment**	*If, No Treatment Reason***
Poor vision/cataract/other eye impairment	1. Yes	2. No	1. Yes	2. No	1. Yes	2. No		
Lung problem/respiratory Problem / asthma	1. Yes	2. No	1. Yes	2. No	1. Yes	2. No		
Tuberculosis/other chronic fever	1. Yes	2. No	1. Yes	2. No	1. Yes	2. No		
Diarrhoea/gastro enteritis/ Stomach ulcer	1. Yes	2. No	1. Yes	2. No	1. Yes	2. No		
Skin disease	1. Yes	2. No	1. Yes	2. No	1. Yes	2. No		
Angina / chest pain / cardiac Problem	1. Yes	2. No	1. Yes	2. No	1. Yes	2. No		
High blood pressure	1. Yes	2. No	1. Yes	2. No	1. Yes	2. No		
Arthritis / rheumatic / joint pain	1. Yes	2. No	1. Yes	2. No	1. Yes	2. No		
Back pain / slipped disc	1. Yes	2. No	1. Yes	2. No	1. Yes	2. No		
Neurological or mental problems (Depression)	1. Yes	2. No	1. Yes	2. No	1. Yes	2. No		
Cancer (of any form)	1. Yes	2. No	1. Yes	2. No	1. Yes	2. No		
Dementia/ memory loss	1. Yes	2. No	1. Yes	2. No	1. Yes	2. No		
Frailty / general weakness / run down condition	1. Yes	2. No	1. Yes	2. No	1. Yes	2. No		
Injury and related disabilities	1. Yes	2. No	1. Yes	2. No	1. Yes	2. No		
Burn and related disabilities	1. Yes	2. No	1. Yes	2. No	1. Yes	2. No		
Diabetes and other problems like prostate / dental etc.	1. Yes	2. No	1. Yes	2. No	1. Yes	2. No		
Others (specify)	1. Yes	2. No	1. Yes	2. No	1. Yes	2. No		

* Treatment

1. No treatment
2. Home treatment
3. Government hospital,
4. Private hospital
5. Traditional medicine

** Reasons for no treatment

1. No money financial difficulty,
2. Lack of family support,
3. No Help to go to hospital,
4. Others

10.2 In the last two weeks, do you have any of the following disease?

S. No	Disease	Yes	No	If Yes, do you need treatment		If yes, did you get treatment		If no treatment, reason
				Yes	No	Yes	No	
1	Persistence cough							
2	Wheezing							
3	Blocked nose							
4	Breathlessness							
5	Skin infection / Disease (eczema, rashes)							
6	Body weakness							
7	Fever							
8	Malaria							
9	Headache							
10	Cholera							
11	Diarrhoea							
12	Others (specify)							

XI. EXPECTATIONS

11.1 At this age and physical condition what are your expectations from your family?

11.2 What are your expectations from the community?

11.3 What are your expectations from the Government?

11.4 What are your advice / suggestions for the youth and youngsters?

11.5 What is your opinion on the increase in the longevity of human life?
1. Good 2. Bad 3. No opinion

11.6 If Good, how?

11.7 If bad, why?

11.8 Do you get the basic needs to lead a healthy life at this old age period?
1. Yes 2. No

11.9 If No, why?

11.10 What are the basic needs, which you feel that you have deprived of at this old age? Whom do you feel to provide them to you?

S. No	Basic needs deprived of	Whom do you feel to provide them to you?
1		
2		
3		
4		
5		

11.11 Do you know that as per law, every citizen is required to take care of their parents at old age?

1. Yes 2. No

11.12 Do you prefer to complain and file case against your children if they fail to take care of you?

1. Yes 2. No

11.13 If your children neither take care of you nor give any money for your maintenance, would you file case against them?

1. Yes 2. No

11.14 If No, why?

11.15 What is the present level of your affection to your children compared to your level of affection at your young age?

1. High
2. Same
3. Poor

Name of Investigator :
Signature of Investigator :
Date

INDEX